The Art of Play

The New Genre
of Interactive Theatre

Gary Izzo

HEINEMANN
Portsmouth, NH

Heinemann
A division of Reed Elsevier Inc.
361 Hanover Street
Portsmouth, NH 03801-3912

Offices and agents throughout the world

Library of Congress Cataloging-in-Publication Data

Izzo, Gary.
    The art of play : the new genre of interactive theatre / Gary Izzo.
       p. cm.
    Includes bibliographical references.
    ISBN 0-435-07036-3
    1. Improvisation (Acting) 2. Participatory theater. 3. Theater audiences. I. Title.
    PN2071.I5I98   1997
    792'.028--dc21
                                        97-27533
                                              CIP

Editor: Lisa A. Barnett
Production: Melissa L. Inglis
Cover design: Jenny Jensen Greenleaf
Manufacturing: Louise Richardson

Printed in the United States of America on acid-free paper
01 00 99 98 97   DA   1 2 3 4 5 6 7 8 9

*This book is dedicated to
the inner child in us all
and to Lola.*

Contents

About the Author

Gary Izzo is one of the first directors to experiment in the interactive genre. He began his work in Renaissance festivals in the 1970s. As a teacher, he has trained hundreds of actors in interactive and participatory theatre. As a director and producer, he has presented outdoor interactive festivals, participatory plays, murder mysteries, and interactive convention show concepts, having founded Creative Entertainment, Inc., a company dedicated to the exploration and production of audience-inclusive theatre styles.

He has worked for many years as a show director/ writer and an entertainment consultant for the Walt Disney World Co. and was an early influence on Disney's use of live actors in interactive shows. He has designed and developed numerous interactive attractions for Disney and introduced interactive theatre as a convention entertainment concept.

For more information about lectures, workshops, show design, and development consultation by Gary Izzo, please write to Interactive Artists, P.O. Box 780212, Orlando, FL 32828.

Preface

T he form and content of theatre has always been shaped by what its culture needs to express itself. New theatre forms emerge from changing cultural conditions or attitudes. The information age we now revel in has connected us intellectually and separated us physically. We were once content to gather in community to watch an alternate reality played out upon a stage. We watched life dramatized before us while we were safe and disconnected in our seats, living it only vicariously from a distance. Ever since the written word was popularized, theatre has been a physical representation of the imaging process we experience when we read. Now, it seems, watching is not enough; we must *take part*. We seek now to play out our lives *ourselves* upon the stage, still within the same safety of make-believe.

Not surprisingly, even the software of our information age strives to be interactive. Yet ideas will never replace touch. We must still connect as human beings. Thus the place of live theatre in our culture will remain undiminished, but it will, as it must, adapt. This book discusses the process and technique of "interactive" theatre, a new form of theatre that places the audience on the stage and in the midst of the drama. Unlike its "participatory" cousins, interactive theatre is both inclusive and *reactive* to its audience. It *changes* in response to the audience's influence. It also creates, or re-creates, a bond of community, and thus restores, if only for a few hours, our lost sense of belonging.

This volume describes the theory and technique of the interactive process. It concerns itself with what the interactive genre is—how and why it works. A companion book entitled *Acting Interactive Theatre* gives guidance for developing and performing an interactive production. It is a more practical guide to the interactive process, intended for the actor, director, and teacher. References are made to exercises from this companion book throughout the text.

Acknowledgments

I would like to thank those actors whose loyalty and trust over the years gave me the strength to explore and whose creativity and faith inspired and defined my vision. I would especially like to thank Nancy, my tireless wife, for her loving support and valued partnership in this and all projects. My thanks to Gerry and Ginny for allowing me to experiment. To Dial goes my great gratitude for his unending guidance; to Doug and Baj for their friendship and support; and, most gratefully, to Hantor and Alessa for their mentorship and inspiration without which this book would never have been written.

Part I

Defining a
New Genre

What Is Interactive Theatre?

Stepping Through the Looking Glass

My first experience in the theatre was as a member of its largest and most important component: the audience. When I was nine years old, my parents took me to see a production of *Man of La Mancha* while we were vacationing in Boston. The production was staged in the round. I remember looking past the stage, to the far side of the vast arena, and seeing rows of attentive spectators seated quietly in the air-conditioned dark. The audience seemed huddled round the stage like cold campers around a fire, while the stage glowed warmly with the passionate adventures of Don Quixote.

At times I was aware of my place in the theatre and at other times I was totally absorbed in the pageant unfolding within the circle of light below me. I was astounded by the magic of it—its power to move me. Within its orb the world of Don Quixote moved with perfect order. It wasted not a single sound, movement, or thought. It had a harmony, a beauty, a perfection all its own. All appeared so real and so close.

I was stricken with the notion that nothing separated that world from mine but a wide expanse of air and light. It seemed to have no borders. I felt a yearning to be there, to be inside that circle. I experienced for the first time the

power of the theatre to lure the soul. I felt that tug of the spirit—
its call to escape and join the illusion.

I thought to myself, "What if I could be there? What if I got up
out of my chair, walked down the aisle, and stepped onto the
stage fully prepared to help Don Quixote and Sancho save
Aldonza from the muleteers? What would happen? Would they
throw me a sword and cheer me on, or would they stand and
stammer in surprise and anger as the house manager ushered me
off the stage, back to my seat and my mortified parents?" That
nine-year-old felt the latter was the more likely, so I didn't attempt
it, but the thought hung in the air like the sea of faces beyond the
stage. Why must we be content only to observe? Why must the
powerful spell of the theatre be held always at a distance, and why
must it always dissolve when we reach out to touch it? This is the
great mystery that I have carried with me from my first play. It has
remained my deepest fascination with the theatre.

I became an actor because actors were the privileged few who
could play within that sacred space. Later on I wrote, directed, and
produced for the theatre because those roles more so involved the
stewardship of the illusion. My work has always been to some
degree occupied with the notion of audience intimacy, much of it
experimenting with the breaking of the so-called fourth wall and
on some level inviting the audience onto the stage.

When I was twenty years old and still in school, I was given my
first professional directing job at a then-little-known phenomenon
called a Renaissance festival. I was to direct a small company of
actors doing excerpts from Shakespeare and Molière on an open-
air stage. The fledging festival was in its third year. With the recent
death of the owner, the festival's management fell to his nephew.
By his own admission, he knew more about the restaurant business than the running of an arts festival. As a result, he gave me
carte blanche in producing the festival's entertainment.

As I walked the grounds with my new boss, he told me of his
experiences at a Renaissance festival in southern California. His
favorite part was the actors dressing up as Elizabethan characters
and roaming the lanes of the festival, cavorting with the paying
customers or "patrons," as we later called them. As we walked
about, some *what if* questions came to mind: "What if we added
a troupe of actors solely to wander the lanes? What if we cast the
full spectrum of Elizabethan society, from nobility through gentry
down to the lowest beggar? What if we developed scenes, or routines, to play out among the crowd in such a way as to include
them in the action?"

Then I thought, "Why not treat our patrons not as spectators, but as Elizabethans themselves? And why not treat everything within the confines of the site as though it really were a place in Elizabethan England? Each patron could be invested with being an Elizabethan and be given a name and an identity, or *role*, to play along with the characters." I thrilled at the thought of actually being able to experiment in a completely interactive theatrical space. I asked my accidental arts manager what he thought of the idea, and he shrugged the one reply every director craves, "Sure, whatever you want." Thus began my involvement in interactive theatre.

Interactive Theatre Is the Art of Play

Interactive theatre *is* the art of *play*. There is no simpler or more accurate definition. I am speaking of *play* in the ordinary sense of childhood playing, not in the theatrical sense of a play. It has been said that art is the creation of a thing of beauty and order through the employment of a specific technique. Play is a thing of beauty and order employed through a specific technique. Defining that technique is the purpose of this book.

A number of years ago, as I concluded an opening rehearsal with a new ensemble, one worried-looking actor, whose previous experience had all been on the stage, raised his hand and very sincerely asked, "Is it art?" The answer is *yes*, a very fine art, one that challenges an actor to play by very different rules.

What is true for the stage is not always true for interactive theatre. The actor must unlearn much of what he or she knows and relearn performance from a different perspective. The improvisation involved requires retraining the mind to process information differently, and the actor must change his or her assumptions about how theatre is performed and presented. The end result allows the actor to return to the stage with more confidence, flexibility, and power than is often attained in years of stage work.

THE NEED FOR PLAY

The rise of interactive styles of entertainment reflects a need for the play element in today's culture. The paradigms we have for the way we live are shifting. The information age has accelerated our lives to a breakneck speed, with the relentless onslaught of information far outstripping our ability to assimilate it. We must spend more of our time sifting and choosing to keep ourselves grounded. The once methodical and predictable marketplace, which measured quality by uniformity and dependability, has changed to one in which only the newest and the fastest win. More time must be spent in the workplace. Both spouses must work for the same standard of living their parents enjoyed. The family unit is strained. Communication diminishes and the art of conversation is lost. Job mobility increases. Families move, separating friends and relatives; community disappears. Sources of support become increasingly external and impersonal.

We know ourselves through our relationships with others. They are the mirrors in which we see our true selves reflected. Without human contact, we lose touch with *self*. Our ancestors lived for millennia in communities, villages, and tribes. They knew themselves within the context of a community they could *touch*.

Today we live our lives in *boxes*. Our homes are boxes laid out in developments or in apartments in which most of us hardly know who lives two doors down. Twenty years ago, mothers conversing across their yards as they watched their children play held society together. Mothers became friends, so their families became friends. Now those mothers are working, and the children are in day care; no one is in the yard.

The interaction within the community of our great-grandfathers was based on mutual support for survival. Our survival now comes from an office, another box miles from home. Many of us spend as much as two hours a day driving to and from that office in yet another box. To play music, one doesn't learn an instrument—we turn on a box. To watch what is happening in our town, we don't step outside our door; we watch a box. And we spend as many as thirty hours per week watching our entertainment from that same box.

My intent here is not to paint a dismal picture of our modern lives. I find life fascinating and exciting on the whole. What I am trying to point out, rather, is that our lives are so impersonal that we are *dehumanized*. We are so separated from simple human contact that we are losing our sense of self. The counsel we all need to cope with life once came as a gift from our elders; now we pay for it from professionals or suffer without it. We hunger today for the mirror of human relationship and personal interaction. We yearn to play.

It is not as though there is no time for play; we do find the time because it is part of our nature to play. Games and entertainment are play, and they abound today as at no other time in history. The problem is not the amount of play but what is missing. Sports, video games, television, movies, even the theatre reflect either the aggression and competition in our lives or our disconnection from one another. What we are missing is simple creative play, the first play we ever knew, the play of connection, experimentation, and discovery, the play of make-believe. If we are to understand the nature of interactive theatre, the reason for its growth and importance, we must first understand the nature of this kind of play.

The Nature of Play and the Child

To understand the nature of play, we must examine it in its most essential form—the child at play. Play is a natural state. Whatever instinct or force of nature is at work in play, we are born with the knowledge of it. Only the absence of play is created. Our lack of awareness of play, or our inability to play, is a function of what we learn as we grow older. As our knowledge of the world around us grows, our connection to play is eclipsed by the pressures of finding our place within it. To see it clearly, we must view play before, as Shakespeare would put it, "the thousand natural shocks that flesh is heir to."

PLAY IS NOT A CREATION OF MAN

Play is not a creation of man nor is it a product of his civilization or culture. It exists outside culture and is older than civilization. This is demonstrated, in part, by the fact that animals play just like people. Play is as evident in the cavorting of young dogs, for example, as it is in the roughhousing of children. In both, there is an invitation to play, by posture or sound; rules are created and adhered to; there may be a pretended fierceness or seriousness; and at some point the agreed-upon play ends and normal life resumes.

In his book *Homo Ludens* (which means "man the player"), first published in 1944, Johan Huizinga sets forth a lucid explanation of the nature of play: "Summing up the formal characteristics of play, we might call it a free activity standing quite consciously outside 'ordinary' life as being 'not serious,' but at the same time absorbing the player intensely and utterly. It is an activity connected with no material interest, and no profit can be gained by it. It proceeds within its own proper boundaries of time and space according to the fixed rules and in an orderly manner. It promotes the formation of social groupings which tend to surround themselves with secrecy and to stress their difference from the common world by disguise or other means" (Boston: Beacon Press, 1955, 13).

Clearly, for the player, the only real motive for play is the sheer enjoyment of it. Whatever psychological, physiological, or biological benefits there are to playing, we play merely because it is *fun* to play. The concept of fun is so basic a quality of life that it is irreducible to any other mental category. Even so, many languages do not have a word for it. Yet this fun, this intensity, this absorption, this power to move characterizes the very essence of play. Play is an absolute and primary aspect of life, familiar and instantly recognizable to all: adult, child, and animal. The function of interactive theatre is to provide the participant access to this fundamental component of existence.

Whether play is entered into singly or as a group, it remains an individual's free choice. Play *is* freedom. It exists outside the boundaries of time and responsibility. We play in our "free" time, our "spare" time. After the obligations of our days are met, we use our "after hours," our "off hours," to play. Play to order is no longer play.

Play serves no material need, yet we do need it. The absence of it subtracts nothing from our pursuit of food and shelter. However, the quality of our lives would surely be lessened by its absence. The curious thing about play is that the need for it is urgent only to the extent that the *enjoyment* of it makes it a need. Unlike our day-to-day existence, play can be deferred or suspended at any time and then resumed just where it left off with the same intensity as before, even if days have gone by.

Play is stepping out of "real life" into a temporary sphere of activity with qualities all its own. Play is "only pretending," "only for fun." It has no bearing or effect upon our real world. Yet, this quality of only pretending does not prevent play from proceeding with the utmost seriousness. There is always a great intensity during play, an absorption and devotion that matches anything we pursue in our real world. Whether it be children playing hide and seek or a stadium full of spectators at the Super Bowl, play has the power so to enrapture as to abolish, temporarily at least, that "only pretending" feeling. At any time, a game can wholly run away with its players, and a sense of abandon can so prevail that the normal appetites of life are suspended. One is seldom too hungry or too tired when the game is afoot. Play is self-sufficient—a temporary activity satisfying in itself and ending there.

ALL PLAY EXISTS IN PLAY-SPACE, OR "TEMENOS"

All play takes place within a "playground," a space marked off beforehand either physically or mentally, deliberately or as a matter of course. The ancient Greeks' word for such space is *temenos*, the sacred circle. It is a sacred spot cut off and hedged in from the "ordinary" world, a consecrated spot, a hallowed ground within which special rules obtain. A temenos exists on the stage, the playing field, the altar, or in the courtroom. It is not, of course, the physical construction of these spaces that creates temenos. It is our collective regard for their purpose that imbues them with the quality of temenos. Whether the rules within be of law, religion, contest, or make-believe, they are by definition sacred places, temporary worlds within the ordinary world, set apart for and dedicated to the performance of an act apart. Thus temenos is a sacred spot, not in the religious sense, but in the sense that it is a thing regarded with the same respect and reverence accorded holy things; a thing venerated and hallowed, secured against defamation, violation, or intrusion; a special, protected, and inviolate space.

Wherever there is play, there is play space. Observe children at play and you will soon see this sacred circle. It may be the sides of a sandbox, the perimeter of a backyard, a section of woods, or the confines of a playroom or tree house. Children know when they enter their play space, and for as long as playtime lasts, only that which pertains within has importance.

PLAY ALSO EXISTS IN A TEMENOS OF THE MIND

A temenos not only is created in the physical world but exists, too, in the mind. Observe a child alone at play and you can almost feel his or her temenos of the mind. A little girl having tea with her dolls plays safely within a fancy Victorian parlor in her mind. A little boy playing with his action figures does battle in the Gettysburg of his imagination. My favorite depictions of mental temenos occur in the comic strip "Calvin and Hobbes." The character Calvin is the quintessence of the playful imagination. He can create a reptile-laden, primordial swamp out of a pool of spilled milk.

While writing this book, I had a visit from my precocious six-year-old niece, Nicole. I was in my study playing computer games instead of writing. Nicole came in to see what I was doing and, after a time spent "straightening" my office papers for me, declared that this place was now an arcade and that she was the manager. I obliged her by agreeing that it was indeed an arcade. She ran out of the room and gathered up a Game Boy and extra cartridges that were lying about, brought them back, and neatly stacked them on my computer table as additional games for the arcade.

Nicole then set about the task of managing her arcade, with me as the sole patron. She did additional paper straightening, and found a clipboard and a pencil. She then conducted a few conversations with other clients using my office telephone. Through the course of our play Nicole made the room entirely her own. It was no longer my study, it was her arcade. Everything in the room was utilized in her play: the desks, the chairs, the telephones, even the closets were all remade in her imagination into her very exclusive arcade. Hers was a temenos of the mind as surely as if she were on a playground.

Nicole informed me that my study was not just any arcade, but a very special one only for the super rich (a true child of the nineties). She then charged me the surprising membership fee of two million ten hundred dollars in order to continue to play. I had to sign in on her clipboard, then pay up. Nicole explained that although her fee was high, membership came with many extras, namely her undivided attention as manager. Clearly, Nicole's temenos was no ordinary place.

After a while it became necessary for her to leave the room for a few moments. Leaving the room meant leaving the play space, and Nicole wanted none of it disturbed in her absence, so she created a few simple provisions. She placed her clipboard outside the doorway, became quite serious, and explained to me that while she was out *no one* was to enter the room without first signing in and paying up, "even if they were an *adult*." I promised my most sincere promise, and satisfied, she left, shutting the door behind her.

While she was gone, her older sister Danielle came by and asked what was going on. I dutifully informed her about our arcade, and she readily signed in and paid me the two million ten hundred dollars. When Nicole returned, she was satisfied to find that the list had been signed and the money paid. Her arcade was still her arcade; the play space had not been intruded upon by the outside world.

As an outsider, however, Danielle still had to be informed of the rules in order to play along. When Danielle announced that she was the manager of the arcade, her assumption transgressed Nicole's established rules and took Nicole's role in the game away from her. Nicole became quite agitated, and just before her tears started I handed Danielle the Game Boy and invited her to be a patron with me, instead. She agreed, and the game resumed.

PLAY HAS ITS OWN UNIQUE AND UNALTERABLE RULES

Inside the playground, whether in space or of the mind, an absolute order reigns. No matter how peculiar the rules of play are in comparison to ordinary life, they have their own unique rationale. The ordinary world with its subjectivity, uncertainty, and shades of meaning is in sharp contrast to the play world's simplicity and harmony. Into an imperfect world, play brings a sort of temporary, limited perfection. I think this accounts for some of our need for play. Much of the joy experienced in play is the experience of that perfect order and harmony; this is how play creates *beauty*. Rules in the play world are absolutely binding and allow for no doubt. The slightest deviation from them spoils the play, alters its character, and makes it worthless.

When I was a child, anyone who broke the rules or ignored them was called a "spoil sport." The worst thing any game can have is a spoil sport. The spoil sport should not be confused with the "cheater." The cheater pretends to be playing the game by the rules and, at least on the face of it, still acknowledges the temenos. This is the important difference between the two. The spoil sport, by breaking the rules of play, shatters the play world itself and play can no longer continue. He robs play of its illusion and must be cast out. Little wonder that society in general is more lenient toward the cheater than toward the spoil sport. Cheaters can get by if they are careful, but a spoil sport can never play. Danielle, as a newcomer to Nicole's arcade game, had not yet fully understood the rules; she transgressed them when she insisted she was the arcade manager. This act "spoiled" our game. When the temenos is broken, play must come to a screeching halt.

Children seem to know and accept that during play one must always adhere to the rules. If one picks up a stick and says "This is a sword," all others need to agree and accept that it is so, and it *is* so, and it *remains* so. Players can always add to the rules; one might say, "Now this sword has the power to heal dead people." Again, all others need to agree that it is so, and so it *is*, and *remains.* If when confronted, another player were to say, "That's not a magic sword at all, it's just a stick," he would be denying the rules of play, and the immediate response would be, "That's not fair." He is in danger of collapsing the play space and being a spoil sport. He must either agree to the rules as agreed upon and established, or be ejected from the game.

There is no reason to change a rule or to judge a rule as proper or improper. As children we all created our play space, developed the rules, and then followed them, because following them was fun and there was no reason to change them. We assisted each other in understanding our shared play reality. We informed each other of who we were, what we were doing, where we were, what we had in our hand, etc. "Now I am Lancelot and you are Queen Guinevere, and this is the cave where the dragon lives." Each player accepted the new creations of the mind from their fellow players because there was no reason to deny them. To deny it would only halt the play.

PLAY ALWAYS HAS AN ELEMENT OF TENSION

In play, the player always wants to resolve something, or achieve something difficult, or somehow end a tension. It tests the player's courage and resourcefulness and even spiritual powers such as patience and—always—fairness, because no matter how badly the player wants to win he or she must always stick to the rules of the game and "play fair."

PLAY REALITY IS A HEIGHTENED REALITY

In addition to resolving tension, the subject of play always involves a heightened reality, a situation larger than ordinary life. It is always dramatic in nature because of its condensed action and heightened, or "high-stakes," situations. Play-life is always more interesting than ordinary life because fascinating things happen. Even Nicole's quiet make-believe game of arcade had a heightened reality to it. It wasn't just an ordinary arcade; it was a very special arcade—one you would never see in ordinary life. Also, it never takes long in play for something climactic to happen. Often play is a series of climaxes, one after another, each one more dangerous and incredible than the previous. It is no accident, then, that an evening of staged drama is called a play.

Play-space is a space in which situations too terrible to endure in ordinary life can be experienced and explored in safety.

Despite its awesome perils, the magic circle of play is always safe. Play-space is the place where we experience our existence without the burden of fear. Each move we make in ordinary life, no matter how small, has a permanent effect upon us. The fact of that *permanence* is the basis for the fear in our lives. Once done, a thing cannot be undone, and, often, fear paralyzes action. Play-space is *impermanent.* We may undo or replay our experience over and over again. We can discover ourselves without the danger of loss. In play there need be no fear, and without it play experience is always a joyous event.

Another curious thing about play is its relationship with time. When a player enters into play space, he or she knows that it is also "play time." It is time outside the ordinary world, separate and distinct. Time has no bearing on play; it is timeless, having no past or future. Play is always a here-and-now endeavor. For a player absorbed in the game, the passage of time seems altered, and a player emerging from his or her absorption in play is like a person waking from a dream, unaware of the time that has passed. The adage "time flies when you're having fun" thus speaks simply and accurately of this unperceived passage of time during play.

Play Tends to Build Community

Within the experience of play, players develop a bond, a shared sense of "being apart" together. The bond retains its magic beyond the duration of the game, and a desire to renew that bond binds the players together and draws them to reunite again in play. Thus the relationship between individuals within the temenos tends to be different from their relationship in the ordinary world. Within the temenos individuals relate to one another on a more basic level than in ordinary life. Bonds formed within the harmony of play space can be truer and stronger than those known in the ordinary world. One might paraphrase a well-known adage as "the family that plays together, stays together" or, perhaps more accurately, "those who play together create family."

Thus play loves to shroud itself in an air of secrecy. "The others outside don't concern us now; we within the circle have our own special way." This feeling of differentness expresses itself in "dressing up." Players "disguise" themselves from their ordinary appearance. Costumes, masks, and badges mark a player's difference from those outside the circle. Like the actor, the disguised player plays a different part; he *is* another being.

PLAY IS EITHER A CONTEST OR A REPRESENTATION

All play is either a contest for something or a representation of something. *Contest play* strives for winning or achieving. A gambler at a blackjack table engages in contest play, as does the football player or the child playing marbles.

In *representation play*, players strive to move beyond their ordinary selves so that they almost believe they actually *are* what they are portraying, but without wholly losing consciousness of ordinary reality. This is the "play" of the actor. Huizinga believes that this representation play is "not so much a constructed sham reality as a 'realization in appearance': 'imagination' in the original sense of the word" (1955, 14). By this he means imagination as the act or power of forming mental images of what is not really present. That little girl having tea with her dolls *becomes* her mind's image of a fine Victorian lady. Representation play is one way we manifest our desires into reality.

OUR LOST PLAY

Play is not a learned ability but a basic facet of our nature. The child need not *learn* how to play. The child already knows; he or she plays naturally, not as a learned behavior. As we grow to adulthood we lose some of our ability to play because we learn judgment, denial, and fear. Yet play maintains a place in our adult lives. To lose our ability to play entirely would be to lose our humanity. Play is part of us; we are "homo ludens," man the player. In our modern society, however, we do lose a significant aspect of play because, in our lives, play manifests itself mostly in contest play. We see it in games of mental power or physical strength or agility—in board games, on the tennis court, on the golf course. This is the play of winning and of achieving a goal. It is a healthy and vital part of our lives, but what is missing is the play of representation.

Where does only pretending manifest itself in our adult lives? I don't know many adults who still run around their backyards playing cops and robbers. For most adults, then, art becomes their representational play. However, we who are involved in the visual or performing arts have ample opportunity to explore this fundamental aspect of our lives, but most people in our society— and we artists forget this—are not involved *in* the arts. They go to museums, attend plays, motion pictures, turn on their television sets, and they *watch*. When viewing a motion picture they may play the role of the hero or heroine they watch, but they do so vicariously. They are not engaged in the process of the experience, because they make no choices. The story unfolds in a predestined and unalterable way. Thus *watchers* are not actualizing their representational play. They cannot use the uniqueness of their own minds and hearts to affect an outcome, and so they miss the echo of themselves otherwise revealed in the course of their own play. The cost is to lose their own self-awareness. Leo Frobenius said, "Man *plays* the order of nature as imprinted on his [or her] consciousness" (in Huizinga 1955). If he does so, he is to understand himself.

If the child needs to play out the complexity of life within the temenos, then the adult has no less need to do so. The struggle of self-awareness never ends. A lack of the awareness of who we are breeds a lack of self-esteem, of confidence, and of purpose. The magic of interactive theatre is its ability to actualize the individual's unique creative power, that ancient and essential quality of the human spirit to play itself out upon the world around it.

Interactive Theatre and the Temenos

The parallels between the nature and qualities of play and the rules of improvisation and creative thought are so striking that one is tempted to say they are one and the same. In both there is a need for setting rules that are apart from those of ordinary life. There is also the need for accepting ideas without judgment and for altering an action through the affirmation of ideas rather than the negation of them. Most of all, both call for the creation of a space in which judgment does not exist—the temenos.

THE INVITATION TO PLAY

Interactive theatre begins with the creation of the temenos. It is first created within the acting ensemble, and then that magical circle of safety and nonjudgment is extended out to include the audience. The acting ensemble says to its audience, "We are sacred ground; we are safe and apart and may be who we choose." The audience is then invited into their space not knowing the rules and having to be taught by the ensemble. The ensemble must make them feel safe, teach them the rules and boundaries, affirm their unique individual natures, and invite them to play. For the audience members, it is like being a kid in a new neighborhood and being warmly welcomed. "Oh, you don't know how to play kickball? That's OK, we'll show you. You'll be good at it. We want you on our team."

I've often described interactive theatre as a sandbox in which the members of the ensemble are the box's keepers. Their job is to greet the audience, hand them their pail and shovel, and invite them to play in a pageant of human behavior. Thus in interactive theatre, with our image of play as a circle, the audience players face inward and the actors face outward. Both the audience and the actors are *apart* together, and the world is at play. But the term *audience* seems inappropriate for interactive theatre. It implies a group of aloof watchers. The word literally means "those assembled to hear." I prefer to refer to the audience as "guests." What else would you call someone you invite into your private space?

Play with Wisdom

We value or even envy a child's ability to play so easily, unencumbered by life's "slings and arrows," which we adults have endured. However, children have a limitation that adults do not. Children are self-centered, not in the sense of their being proud, but in the sense that they lack awareness of the world around them. They are the center of their own universe. Becoming an adult means expanding our own awareness to include others and gaining understanding through our relationships.

Adults forget the sacred circle of play when they learn judgment, denial, and fear. However, as adults rediscover the temenos, they can use their greater awareness of life to choose what they play out, or place, within the temenos. The child may play naturally, but the adult may play *well*. If we rediscover our temenos, we can choose to experience love, acceptance, support, and affirmation of the good in us. We can "play" at the finer qualities of our existence. The temenos has an awesome power for creation in our lives, but, unlike children, we adults may choose, with wisdom, what we create.

The Empowerment of the Inner Child

If the temenos of the stage widens to include the audience, then those "watchers" can themselves run with Don Quixote and Sancho and truly share in their adventures in an active and vital way. It is the pretending of our youth made whole again, and it has a great power to move the soul. I've always considered interactive theatre to be a theatrical entity, but it oftentimes seems to transcend the purely theatrical. At times it becomes something else, something far more basic. Take average people and put them in a place that allows them to exercise their imaginations without constraint, and they will be childlike and experience freedom and innocence again. Put them in a place of human contact, humor, and playfulness where they are celebrated, without condition, simply for who they are, and you will see something within them *expand*. This widening is the magic of the heart opening up, and the rediscovery of innocence and wonder. Interactive theatre takes people who have forgotten how to be spontaneous, creative, and uninhibited and permits them to be that and more.

Any stage play of quality does more than entertain; it holds a mirror up to nature, as it were, and offers a glimpse into the human condition. Each work of the theatre contains some kind of insight. The power of the theatre of the stage lies in its ability to deliver this insight through a vicarious experience. Interactive theatre actualizes the experience, making it felt all the more. The unique "message" of interactive theatre lies in its ability to reintroduce the watcher to his or her own inner child.

The Impact of Interactive Theatre on Its Audience

Life within the temenos can be very pleasant and very healing. When you are welcomed into a place where you are not judged, where you cannot make a mistake or be inferior, where you are considered special just the way you are, your mind reacts as if to fond memories of dear friends and happy events. It doesn't matter that it is a make-believe world, a good play still has the power to move and enlighten even though it is not real. The subconscious doesn't know the difference, and neither does the heart.

A guest who spends time in the sacred circle relinquishes inhibition and doubt and finds the freedom that leads to empowerment. A guest will begin to feel vital and *valid*. How else could you feel when you are in complete command of your reality—when the world around you values you without reason or condition? In good interactive theatre, there is always a subtle but significant affirmation of self.

Over the years, I have seen the impact of this kind of affirmation. An actress friend once played a peasant at my Renaissance festival and spent part of one morning playing to an elderly woman who had come to the festival alone that day. The actress listened to her, incorporated what she said into the festival reality, and they both had a great time with it. By chance, they kept running into each other, and the actress built on the reality they had created together. At the end of the day the woman was still there. She pulled my friend aside and, with tears in her eyes, thanked her for taking time with her and *listening*. Her husband had died some years before, and she had no family. She told the actress that she was the first person in many years to "really communicate" with her.

Another fine interactive actor, who has worked with me for many years, once played a friar at the Sterling Festival. He was fond of the technique of involving children, then looping in their parents, who then could not refuse. Children also seemed to take a strong liking to the ebullient Friar Pinch. One day he met a very sweet little girl of five and her mother. She was an extremely reserved child, the kind who wraps her arms around Mommy's leg and buries her head. The actor was determined not to give up. He spent much time and most of his "bag of tricks" on the girl. The mother was calmly indulgent, almost aloof. Eventually the actor got the little girl to play by focusing on his drawing in the dust with a stick. The two of them played at their drawings and, eventually, the girl began conversing with the inimitable Friar Pinch. With a temenos established, she was soon sprightly and talkative.

However, since that interaction hadn't drawn a crowd, the actor decided to move on. He said his good-bye to the little girl, and only then saw the strange expression on her mother's face. Unsure of what it meant, he sheepishly signed off and headed down the lane. He didn't get far before the mother caught up to him. She took his collar in both her hands, drew him to her, and in a very intense tone of voice said, "You don't know what you've *done*!" The actor was terrified and, as he saw his job flash before his eyes, uttered a barely intelligible stream of apologies. To which the mother replied, "No! You don't know what you've done to my little girl!" The actor, who was by now convinced he had nothing left to lose, asked her what it was that he did. The mother replied very slowly and deliberately, "She . . . doesn't . . . *talk*!" Indeed, the little girl had *never* uttered more than a few words to her mother, and *never* to any one else.

In another instance, one of my instructors played a clownish Spanish manservant between stage performances. This actor, whose mother was confined to a wheelchair for many years, was fond of playing to the handicapped. His great genius was in how he treated them with the same irreverence he treated everyone else. His philosophy was that the handicapped do not want to be treated differently. It worked. It didn't matter how debilitating the disease, he would always command them to get out of their chairs and let someone else ride for a while.

One gentleman in particular and his friend would come to the festival every year to see the actor's show and have a pleasant conversation with him. One season the man's friend returned to the festival alone. He found the actor and told him that his friend had died during the year and that he had asked him to return to the festival to deliver a message. Through the voice of his friend, the man in the wheelchair told the actor that his one regret in leaving this world was not being able to see him one more time. He thanked him for making him feel *human* and for putting laughter into his life of pain. He said that his yearly encounters with the actor reminded him of what joy was, and gave him the strength to continue his struggle for life. Finally, he said he would take his gift with him.

These are very nearly the words he spoke. The actor was so overcome that he had to sit out part of the festival that day to regain his composure. He told me later that he was moved by the kindness of this man's words, but what completely overtook him was the *shock* of how what he considered to be mere playful banter could have such an enormous effect on someone else's life.

Of course, these stories are some of the more remarkable effects of the temenos. There are less impressive tales I could tell, but they would be no less significant. I began a tradition at the Sterling Renaissance Festival of having the entire cast lead the last guests of the day out through the front gate after the final "pubsing." I wanted a sort of curtain call for the ensemble. Since I never let actors break character, even after the performance, it was a way of allowing them to get their kudos without having to shatter the illusion we so painstakingly create for the guests. It also had the added benefit of drawing the guests out of the festival so that we could close. I would have them line up on the "real world" side of the lane, forming a gauntlet. There they would bid farewell and Godspeed to the last, best guests of the day. Those times are the most impressive to me because I could always see among the crowd a glow, a sense of calmness, and an outward energy.

I will still stand sometimes and look at the faces of the guests flowing by, and understand the shock my instructor felt with the man in the wheelchair. The guests resemble, for all the world, pilgrims flowing from a shrine. It truly feels as if you're in the presence of people who have witnessed a miracle; it is so real it's frightening. In a sense, though, they *have* come from a sacred place, because the temenos is a sacred place. The power of play runs as deep as our souls; perhaps they have seen a miracle—the miracle of themselves.

Audience Inclusive Styles 2

*L*et us be clear on what we mean by interactive theatre. There are many styles of theatre that are on some level inclusive of the audience. Many people confuse one with another or simply lump them into one category. Understanding the dynamics of each is necessary to appreciate what interactive theatre is, and what it is not.

Intimate Theatre

A production is said to be *intimate theatre* when the traditional proscenium stage is altered to bring the action on the stage closer to the audience. The thrust stage, theatre-in-the-round, and the various forms of environmental theatre all employ unusual stage configurations, or no stage at all, to bring about this change in style. Yet all may retain the barrier, or *fourth wall,* between the real life of the house and the illusion onstage. The dynamic between actor and audience remains the same as that in traditional proscenium-style theatre, except that the audience is physically closer to the action onstage.

When a production "breaks the fourth wall," it spills out into the real world of the house. This sometimes takes the form of actors leaving the stage and entering the auditorium. Here again, the effect is in the illusion's proximity to the audience. The production continues undisturbed in its preplanned order. Its harmony is never breached by any spontaneous act on the audience's part. The important difference here is that the production, if you will, is aware of the audience's existence. The audience is addressed and acknowledged by characters in the play as though they belong there, yet the characters always remain within the context of the play's reality.

Audience Participatory Theatre

Audience participatory theatre takes this notion a step further and opens the production up to the spontaneous actions and responses of the audience. In participatory theatre the audience can cheer for the hero or boo at the villain. One or more members of the audience may be brought onto the stage to perform some action integral to the scene. The effect of participatory theatre for the audience is the thrill of seeing one of its number take part in the production, that is, join the temenos. The audience at large identifies with, and lives vicariously through, that audience member just as they would for any other character in the production, except that particular identity is one step closer to themselves. The feeling is, "That could be me up there." Once theatre becomes participatory, the stage itself gains an identity rather than being a forgotten convention.

In participatory theatre the production is not only aware of the existence of the audience, as in intimate theatre, it is also aware of *itself* as a play. Characters in the production are aware of themselves as characters in a fiction, which is one of the two conditions that make theatre participatory. Although it can be said that there is interaction between performer and audience in participatory theatre, it is not truly interactive. Participatory theatre is predetermined and prerehearsed much like any other theatre. There is a fixed outcome to the story. Like any play, that outcome is arrived at through a finite number of scenes that must be presented in a certain order, one after the other. Each of those scenes contains one or more plot points that direct the action toward that fixed outcome. Neither the outcome nor any of the plot points may be altered without changing the story.

The other condition that makes a play participatory is that the outcome remains unchanged. In most participatory theatre, the audience member's inclusion in the production is, for the most part, predetermined and often rehearsed (at least among the actors). It achieves the effect of participation while still allowing the production to continue in its preplanned order after the participation concludes. The audience member, ignorant of his "role," is prompted by characters in such a way as to capitalize on his or her actions and reactions to create extra laughter and interest. The skill of the improviser enters at this point, to ad-lib around the unavoidable variables engendered by any audience member's inclusion in the production. The audience participant responds or reacts to the production but does not *alter* it.

Variety Entertainment

Variety entertainment is a form of participatory theatre. Some people still think that variety was an entertainment fad from the late nineteenth century that died with vaudeville. In truth, the variety form is ancient; its roots run as deep as theatre itself. As long as there have been balls to juggle, ropes to walk, or any trick that fascinates, there has been variety. In recent years there has been a resurgence of variety arts; this time around it's called "new vaudeville." The impetus for its revival came from the expansion of the Renaissance festival circuit that began in the 1960s. Groups that have popularized this art form, such as Penn & Teller, The Flying Karamazov Brothers, and Avner the Eccentric, began their careers performing at Renaissance festivals.

The difference between variety and participatory theatre is that variety revolves around an act of skill. There is no story told in variety per se; the wit of the artist alone connects one feat of skill to the next. The variety performer is entirely aware of himself or herself as a performer on a stage; there is no illusion presented and no belief to suspend.

What distinguishes new vaudeville from old vaudeville is primarily its inclusion of the audience. New vaudeville artists work close to the audience and very often incorporate participation into their routines. Also most new vaudeville performers present an air of detachment, modesty, or humility concerning their act.

They often place themselves, figuratively speaking, between the audience and their stunt, as though they are mere stewards of their skill. This is their way of encouraging participation, by being "on the audience's side," if you will.

Improvisational Comedy

Improvisational comedy has grown since the days of Nichols and May to become a major feature in popular entertainment. In this performance form, a particularly witty ensemble of comics takes suggestions from the audience as variables in improvised scenes. These theatre games, or "structures," are designed to create the sort of absurdity, irony, or juxtaposition that creates laughter. The structures support the improvisers by providing a basis for comic action. The more outlandish the audience suggestions, the more comic opportunities are presented to the improvisers. Structures provide a safety-net for the genius of the improv comic, particularly when genius fails. With the proper structures and a competent ensemble, an entire evening of *almost* certain laughter can be created.

Improv comedy is participatory only insofar as the audience suggests what may happen on the stage. The professionals then take over and do the performing. Rarely are audience members brought onto the stage. There is no room for an amateur in working an improv structure, because the scene will only be as strong as its weakest link. The production of laughter is the only goal, and to that end a material participant from the audience would hold the show back.

The thrill of live improv is knowing that what you see is a spontaneous creation. Much of the gratification comes from watching the ensemble work together in a seemingly rehearsed state of harmony and support. The audience's personal connection to the show comes from watching its suggestions played out on the stage.

Street Theatre

Street theatre is a broad term used to describe any entertainment given outside the normal confines of a theatre. It is usually participatory and can contain any or all the styles of variety, improvisation, storytelling, dialogue, music, pantomime, or scripted play. It has its roots in the minstrelsy of the common player, who performed in the streets of Britain from the fourteenth to the sixteenth centuries. Today one can find street theatre at outdoor festivals, concerts, and in the streets and parks of any city. It is a catchall term and thus defies too detailed a definition.

Interactive Theatre

In interactive theatre, the stage is an *environment*—one that encloses both audience (or guest) and actor alike. Environmental theatre need not be interactive, but interactive theatre is always environmental. Each guest, singly or as part of a group, is endowed with a "role" to play. The outcome of any "scene" may change completely, depending upon the nature, actions, or response of the guest. These actions or responses, whether solicited by the actors or not, continually alter the unfolding drama. The guest is as responsible for the outcome as is the actor. This is what separates interactive from participatory theatre. It may sound chaotic, but there is still structure and order in interactive theatre.

Unlike participatory theatre, the interactive play is no longer aware of itself as a play. Interactive characters exist without any acknowledgment of themselves as characters in a fiction. The interactive production isn't even aware of the audience per se because it views it as part of its own reality. Audience members are merely fellow characters within the illusion.

It may be difficult to conceive of interactive theatre as theatre at all until one considers that all the basic elements of drama are present and at work. Subject, setting, character, plot; the unities of action, time, and place; theme, conflict, and resolution are all still-vital elements of any interactive play, although they may be presented in unfamiliar ways.

That which is *only* spontaneous is merely play. Interactive theatre rightly retains the label of art, because its aspect of the sublime is made manifest by other than accidental means. There is much premeditated action in interactive theatre. Structures are prepared and honed as with any art, but the *medium* of interactive theatre is the spontaneous, because interactive theatre is designed not to be *observed*, but to be *experienced*.

Because of its spontaneous and unpredictable nature, interactive theatre roots itself in the technique of the improviser.

However, interactive play is always led by the actor, so the general terms and content of the scene are always within the actor's control. The actor first encourages, then—through his interaction—teaches the participant to improvise with him. He then gives the participant a palette of ideas with which to play. In this way the participant cocreates the scene with the actor, but on the actor's terms, and within the general goals of the performance.

Truly, interactive theatre brings the audience member from the audience onto the stage, to play alongside the player within the temenos. Interactive theatre, then, can be defined as theatre in which the audience actively and spontaneously cocreates, with the actor, the unfolding drama.

Theatre Without a Stage 3

*I*nteractive theatre doesn't play by the same rules as theatre for the stage. An actor who wishes to learn interactive theatre technique must first come to terms with the differences between stage work and interactive theatre work.

Generally, a stage actor has every spoken word written for him; his part in the drama already has form and purpose. The interactive actor supplies the words to a well-formed outline or, in some cases, forms even the outline as he goes along, deciding what the scene is, how it develops, and how it closes. Thus the interactive actor must, to some extent, play the part of dramatist.

The stage actor knows his or her placement on the stage, when and where to move, to look, and where the audience is at all times. The interactive actor doesn't have the advantage of preplanned movement. The staging for stage work directs the audience's focus to the particular point of action they need to see, at the right time. An actor in interactive theatre has to do that on his or her own. He has to learn to adjust his movement to direct the audience's focus so they understand what is going on.

A stage actor takes for granted that the audience is in a fixed location. In interactive theatre the guest is rarely in a fixed location. This compounds the problem of directing an audience's focus. The interactive actor often has to gather and hold the audience as well as guide their focus.

The stage actor can enter or exit whenever he or she needs to punctuate the beginning or ending of a scene or broaden the scope of action. The character can storm out of a room after a lover's quarrel, then return to find his love in the arms of another person. This doesn't often happen in an interactive environment because timely exits are rarely handy.

Finally, the stage actor has a stage to stand on, a raised platform that everyone can see. This doesn't always happen in interactive theatre either. The interactive actor may at one time or another be without the advantage of a stage, lighting, scenery, special effects, sound amplification, or music. As a result, the interactive actor must learn to create and sustain the illusion and mood of the scene through his character alone.

One of my acting professors used to rail against the trappings and technical accoutrement of the modern stage. He used to say that the true art of the theatre can happen without sets, lights, or even costumes and grease paint. "All a real actor needs are the boards to stand on!" he would say. The art of interactive theatre takes that aphorism seriously. Indeed, it even takes away the boards!

I tell my students that in interactive theatre the actors "carry the stage on their backs." All the essential elements needed to make theatre happen are incorporated into their characterization and made active through improvisation. They are not dependent on any exterior support systems to aid them. Actors must create the illusion of reality with their body and with their voice. They must gather, focus, and hold their audience. The actor must create the scene, make it fun, and give it meaning, context, and resolution.

The Impact of Interactive Training on the Actor

They say of the Big Apple that if you can make it there, you'll make it anywhere. If you can make it in interactive theatre, you'll at least be *comfortable* anywhere. More than anything else, interactive experience gives an actor self-reliance. The improv experience alone will give an actor great poise in a stage crisis; if nothing else he or she can ad-lib.

A facility with ad-lib is not the only benefit of improvisational training. An actor learns to *listen*; this skill is more undeveloped than many actors would like to think, yet it is so essential to natural-sounding dialogue. An improviser learns to control the mind and free the imagination. Actors must literally learn to think in a different way. They become more aware of, and so more at ease with, their creativity. They gain the confidence to make mistakes, take risks, and dare to excel.

Often confused with improvisation technique, interactive technique teaches an actor presence. The outward energy needed for interactive acting shows the actor how to fill the stage, even when the interactive stage is quite large. It demands *believability* in the actor on an almost cellular level. When performing at arm's length to your audience, you must learn to *think* like your character and *react* like your character. Even the way you focus your eyes can affect your believability with the audience. Thus interactive actors learn to be sensitive to their audience like no other actors. The constant inclusion and adjustment involved in negotiating their way through an interactive scene requires actors to be wholly outward in their approach. Internalization in interactive theatre means to disappear completely. An interactive actor in performance is his own dramatist and director. Nowhere else will actors learn to be so *responsible* for their work, and nowhere will it be more readily apparent when they succeed or fail.

I have a file of letters from student actors who have spent a summer at my festival or a year at a theme park. They all say the same thing: "I learned more about myself as an actor and as a *person*, in a few months of interactive theatre, than I did in four years of college." This, I am certain, has more to do with the "trial by fire" of interactive performance than it does with my teaching prowess.

My favorite feedback comes from actors who tell me that they are no longer nervous at auditions, that they used to hate them but now look forward to them. I often attend regional "cattle call" auditions, and I have hired many good actors who had given dreadfully self-conscious auditions. It is gratifying to see them audition a year later after having worked in interactive theatre. They virtually shine with confidence and ease, and producers who never took a second look the year before practically line up to call them back.

Where Is My Seat?

Now let's look at interactive theatre from the audience's point of view. What is assumed on the audience's part? If I were to go to a theatre to see a conventional play, I would expect to walk into a climate-controlled auditorium and see a play from beginning to end. I would expect to sit in a comfortable seat reserved for me. All seats face the stage, where the entire action of the play will take place. The lights dim around me so that all my focus is on the stage, and all I have to do is look ahead. The set is beautifully lighted and designed to create whatever scenic image best suits the action of the play. All lighting, music, and stagecraft have been prearranged.

As a guest for an interactive show, I may not be going to a theatre at all. I will arrive at an environment and will be encouraged to treat it as real life. I observe the action as I observe action in real life: firsthand, not from a distant seat behind the fourth wall. I find my own way through the environment, viewing what I choose. The show happens *around* me, and *to* me.

As an audience member for a conventional play, all I need to do is sit back in my seat and suspend my disbelief. Interactive theatre, on the other hand, tells my subconscious that this is really happening because it responds to my presence. I have an effect upon it. My life and this theatrical life unfold at the same time, making it a here-and-now experience.

Modern audiences recognize and come to expect the more common formula of conventional entertainment; they know its structure and are secure in their expectations. Interactive theatre gives them a new and unfamiliar form that often throws them off balance and challenges them to see entertainment in a new way.

Action and Style 4

Illusion and Belief

A unity of action, time, and place must be observed throughout the interactive event. But in addition, there should not be any break in the flow of action from scene to scene, as with scene changes in a stage play. Beyond the impracticality—and danger to the audience—of blackouts and scene changes on an environmental stage, there is the matter of audience belief.

THE SUSPENSION OF DISBELIEF

The theatre phenomenon known as *the suspension of disbelief* is the mental process that allows us to enjoy a play or a movie. The creators give us credible means by which we can believe that Robin Hood is really Robin Hood, instead of an actor; that the surroundings really are Sherwood Forest, instead of a set made of wood, wire, and paint. Something in our minds says, "OK, I know this is not real, but just for fun I will allow it to be real for me." Only then can we truly be afraid that Robin Hood may lose his head to the Sheriff. However, there must be a credible and sustainable illusion in order for our minds to allow such belief.

The credibility of that illusion is much harder to achieve and maintain in interactive theatre. It is one thing to have the mind accept that "they onstage are Romans in

31

Rome" and quite another to accept that "I am a Roman in Rome." When the stage action surrounds and incorporates the audience in this visceral way, audience members get much closer to the feeling of "real life," and there are more barriers to the suspension of disbelief.

A CONTINUOUS ILLUSION

When a scene change takes place in a conventional play, the continuity of the illusion is broken. If the swoosh and thump of moving scenery is heard in the dark, audience members are reminded that they are watching a play. They must recapture their suspension of disbelief as the lights come up. A smooth scene change, however, will leave the mood undisturbed and allow them to re-suspend their disbelief easily. In interactive theatre, this is much more difficult to achieve.

Any attempt to change the scene or time frame during an interactive event breaks not only the illusion of the production but of the guest's role as well. Part of the joy of an interactive show is walking around believing you are someone else, someone in a different time and place. If you are suddenly reminded by a scene change that you are really *yourself* in the present, you feel betrayed and you are to that extent removed from the show and its characters. It is hard enough to let yourself believe you are someone else. Who wants to be reminded every twenty minutes that you're not? For this reason, all action in interactive theatre is continuously in the *here and now*.

The Unity of Audience

There is a unity rarely spoken of in conventional theatre, yet it is as essential as the unities of time, place, and action. I call it the *unity of audience*, and in interactive theatre it is a critical factor in how the action proceeds. Unity of audience ensures that the production controls what the audience sees, when they see it, and that everyone sees everything. The tricky thing about an interactive show is that there is *no* unity of audience, at least not all the time. In fact, action in interactive theatre proceeds in a variety of ways, depending on how the production is set up.

Nevertheless, action in an interactive show is still tied somehow to the notion of audience unity—who sees what and when.

The interactive genre doesn't necessarily *need* audience unity, and it is this uniqueness that lies behind the trepidations of the theatre community with regard to interactive theatre, even to their denial of it as theatre at all. Let's take a closer look at how the interactive genre adapts itself to an existence without the fundamental assumption of audience unity.

THE FLOW OF AUDIENCE

Interactive theatre is always environmental. The fact that the audience as a whole is regarded as part of the theatrical reality *makes* it environmental, regardless of how it is staged. The space is populated with characters, and audience members, who for all practical purposes are also characters. The audience may move through the space at will. Exercising that will, after all, is what it's all about. It may seem intimidating to consider all the ways an audience can flow through a theatrical space, but one doesn't need a degree in fluid dynamics to figure it out. Audiences actually boil down to a manageable set of variables.

First, an audience can be either *closed* or *open*. A closed audience is one in which everyone arrives together and leaves together, such as in conventional theatre. An open audience is one in which audience members arrive and leave at will, seeing as much or as little of the whole production as they wish. Second, the performance space itself can either be a *single* space, where the entire audience inhabits one space only, as in a ballroom, or a *multiple* space, as in the many rooms of a castle or mansion. Last, the audience's movement within the space may be *controlled* by the production or left *free-roaming*. Controlled flow means there is a unity of audience, such as in an interactive murder mystery that takes place in each room of a mansion (multiple space). The whole audience can be broken up into smaller groupings, filling all the rooms. Characters guide guests from room to room in such a way that all groups see every scene they need to see in order to understand the whole plot. Thus, most murder mysteries must have a unity of audience (controlled flow) and a closed audience, due to their dependence on plot. Free-roaming audiences make their own way, helter-skelter, through the performance space. Here there is no unity of audience, as for example in the re-creation of an Elizabethan village or a Wild West town.

Surprisingly, there are only eight practical configurations for these six variables. The most common combinations are a closed audience with a controlled flow and an open audience with a free-roaming flow, each in either a single or multiple space.

The Flow of Action

Nonlinear Plots ■ The treatment of plot in interactive theatre is also unusual. For most people, the idea of a free-roaming, open audience is the most foreign. One may wonder, "How can people come and go in the middle of a production and understand how it ends?" The question, of course, implies that there must be a conclusion. However, an interactive show, taken as a whole, need not *conclude*. After all, if the outcome may be affected by audience interaction, then it stands to reason that the outcome cannot be predicted. Without a predictable outcome, a strict sequence of scenes is no longer useful. The conventional plot goes out the window in favor of what I call a *nonlinear plot*.

This nonlinear form, which I refer to as an *interactive event*, is by far the most versatile form of interactive theatre. It is used where there is no continuity of audience from "scene" to "scene" and there is no through-line to the play. The action is geared to a series of "floating scenes," a sort of "plot soup," whereby the audience roams free through the environment experiencing them at random. These random, lifelike encounters collectively create an image of life in our created reality. It is not so much a story being told, but a reality being explored, whether it is the moral decay of the fall of Rome, the vice of the Prohibition era, the creative awakening of the Italian Renaissance, or the pioneerism of the American West. The "scenes" that populate the environment are the characters and activity engendered by the subject. The "story" being told is, as always, the frailty and virtue of the human spirit, and each guest sees a different story.

This nonlinear plot form, or interactive event, can also be put to excellent use where there *is* a continuity of audience. For those who may have doubts about this, imagine an environment in which each character pursues its given activities throughout the event, first as exposition, then as conflict and rising action, and finally as resolution and closure. Each guest pursues his or her own plot by following their chosen character(s) and situations. Even thematic statements are built into the character's activities. The activities given to the actors, how and to what extent they are rehearsed, and how they are employed, will be addressed in later chapters.

Linear Plots ■ A conventional, or *linear plot*, is a set of predetermined plot points leading to a specific outcome. It is the kind of plot we all know and love. A linear plot is used in what I call an *interactive play*. So that we don't trip over our terminology, an interactive play can be considered an interactive event, but not the reverse. Many so-called interactive murder mysteries are, in reality, interactive plays. They use the framework of a traditional play within an interactive setting. Audience members can manipulate the course of individual scenes, but the plot itself is protected either by the actors' manipulations or by planned disclosures that leave no room for doubt. Whatever happens, the plot points are always hit, and one or more predetermined outcomes are always reached.

I describe interactive plays as "interactive events clinging to conventional theatre for security." It is a sort of hybrid form that is nonetheless fascinating in its complexity. It is more often embarked upon, I think, due to a lack of awareness of other possibilities and because, at this point in the genre's growth, audiences understand it better. It is also simpler to package and rehearse.

The most challenging aspect of using a linear plot is keeping it on track without being obvious about it. The transitions from improvised interaction to scripted scene must be seamless so as not to challenge the guests' suspension of disbelief. The more carefully scripted the scene, the more difficult it is to make it a natural extension of the current action. It is better to script loosely, using scenario and character development rather than dialogue. This, however, takes good improv and good character technique—both of which will also be addressed in later chapters.

Whether tightly or loosely scripted, key actions must take place to advance the linear plot, and they must be done without breaking continuity. Despite the spontaneity of interactive theatre, key moments are often carefully rehearsed. What makes this rehearsal worthwhile is that a more heightened theatrical reality can be presented. These highly theatrical moments, such as a heated debate, a sword fight, or a daring rescue, are the stuff of the theatre and require polish.

Mixing Styles ■   In the mid-1980s I owned Creative Entertainment, Inc., a company dedicated to the performance of all forms of audience interaction. One of our most popular convention events was re-creating a Renaissance feast, using a combination of nearly every interactive form my colleagues and I could think of. We staged it in the environment of an Old English feasting hall. Each guest was endowed as a well-known and honored visitor. Servant characters exploited the demands of pleasing the persnickety king for his holiday feast. The evening was filled with interaction between the rakish servants and the king's too-well-known visitors. To provide rising action, we added a linear plot, wherein the king's favorite acting troupe met with trouble and could not attend the feast. Prompted by the queen, the servants posed as the absent troupe of players in a desperate attempt to fool the king—hoping to keep their livelihoods and their heads. Their normal foolery was heightened by the addition of their disguises and carefully rehearsed tricks designed to deceive the king.

In addition, they actually performed the entertainment, or attractions, adding dances, songs, and theatre to the evening. The theatrical offering was itself an audience participatory show in which guests had parts to play. We accounted for this by stating that there were not enough actors to perform the king's favorite play. So a participatory play took place within the context of the interactive feast. The conventional plot reached its climax when the servants were finally discovered, and the twist was that all along the king had arranged for the actors to be missing, as a holiday prank to keep his servants honest. The lesson we learned here was that you can successfully mix your styles, but only if you are deadly serious about not mixing your realities.

Interactive theatre may tell a story, but in its purest form it reveals its subject or theme through the characters who live it. Its soul lies not in its plot but in its extraordinary characters. The real interaction takes place between guest and character, not guest and story line.

Style

The style of action in interactive theatre should never be confused with what we call "living history." Living history strives to recreate life in an historical period exactly as it was lived. Places like Williamsburg, Virginia, and Plimoth Plantation, Massachusetts, stage environmental towns from early America, interactive in nature, but not theatrical. It is more an historical study than theatrical production.

If you want to see what the colonial blacksmith's life was like, for instance, you can go to the blacksmith's shop. There he will be, working his metal in as historically accurate a setting as possible. Perhaps you will hear some idle conversation in a historic dialect as he answers questions. On a daily basis, that black-smith's life is no more exciting than yours or mine—probably less so. Living history seeks only to open the door on the actual past, to show you history in a visceral way, and to let you feel what it was like to live in that time. It is fascinating in its own way, but it is not drama.

INTERACTIVE ACTION IS DRAMATIC ACTION

Interactive theatre is a *dramatic* re-creation of life in another time or place. As in any drama, the action presented is distilled from daily reality; it is "life in essence." All the extraordinary events and insights of life are pressed together into a potent and compelling package. A colleague likes to refer to it as "just the good stuff." In a dramatic re-creation, our little visit with the blacksmith may entail watching his only anvil split in two, hearing him and his wife argue about their daughter marrying an Indian chief, or see-ing the jealous town magistrate demand a hundred new horse-shoes by sundown.

INTERACTIVE ACTION IS POSITIVE

In addition to being dramatic in action, interactive theatre also presents a style that is positive in nature. This is not to say that interactive action is all hearts and flowers and happy endings. We can be as pithy in interactive theatre as in any other genre, but because interaction is the goal, a temenos must be created. For that, the environment must be positive and safe or else play can-not happen.

If we were to re-create the Elizabethan Renaissance, for instance, we would need to re-create the pageantry and pomp and the sense of exploration, discovery, and new ideas. We would also re-create the cultural diversity, poverty, and igno-rance of the time. We would not, however, re-create the cruelty and harshness of life in Elizabethan England. An *actual* re-creation of an Elizabethan town would include oppression, big-otry, public humiliation, torture, disease, and an all-pervading stench. An interactive environment with real sewage running down the side of every street or with the sight of animals being slaughtered may impress those who enjoy shocking their audi-ences, but it would do little to encourage playful interaction. Remember, play exists outside cultural bias and judgment. To inspire it, our themes must retain an air of innocence.

INTERACTIVE ACTION IS QUINTESSENTIAL ACTION

In interactive theatre we take the best of what we remember. Creators of interactive shows must carefully consider the audience's general perceptions of the era presented. The starting point of any interactive show is the audience's preconceived assumptions about the period and subject matter presented. One must ask, "What are my audience's *collective impressions* about the subject? What do they know about the period? What are the clichés they will recognize?" The creator must come to understand the quintessence of the show's subject, as the audience understands it. Only by starting there can he or she be sure that the audience will recognize and react at the level required for interaction.

We need not completely pander to the audience's preconceptions, however. It is part of our duty as dramatists to enlighten and expand awareness in our audience. It is also allowable to "stretch" their perceptions a bit, without losing them of course.

Coming to terms with the audience's collective impressions was the first task I had to tackle in developing the "Streetmosphere" show at the Disney-MGM Studios. Streetmosphere opened in 1989 and became the model for interactive productions in theme parks across the country. It was an interactive event that took place at the mouth of the park, on a re-creation of the Hollywood Boulevard and Vine Street of the 1930s and '40s. Starlets, has-beens, hopefuls, and other folk of tinseltown engaged guests in encounters from Hollywood's Golden Age. Streetmosphere was a unique expression of the interactive genre. It enjoyed a successful seven-year run, was seen by millions, and proved that interactive theatre has a mass appeal. It also inspired a thriving and lucrative interactive convention market at Disney that continues today. Sadly, a parkwide concept change in 1996 reduced Streetmosphere to the standard theme park fare. Adjustments for a crowded park finally relegated it to clowning-style line entertainment under the same name, despite the name *Streetmosphere* being later trademarked by another company.

Before its inception, I had to determine what the park's international audience's collective impressions were of the Golden Age of Hollywood. It was soon clear that the Hollywood the world remembers is the Hollywood it saw on the silver screen. To find the look, style, and rhythms of the show, I went to the films themselves and the popular tabloids and newsreels of the period. There I found all the necessary stereotypes and clichés I needed for a world audience's common perceptions of Hollywood's heyday.

However, the Hollywood the world remembers is also the Hollywood the studios *wanted* them to remember. My research showed that the studios, which at the time had complete control of their stars' careers, staged their public images as carefully as they did their films. Thus people have both a strong conception and a misconception of what Hollywood was. Part of what I enjoyed about Streetmosphere was that we, in a playful and comic way, got to tweak the audience's ideas about the *real* Hollywood.

The style of interactive theatre, then, is positive in nature. It is the best that we remember of a period or place, in order to support the creation of temenos. It is dramatic action, the distillation of life's highs and lows. It plays off the audience's collective impressions or assumptions about the subject because interaction begins with the guests' understanding of what surrounds them. Interactive style also means stretching the audience's perceptions for the sake of insight.

The 5
Performance
Environment

*I*nteractive theatre is a process-oriented form of theatre. In stage work, the process of rehearsals yields a polished end product—the play, the finite result of the process. That result is then repeated in precisely the same way thereafter. In interactive theatre, the process *is* the result, which means that the *process* is honed and polished and the results are different for each performance.

Defining this process without a result as a fixed point of reference is my great challenge in this book. To do it, I will create a model interactive show to which I can refer. In order not to be jaded by my own past work, I have selected a totally new subject.

I have long thought that a show based on the American Wild West would make a tremendous interactive event. It is certainly one that would be fun to play with here. So, together, let's go through the entire process of interactive production using a Wild West theme to give a clear picture of all the major factors required for an interactive experience.

Remember, though, that I am attempting to describe a living, creative process with a contrived model. It is imperfect at best, but at least it should provide a good context in which to understand the process. I will be describing somewhat empirically what is essentially an artistic and ephemeral venture. It is in a dimension apart from conventional stage work; to see it clearly, you must be willing to flex your perceptions of theatre just a bit.

Subject of Show

Every interactive show must have a subject, just as any play, book, or movie must have a subject. The subject is whatever is dealt with or explored by the show, such as the Golden Age of Hollywood, the English Renaissance, the wedding ritual, the solving of a mystery, or, in our case, the Wild West. The subject determines the themes to be examined, and the general setting that the audience will be transported to.

CHOOSE AN EXTRAORDINARY SUBJECT

One can explore any era, but it is wise to choose a period that is both somewhat familiar to the audience and extraordinary in some way. Choose a subject that fires the imagination: periods of history in which life seems to have been lived to the fullest, ones filled with danger, excitement, discovery, and adventure—the stuff of the theatre. This is important because the subject plays a major role in the show. Everything supports, reveals, and elucidates the subject.

THE SUBJECT SHOULD NOT DEPICT THE PRESENT

The subject should depict a setting of the past or future. The one setting that should be carefully considered before being explored is the present. It really makes no sense to "transport" someone to the present day. It is difficult if not impossible, as a guest, to play along with an alternate reality with which you are so intensely familiar. Something as familiar to you as your own life is hardly a place to start. The temenos is an escape from real life; there is no magic in being transported to where you already are. It's like saying to your child, "Let's play homework." People are far too close to the stress and mundane concerns of the present for it to be an effective backdrop for interactive theatre.

Yet, on several occasions I have attempted to depict the present in an interactive event with resoundingly bad results. Most times, guests didn't even realize that they were speaking to a character and not a real person, despite that character's comically outrageous behavior. When they did find out, they were too embarrassed to play.

I was one of three show directors who opened Streetmosphere at the Disney-MGM Studios. After a troubled opening, I alone stayed on for a revamp in its second year. Some of our early characters, mandated to us through a process I call "corporate theatre" (an oxymoron), were modern-day autograph hounds who would try to make guests feel like stars by making a big deal about them and asking for their autographs. This idea turned out to be as clever as a lamp post, because theme park guests encountered our characters outside any discernible context. Determined to make them work, we made these characters as odd and inviting as we could, but some people *still* didn't get that they were characters. We kept getting complaints about "obnoxious guests" and finally terminated the characters when one actor was nearly punched out. So, for an interactive event that the guest "discovers," I recommend extreme caution with a present-day subject.

I do confess, however, that I have produced interactive plays, such as murder mysteries, set in the present and they were successful. But they are still the exception to the rule. In interactive plays the audience *expects* to see characters, and a controlled-flow audience and linear plot make characters hard to miss. Why, then, would a present-day setting be undesirable under these conditions? For one thing, the action of a show set in the present is subject to much more scrutiny in terms of plausibility. For instance, if a character is killed by a certain type of poison, is there an antidote we don't know about? Will there be a doctor in the audience who knows that there is? Does the plot *depend* on a poison with no antidote? When the paramedics arrive, will they follow standard procedure, or will they be accused of being impostors?

Now, if I set my play in turn-of-the-century London, for example, chances are good that no one will know exactly what the characters *should* know. They will accept what is presented as true without question. In present-day settings, the action must seem *absolutely* real, and this can be a great burden in creating extraordinary action.

In addition, if the guests are asked only to play *themselves*, they are not only cheated of the fun of make-believe, but the baggage of all of their inhibitions comes along for the ride, and interaction is encumbered. An interactive play set in the present in which guests are endowed with a character is somewhat better, but *each* guest must be so endowed with a character for any significant change to take place in the audience's consciousness as a whole.

DEFINING THE SUBJECT

Let us begin the process of developing an interactive show. We will create an interactive event based on the American Wild West. But already our Wild West idea is too broad to be useful as a subject. It needs to be more keenly focused. A subject too broad will lose definition for the audience. Like a ball too large to grasp, it will prove too unwieldy to use effectively.

What are we really talking about when we say the American Wild West? A little research will tell you that the era of the American West spanned some fifty to seventy-five years. It encompassed such events as the exploration of the West, westward expansion, the Gold Rush, Indian wars, Mexican wars, railroad expansion, and immigration, among others. What criteria shall we use to narrow our idea to a workable subject? For inter*active* theatre, it is always wisest to use the most active choice.

The discovery of gold was the catalyst for the rapid expansion of the frontier. Let's focus, then, on the Gold Rush era. Now let's choose a time frame of, say, 1849–1870, a twenty-one-year span. This will give us enough historical leeway to portray much of the juiciest action without worrying too much about scholarly audience members looking for anachronisms. I have also found it best to have the company play a specific year, using the current day and month for each performance. It gives us a fixed point in history from which to dig up some anecdotes and stories that we may find useful. A year chosen toward the end of the span helps justify a character's knowledge. Just as we can readily recall specific events of the past twenty years in our own lives, so too can the characters.

Perhaps the most fascinating and dynamic activity, and arguably the most expedient choice for revealing the varied aspects of the Wild West, is the frontier town. "Boomtowns" were established near mining claims or on anticipated rail routes to take advantage of the inevitable commerce those developments would bring about. Not all claims were rich, however, and not all anticipated routes were founded, so many boomtowns quickly became ghost towns. But the almost comical velocity with which they were begun, and the fierceness of their founders' energy, determination, and independence, truly characterized the spirit of the West.

We choose now to make our subject more specific: the boom-towns of the Wild West, during the Gold Rush years of 1849–1870, with the cast referring to the event's year as 1865. This should not be seen as a limited choice but rather as a *focused* choice—one that will actually engender more ideas and activity than the broader subject of the "American Wild West." This idea of freedom through structure is endemic to nearly all of the choices we will make in developing our show and its characters. Specifics yield more than generalities.

Environment

The environment is the physical location where the interactive show takes place. It is really the first and one of the more important production choices to be made in an interactive show. The environment makes up the boundary of the temenos. Within it the guest will be invited to play and to explore through the actions and inter-actions of the characters all the themes of the subject. Before we define the environment for our Wild West subject, a few things need to be said about what is required of an interactive environment.

THE ENVIRONMENT MUST REVEAL THE SUBJECT

The environment must reveal the subject of the show in a mean-ingful way. It must be a place where the many activities indica-tive of the subject can occur, a place where all the necessary actions of the characters can reasonably be played out. Nicole used her imagination to create any space she needed in her make-believe arcade, but in the theatre we have only the stage we build. We must create physical space that anticipates as many different actions as possible.

For instance, if the subject were the film industry in the Golden Age of Hollywood of the 1930s and 1940s, as it was for my Streetmosphere show, it would be advantageous for the environ-ment to depict the corner of Hollywood Boulevard and Vine Street. This quintessential Hollywood location is recognizable to nearly everyone and is the origin of the adage that "If you stand on the corner of Hollywood and Vine long enough, everyone in the world will walk by." Not surprisingly, that is where we set the show.

This environment supported the subject of the Golden Age of Hollywood in a number of ways. Grauman's Chinese Theatre is on

Hollywood Boulevard, as are many other landmarks of the old Hollywood. Thus on Hollywood Boulevard many activities indicative of the subject can take place. Filming can be done out on the street, stars can be seen walking their dogs, talent agents can be seen swinging deals, film directors can direct and audition talent on the street, gossip columnists can intrude to get the dirt, and citizens such as cops and cabbies can ply their everyday trades in the face of their town's unique fame. It is a place where a plethora of quintessential "Hollywood" activities can easily be played out.

If the location itself limits the number of related activities, then the show itself will be narrowed. For instance, if we had chosen the inside of a sound stage for a Hollywood environment, it would severely limit the amount of activities that could be depicted. We could certainly do all of the filming activities there, but we would not see everyday citizens coping with this unusual industry and, therefore, we would lose an important reference. We could see stars and directors on a film set, but not their private and social lives. The street, on the other hand, connects everything in Hollywood. It connects the apartments, the five-and-dimes, the sound stages, clothing stores, police stations, and service garages—all aspects of what we know as Hollywood.

THE ENVIRONMENT SHOULD BE EASILY RECOGNIZABLE

The environment's physical location and ambiance must strongly, clearly, and immediately suggest the subject. It is not enough that the audience gets just "Hollywood, California" or "a 1940s street corner," but it must get both *together*.

The environment should be clearly identifiable on its own. It should reveal the period in history and even give a sense of the theme of the show—without a single character or performer present. If the environment doesn't make the statements that it needs to, the characters will find it more difficult to create and sustain any illusion. It is all of the *exposition* the actors will get, outside of their own characterization. One should never stage an interactive event banking on the hope that the audience will naturally *assume* what the environment is meant to represent. The environment must speak for itself.

THE ENVIRONMENT SHOULD BE LOGISTICALLY APPROPRIATE

Another criterion to be carefully considered is whether or not you can reasonably fit the required size of your audience into your chosen environment. Attendance and capacity considerations are unfortunate but are the realities of life in the theatre. The wonderful thing about a street is that it is a large and open space that people can flow through. Other factors, such as whether or not the space is indoors or outdoors and whether the production calls for a unity of audience, may suggest certain settings and eliminate others.

ENVIRONMENTS MAY BE INDOORS OR OUTDOORS

One of my favorite designs for an indoor interactive play used the subject of speakeasies of the 1920s. The environment was a large multibalconied room with a large bar in the center and a dance hall–style stage at one end. It was themed as a converted boiler room, which I chose in order to convey a sense of the "underworld" and to represent the simmering pressure of the Prohibition era. The environment included gambling tables, a lounge, and a haze of "cigarette smoke" that hung in the air. Guests entered at the top floor of the building through a little dress shop, where they had to give a password and be let in through a secret door. Identities were given to them on their "ticket," which contained their password. The play involved a bullying gangster and his men, a jealous gun moll, and a femme fatale dance hall girl coveted by the gangster and secretly in love with the honest bartender. Attractions included light hors d'oeuvres and bathtub gin as well as a stage show, police raid, shoot-out, and high falls from the balcony. This was a closed audience and a controlled-flow setup, but it *pulsed*. The police raid cleared the room, and another audience was let in for the next show. Notably, this design can be presented as easily in a nonlinear plot form as it can with a linear plot.

The Renaissance festivals that abound across the country are essentially interactive events that depict the English, and in some cases the Italian Renaissance and medieval feudalism. Here the environment most often used is a festival. In old England a market at a crossroad or "market cross" was erected on certain feast days and a trade fair/festival would take place. It was usually held near taverns, where people could lodge, eat, and drink. There were traveling performers to entertain, goods to purchase or trade, and all classes of society to meet. A master of revels would be chosen, and for the several days' duration of the festival, nobles, commoners, and vagabonds would converge and celebrate.

Such a festival makes a marvelous choice for an interactive event because all walks of life are present and there is good opportunity to show a cross section of society. The fact that it is a festival day when feasting and reveling are going on provides the necessary justification for food and drink and for wares to buy from artisans and vendors, and, of course, it is an outdoor event with a broad space to support a very large audience.

DEFINING OUR MODEL ENVIRONMENT

Now let's get to work and find an appropriate environment for our Wild West boomtown event. The location of our boomtown is California, where the Gold Rush first happened. Settings within this Wild West environment are happily plentiful. We could choose a saloon, an Indian encampment, a ranch, or a gold mine. All of these reveal aspects of the Gold Rush days, but they do not have a broad enough range of aspects to be useful for a show. In fact, our choice in this case is practically made for us by the subject, since boomtowns were little more than one main street. Thus, Main Street would be quite suitable as an environment.

Not surprisingly, in western motion pictures the action invariably happens on Main Street, the center of town. It connects us to virtually all the structures that make up the town. We have an environment inclusive of the full range of activities that we know as the Wild West boomtown. Even actions that may in reality take place outside of town can still take place there, to some degree.

Let us now define our environment in more detail. We have a bank, a saloon (the hallmark of the Wild West that historically had a cathouse above it, but we'll use our discretion here), a general store, perhaps a schoolhouse, a church (a nice contrast to a lawless time), a barbershop, perhaps a doctor's office, a sheriff's office, and a jail. Perhaps we might add other useful buildings: a blacksmith's forge, stables, a boardinghouse or hotel, a clothier shop, and a funeral home. Some of these shops can be functional and truly sell specific wares or demonstrate a skill. Buildings that actually supply food, drink, activities, and merchandise could be incorporated to form an interactive park.

With yet more research, we will acquire additional interesting knowledge and stories of the period. We can then include them in our environment and create a mythology of the space. When an ensemble is well versed in a mythology, guests receive an extra sense of continuity, because they may hear different characters at different times making the same references. One can give greater character to the environment through common memories or anecdotes tied to specific locations. Even the design of the set can disclose parts of a mythology, such as a sign indicating the spot where the town's first sheriff was gunned down. For now, let's give our town a name; we'll call it Vulture Gulch.

Whether producing an interactive event or an interactive play, the process of choosing an environment is much the same. An environment for an interactive play may have additional requirements specific to the actions written into the plot, but it should otherwise fulfill the same criteria.

Event

An interactive show needs a focus to the action created in the environment. A western town merely going about its business is not extraordinary enough for a theatrical experience. We need something to create a dynamic, a flow of action with higher stakes than being just another day. Just as an actor needs an objective for his actions onstage, the "action" for the town needs an objective. There must be a singular context through which the guest understands the activity—a reason, if you will, for the guest to be there, an *event*. The term *interactive event* is derived from this notion.

At Renaissance festivals, for instance, the event usually revolves around the arrival or presence of the king or queen at the festival. The whole town is infused with energy over the opportunity to see and greet royalty, which was quite rare in Renaissance times. Back then they couldn't be seen on television every week. Action in the environment relates to the event, giving a sense of continuity to the guest.

Interactive plays have a plot scenario to focus the action, but they still need an event. The audience discovers the plot only as it unfolds. There must still be an obvious context for the action that the audience is aware of from the beginning. In an interactive play, the event answers the question of why the audience is gathered. It may be a wedding, a party, a crime investigation, a reunion, or any such event.

THE EVENT MUST BE A RECOGNIZED RITUAL

The key in choosing the event, whether it be a conventional or a nonlinear plot, is that it must be a recognized *ritual*. Interactive theatre asks much more of the audience than conventional theatre. It must not leave them guessing about what to think, what to do, and how to react. The role of ritual in culture is to provide a set form or system of behavior so that the individual may know his or her place within that culture. It does no less in interactive theatre.

By providing the guest with a ritualized event—whether it be a celebration, a wedding, a trial, a funeral, an investigation, or a christening—the guest is given a lifeline to what behavior is expected of him or her. Guests know, for example, what weddings are about, they know what should happen, and they have an idea of what might be expected of them or what their place in the event might be. We make them more comfortable by taking away some of the unknowns. When guests feels more secure, they respond better to interaction, and they have an idea of how to respond. Actors must never expect more of their audience than they do of themselves. Even the best improvisers start with some idea of what they're creating.

DEFINING OUR MODEL'S EVENT

For Vulture Gulch, our choice of event will be a celebration of Founders' Day. The town has just been incorporated as a city, entitling it to all the benefits thereof. The day of our show is the day of celebration set aside for all to revel in the great news. We may even add the announcement of the town being selected to receive a railroad spur line. This good fortune usually ensured the future of a town.

As long as we are enjoying the luxury of imagining our setting, let us assume further that our show is situated on an actual railroad line and that a real, vintage locomotive is at our disposal. The main event for the Founders' Day celebration can then be the arrival of the first train on the newly completed spur line. Now our antique locomotive and railcars of the period can triumphantly arrive, providing a nifty attraction and giving the set a visual focal point (called a "weenie" by Disney Imagineers).

The selection of a celebration as an event creates a sense of playtime, which is very important for interactive theatre. Whenever a theme of celebration is used, we are much further along in encouraging our audience to take part. Celebrations are contagious, and they are rituals we all know.

Theme

The theme is the idea or underlying motif that is developed or elaborated upon in the event. There are often a number of themes at work in the same show—sometimes as many as the number of characters in the production. Themes are always tied to character, because it is the actions of characters that develop them. Each interactive character develops one theme. This theme influences the content of the character's activity.

Themes are extensions of the subject. They are the facets of human nature challenged by what the subject suggests or by what we have experienced of the subject. Through these themes, the interactive production speaks its message on the human condition.

HOW MANY THEMES?

The type and number of themes we choose depends somewhat on the style of our production. Our model is an interactive event, and as such it can contain many themes as long as we have the characters to back them up.

In the case of an interactive play, the number of themes would be fewer because of the play's singular line of action. There are only so many themes one can fit into a conventional plot before it becomes too muddy, even if several subplots are used.

In a nonlinear plot, more themes can be explored because the guest encounters them directly through character, not plot. Each character the guests meet develops one theme through his or her actions and interactions in the environment. The themes they see depend on the characters they meet.

DEFINING OUR MODEL'S THEMES

What themes may we employ in our boomtown? Again, research should provide the options. Boomtowns were motivated by greed. They were founded out on the frontier far from civilization and government, suggesting the themes of lawlessness and immorality (surely crowd pleasers). People endured great hardships, undertaking enormous tasks with insurmountable odds, intimating themes such as courage, foolishness, determination, and self-reliance. People came to these towns from all walks of life to build something better for themselves and for their children, evoking a terrific theme: hope. We may choose some or all of these for our production.

Characters

In this context, interactive characters are *personifications* of the themes. An outlaw character may explore the theme of lawlessness in the Wild West, for example, or a mail-order bride may explore the sort of naive hope that characterized many who went West for a better life. Interactive characters must always be quintessential types of the period depicted and easily recognizable by the audience. They are the progenitors of the activities that make up the sum of the world created by the subject. There are many choices that go to make up a character designed for interactive theatre, and I will address them in Part II. For now, a few things remain to be said concerning the performance environment.

CHARACTERS HELP TO DEFINE THE ENVIRONMENT

The characters give life to the environment and make it a real, a here-and-now, place. Their relationship to their environment is more than the relationship of a stage actor to the set. If a character is familiar with the space, such as the owner of the general store would be on his front porch, the actor must always make it clear to the guest that that familiarity exists. His manner, actions, attitude, and rhythms should reflect a man who owns that porch, knows that porch, and is quite at home on that porch. And he must *always* appear that way, not just some of the time. Likewise, if a character is new to town, that character's action must reveal an unfamiliarity with the space in order to clarify that character's relationship to the environment.

The character may react differently to different parts of the space, as will a righteous schoolmarm passing a saloon on Main Street. That schoolmarm must show her distaste, fear, or loathing for that place in order to complete the picture of how she relates to her world. If she does, the audience will understand that the characters are a living part of the setting around them. This means that they must make the environment, in a sense, a character. For only the characters themselves can make the environment come alive.

THE CHARACTER ALWAYS CHOOSES TO BE IN THE ENVIRONMENT

I must point out that the character always *chooses* to be in the environment. He or she is never there against his or her will or by pure happenstance. A character who doesn't want to be there has few reasons to become involved in the environment. The environment won't come running to the actor. Thus a contrary choice here will leave the actor fewer character options.

CHARACTERS HAVE AN OBJECTIVE FOR BEING IN THE ENVIRONMENT

Why is the character in the environment, and why did the character decide to come to that place? A mail-order bride may be coming to Vulture Gulch to meet her new husband. The prospector may have come because of the run on gold. Whatever the circumstances, each character needs a reason to be in the environment.

Moreover, what does the character want from the environment? The schoolmarm may need a place where she feels important. The outlaw may want a place he can control. A saloon girl may want adventure. There is always something for the character to gain by being in the environment. The place the character chooses to be is the one place in the world for him or her to achieve what is desired. Therefore, this places the maximum amount of character activity at the actor's command.

CHARACTERS SHOULD BELONG IN THE ENVIRONMENT

Characters should always be chosen so as to appear to the guest as though they belong in that environment. This may seem obvious, but I have seen shows in which a real stretch has been permitted for the sake of comedy or spectacle—which usually detracts more than it enhances. For example, what if, in our Wild West show, we had a John Wayne fan as a character? Having a movie buff running through an 1860s Western town looking for the Duke may get a big reaction. It may even be a fun, fascinating characterization, but it would actually break down the fabric of the illusion and make it difficult for the audience to indulge in suspending their disbelief.

I've found that audiences have a surprisingly powerful need for consistency and continuity in the illusion. It is not as though a guest will stop at the box office and say, "Hey, wait a minute, my belief in this illusion is being damaged by this character"; it is not something that audience members are consciously aware of. In watching them over the years, I am more and more convinced that audiences require total perfection in an illusion, and where anachronisms or tears in the fabric of that illusion are present, their belief in the show and the characters of the show will lessen.

Characters must not merely fit the period, they must *obviously* fit the period. The period must be respected. If it is chosen *for* the guest, if the production says to the guest, "We are presenting a slice of American history, from this particular period, for you," and then we show that guest a modern character who is obsessed with a movie star who was born well after the period, then we are backtracking on our promise to the guest. Guests will sense that, and their reaction to the show will reflect that lack of respect. As their belief in the show and its characters is lessened, so too is their willingness to participate with those characters.

STICK TO YOUR BARGAIN

We know that if there is an anachronism in a conventional play—whether physical, verbal, or behavioral—it may interfere with the audience's suspension of disbelief. But nowhere is this more apparent than in interactive theatre. The suspension of disbelief is one of the main motivators for interaction to take place. It precipitates the guest's willingness to be involved with the characters. So when the illusion is damaged in interactive performance, the consequences show up in the audience's lack of playfulness.

Some anachronisms in environment are unavoidable and are ultimately accepted as a convention of the production. Any anachronism from the character, however, is merely a matter of laziness and is the least forgivable by the guest. In developing an interactive show, you must decide what you are offering to the guest, define it carefully, then stick to your bargain!

As a footnote to this idea of keeping your promise, one of my pet peeves at Renaissance festivals that seek to portray old English royalty accurately is their presenting King Henry VIII and Anne Boleyn, for example, in a town full of true period citizens but then adding fairies and trolls. Now, although such fantasy characters can be wonderfully entertaining in themselves, they are denied by the greater reality of the show. There were no such things as fairies and trolls in King Henry's time! The people may have believed in fairies and trolls, but their actual presence disturbs the reality of the town. On the other hand, if the festival were presented as a fantasy faire based on, say, Old King Cole and the fairyland, where old English characters mingle with the fairy kingdom, then it could work. The point is to keep the bargain and deliver a consistent illusion.

INTERACTIVE CHARACTERS ARE INSEPARABLE
FROM THE ENVIRONMENT

Another common misconception (usually made by the marketing and promotional people) is that the characters can exist *outside* the environment. This just isn't true because the characters truly are extensions of the environment. Their entertaining activities are dependent upon being within the temenos. It is a clear case of codependency. Take away the Main Street of the Wild West and replace it with the local mall, and the cowboy isn't going to go far in entertaining interactively.

If the idea is promotion or education, whatever is extracted from the environment must stand on its own as entertainment. If I were to promote my Wild West show at the local mall, I would send out the saloon girls' dance number, stage a shoot-out, or have the prospector tell tall tales, but I would not try to represent interactive theatre without the environment. Radio and television spots in the proper context can work, but the operative word here is *context*. An interactive character needs context.

However, if you enjoy a good theatrical disaster, try it. Disney presents a yearly outdoor event for downtown Orlando, at Lake Eola in the center of the city. Once a year Disney gathers up bits and pieces of all its parks and does a sort of outdoor version of Disney World. It's a free event that's really quite nice. My first year, Disney requested that the already popular Streetmosphere characters take part. So, we dutifully marched our 1940s Hollywood environment characters out into the streets of Orlando—starlets, talent agents, cops, and cleaning ladies—despite my pleas against it.

There is nothing so bizarre as watching a 1940s starlet in a modern downtown area trying to get work from passersby, or watching people's reactions as a cop writes them a ticket for stepping on the cracks of the sidewalk. The experience is fairly useless in terms of entertainment (unless you're a director with a good sense of humor), and it can be quite frightening for the actors involved. Plenty happens, but little of it is theatre. I have seen everything from characters being befriended and/or chased by street people, to pedestrians running in fear, to characters being nearly arrested by downtown cops who just don't get it— but why should they?

Performance Elements

By now you may be wondering, Where is the show? Which part is the show? The show is the sum of the action and activities of the character, its action with the other characters, and its interaction with the guest. This action is improvised, because the inclusion of the audience adds variables that can never be predicted, which requires the flexibility and spontaneity of improvisation in order to complete any cohesive action.

In performance, there is really no such thing as improvisation, pure and absolute. A series of structures is always at work. The success of the scene usually depends on how appropriately improvisers select and manipulate these structures, which I call *performance elements*. They are created from improvisation and are fixed at some point to become a repeatable block of action. They create the context for interaction and make up the body of what is rehearsed and maintained for the production.

Performance elements vary in structure and in their level of predetermination. The following seven elements embody most of what the actor creates for, and with, the guests: character action, endowments, *lazzi, conceitti,* encounters, scenarios, and attractions. Chapter 15 outlines these elements in detail, discussing their natures and how to develop them for the interactive production.

UNSCRIPTED PERFORMANCE

When the Disney-MGM Studio opened Streetmosphere, it was a wide departure from the carefully staged and scripted entertainment they were accustomed to producing. The idea that the show would be improvised was a little difficult for some to grasp. So, it was considered prudent by some executives to *script* this improvisation. After all, improv or not, the actors had to know what to say—or so the executives thought.

Despite our best efforts to oppose it, scripts were nonetheless written because in the bizarre world of corporate theatre, an executive's comfort level is sometimes more important than a little wasted effort. Besides, my fellow show directors and I were still amazed that Disney would go for such an unusual show. We thought that if they really understood what they were getting into, the project would never happen.

So good comedy writers, who had no particular experience with improvisation or interactive theatre, were contracted to write the scripts. Now there are two possible ways to go if you *have* to script for interactive characters. Either you realize that you cannot predict the guests' responses and write mere monologues, or you *write in* the audience's response to the script. Both were attempted, but neither of them had a prayer of working. They were dutifully tried and quickly discarded.

There is nothing like watching an actor spout off lines in the middle of a crowd, waiting for a particular response that will never happen, or facing down guests to deliver a monologue to them for which there can be no possible reply. I'm glad to say that those involved eventually did come to respect the art of improvisation as a base for performance action, even if they still didn't understand it.

Even as I would not have you think that scripting is desirable, or possible, in interactive theatre, I would also not have you think that interactive performance is a bunch of costumed actors who run around and say things off the top of their heads to passersby. Nothing could be further from the truth. The actors' work is the result of a carefully executed technique.

Summary

To summarize, interactive theatre begins as a subject. That subject is given precise definition. An environment is chosen that justifies the full range of activities engendered by the subject. An event is created to give focus and dynamic to the activities presented in the environment. That event takes the form of a recognizable ritual in order to provide the guest with a familiar system of behavior. Themes are identified from the subject, and characters are chosen to develop those themes. Performance elements are developed to explore the actions of the characters within the environment and to include the guests.

Part II

Character Development

*T*he characters in a conventional play are the puppets of the dramatist. Clearly, the actor plays a central role in breathing life into the character, but the character says and does what it is told to by the dramatist. The playwright is in absolute control of the character's universe. His or her mind alone guides the action, conflict, and themes played upon the character, and in so doing the writer unmasks his view of our world.

Interactive characters take on much of the responsibility of the dramatist. The writer provides the broad strokes of subject, theme, and character occupation, while the actor's use of character guides and determines most of the dramatic action. Normally, the conventional dramatist paints a complete portrait into which the actor must infuse life. Interactive style, however, requires the writer only to define the environment and its characters. Interactive characters then act like spinning tops on a canvas, each inscribing in their own unique colors their particular pattern, prompted only by the physics of their given shape and momentum.

The process of interactive character development, then, must go beyond the mind of the playwright and create characterizations that are *in themselves* dramatic engines. The aim in this development process is, first, to create an attractive and comfortable characterization that will bridge the audience's barriers of inhibition, and, then, to provide a structure that will fuel the actor's spontaneity, lead the actor into choices of active interaction with the audience, and disclose the subject and themes given to the character to reveal—thus creating the drama.

Essential Qualities 6

We begin this process by examining the qualities necessary to achieve a character that is attractive and comfortable for the guest. At the heart of this is tricking the guest out of his or her fear and judgment in order to empower the guest to play. These essential qualities are thus drawn from the nature of play; they are the sparks that ignite a temenos around the character. Of course, they will be seen only at the end of the process, when there is a character to consider, but we do need to understand them at the outset. Consider them a sort of litmus test for characterization. Once formed, characters must uphold these essential qualities.

Extraordinary

Above all, the character must be extraordinary. The stuff of theatre is life condensed and intensified. Theatrical life is a string of extraordinary events played out by extraordinary human beings. The characters we create must be extraordinary people. The audience does not go to the theatre to see everyday life depicted. We go to the theatre to see how the human spirit reacts to the extraordinary. We can experience this in relative safety in the theatre—we do not have to risk our lives or livelihoods. We can see it played out on the stage rather than live it ourselves. Even as interactive theatre grants the audience license to play it out themselves, guests still do so within the safety of the temenos. The theatre is a sanctuary for the display of the extraordinary.

I usually begin character development workshops by exploring this idea of what is extraordinary in life. I begin with an exercise in which actors present a *real* extraordinary character, a person that they have actually seen or been acquainted with. We then examine their characters for their extraordinariness. The people I have seen depicted in this exercise would be impossible to contrive, which reinforces the idea that truth is indeed stranger than fiction. Oddly enough, a surprising number of theatre professors are depicted. Thus this is a fun way to loosen up a new group of actors and get them to feel comfortable taking risks in front of one another and going "over the top" while remaining believable.

CHARACTER ACTION IS DRAMATIC ACTION

Characters should exhibit great theatrical economy. In any dramatic action we see only the highlights of life, the key elements together, life condensed. Such is what an interactive character's life is like. It is as though in one hour of performance all of the extraordinary things that would happen in weeks, months, or years in an ordinary life are packed together. Our prospector character might in real life pan for months before striking gold, but in the course of the show this gold strike will be found, and found often. A lonely schoolmarm in the Wild West would probably search for years for a husband or to fall in love, but on any given performance day she may fall madly in love, out of love, get married, get divorced, and fall in love again—all in the span of one hour.

Another exercise I like to do with a new group of actors is to have them relate an extraordinary event from their own life or from the life of someone they know. Everyone has had an experience in which life imitates art. Even real life sometimes gets as accelerated or intensified as if it were a play or a movie, and relating life's extraordinary events is instructive.

EXTRAORDINARY CHARACTERS ARE PROPORTIONATE AND BELIEVABLE

In creating an extraordinary or larger-than-life character, it is important that character does not become caricature, but remains believable for the audience. When actors are requested to push the envelope on extraordinary characterizations, the tendency is to take specific aspects of that character and exaggerate them beyond the plausible, creating something more cartoonish than natural. This needs to be carefully guarded against in interactive characterizations. The character's believability is crucial to the audience's acceptance of the play space. A character that will be literally inches away from its audience must be extremely convincing.

Rather than exaggerated, the character needs to be magnified; extraordinary, but balanced; larger than life, but proportionately so. The final test is whether the actor can believe in the character. The actor's own psyche works very much like the audience's. If the actor can believe in the character, chances are the audience will as well. I remind actors to search their created character for that same feeling they had when they portrayed their real extraordinary character in the exercise mentioned above. If they can feel that way about their created character, then they have achieved something proportionate and believable.

Fascinating

The effect of an extraordinary character is fascination. It is the lure that draws and holds the audience. The audience's physical placement and attention are usually not guided by an external plan, other than what attracts its interest at a given moment. In order to capture and maintain interest, characters must fascinate. The most successful characters are those the audience simply cannot take its eyes off of.

Actors will often ask, "OK, fine, how do I create a fascinating character? How do I go about being fascinating?" Usually it is the most subtle and ordinary things that are the most fascinating. Fascination is often a function of how well observed a character is rather than how outrageous it is. The actor must focus on the details of the character: its movements, gestures, idiosyncrasies, and so forth. If an actor makes the details fascinating—even the smallest detail—his or her whole character will share that quality.

In the extraordinary character exercise, I will often ask, "What is it about that character that fascinated you? What are the details that are fascinating? What are physical elements that reinforce that fascination?" I ask the actors to examine the character's intensity, its focus, and its passion to find out what is fascinating about it. These tiny clues into the soul of the character are what intrigues the viewer. It may be simply an idiosyncratic look or gesture that the character does, which reveals volumes about how that character feels or its attitude toward itself or others. These subtle and ordinary elements answer questions about who that character is; yet each answer raises new questions. This mixture of discovery and mystery is what we call fascination.

PHYSICAL DETAILS CAN BE METAPHORS FOR PERSONALITY

One of the most striking things about the extraordinary character exercise is that the fascinating details are often physical metaphors for personality traits—which is surprising when one considers that these are real people being depicted, not theatrical contrivances. For example, people in denial of their own self-importance may raise their hand habitually and shrug as if to say, "Don't look at me, I'm not important." Others may flinch subtly as if being attacked.

I remember one real-life portrayal of a person who had a preoccupation with intensity and emotion. She was the actor's theatre professor. Her trademark gesture was her habit of narrowing her eyes with great intensity, pointing a finger at an actor who had reached the emotional moment she was looking for, and whispering, "Yes! Yeesss!" while nodding her head in a very intense and knowing way. She would then pound her sternum with her clenched fist, very sharply, and say, "I felt that, I felt that!" When creating an event, such behavior becomes a wonderful physical device to show a character addicted to intensity.

All actors must eventually examine their characters from this perspective. They must create the physical details that fascinate and reveal the specific choices that they have made for their characters' personalities.

FASCINATION IS IMPORTANT FOR THE ACTOR TOO

Actors must also create a character that fascinates themselves—a character that they love, and love to play. There is no room for professional Spartanism here. It is important that actors have a great deal of fun with what they create; otherwise the necessary inspiration will not be present. I discourage actors from creating a character they think they *should* create; rather I encourage one that they feel enthused about. I do this as far as I am able, within the casting constraints of the particular show.

Identifiable

Identifiability is character exposition. On the stage, character exposition usually happens before the character makes his or her first entrance. If not, the character's first scene must define who it is. An interactive character has no such luxury. It must wear its exposition on its sleeve.

Exposition is important because the audience likes to know a little bit about where it is being led. Guests are far more trusting and willing to accept when they are not in the dark about what is presented to them. Guests will usually observe a character from a distance first. It's then that they decide whether or not that character is interesting, long before its first words are spoken. So, the character must reveal as much as possible from a distance. The audience should be able to tell at a glance what the occupation of the character is and something of its nature. The more exposition given beforehand, the less has to be established at the beginning of their encounter.

Consider the first two situations: I am a guest standing in the middle of Main Street in Vulture Gulch, and I am approached by a character dressed in overalls who asks me if I would like to sell my claim. Immediately, questions pop into my head: "Who is this guy? What does he want? What does he mean by a claim? And why does he think I have it?" I would probably take a few steps back as I try to assess the situation, and it will probably take a few more minutes of explaining on the character's part before I realize that I am talking to a prospector who is interested in buying a gold mine claim that I am assumed to own.

Consider situation two: I am standing in the middle of Main Street in Vulture Gulch and look down the street to see a frumpy man in dirty leather clothes who walks with a hunch that indicates he is tired, sweaty, and sore. I have the impression that he does manual labor. His expression, manner, and movements seem to be those of a simple man of low education and a casual personality. He is muddy, looks as though he has been outdoors for quite some time, and is carrying a handpick and a prospector's pan on his belt. I conclude that he must be a common man and a prospector.

Now he approaches me and asks me about the claim. I know immediately that he is a '49er who is looking for a claim that I'm assumed to have. I have a much better picture of who he is and why he has said what he has. I also have a better idea of how I might respond to his assumption, because I have some information in advance of the question, a set of criteria from which to go on. I am not caught off guard. Moreover, the actor's job is easier because he has lessened the burden of explaining himself from square one. A good rule of thumb is that a character should be identifiable from forty yards away.

CHOOSE RHYTHMS THAT WILL MAKE THE CHARACTER STAND OUT IN A CROWD

So how does an actor go about making his or her characterization identifiable? One device is the character's rhythms. They must be noticeably different from those of the guests as they move through the environment. There is a distinct rhythm to people milling about an interactive environment. As they amble through its various features and attractions, they do so with a kind of curious, contemplative waddle. Whatever the character's rhythms are, they must never fall into that same cadence.

VISUALLY IDENTIFY THE CHARACTER'S OCCUPATION

How does one telegraph the key elements of characterization? In addition to rhythm, costuming and accessories go a long way in identifying a character's occupation. This is why I placed a hand-pick and a pan on the belt of the prospector character, because those props speak to the guests of his occupation. His costuming of dusty worn clothes also reveals that he works outdoors and is used to hard manual labor, which also supports his occupation. Color and texture in the costuming can also help make the character stand out visually.

A single notion of what the character does must be presented. If, in our folly, we decide that our prospector is also an amateur artist, we might show this by having him carry paint supplies, wear a painter's smock, and be splattered with paint. Yet this picture would be far too confusing. The guest must be able to figure out at a glance what this character does. Whatever physical details go to make the character extraordinary or fascinating must also be telegraphed to the casual observer.

Approachable

All people, no matter where they are from or how they have been brought up, learn from childhood how to defend themselves, both physically and emotionally. Learning the art of personal defense is necessary for everyone, but it is also a double-edged sword. We in interactive theatre get the bad edge of the sword because we must *disarm* the guest's personal defense mechanism, which stands in the way of interaction.

Whenever guests meet a character, they experience fear or apprehension to some degree. It may be fear of that character embarrassing them in public or requiring them to participate in a way they don't want to. They may be afraid of being asked to be creative and not being adequate, of being seen as uninteresting, dull, or a party pooper. Such fears activate the guests' personal defense. They will tend, in the absence of anything that encourages them to the contrary, to say no, back off, and they will close themselves off physically from the character. They will do all they can, initially, not to participate because of their lifelong training.

Such personal defense has never been disarmed by aggressive behavior. It has been overcome, perhaps, but never disarmed. Much interactive technique (which I elaborate in Part V) begins with disarming the guests' personal defense systems. One begins by building a character that is approachable.

Approachability is essential to a successful character because, without it, the actor will be constantly fighting the guests' reticence to play along. Every interactive character must be approachable both physically and emotionally. It must seem to say, "I am safe, I won't embarrass you," and "Don't worry, you will remain in control of the situation."

Many actors misunderstand this concept at first, and think they are being told that every characterization must be all hearts and flowers, particularly those actors tasked to portray "bad" or "ornery" characters. They are alarmed at this idea of approachability, because they can't see how a *mean* character can be approachable at the same time.

One might conclude that if one were playing the "evil" outlaw of the town, he must therefore instill fear and hatred in the audience, that if the characterization is successful, people will be afraid to approach it. If success is measured in playful interaction, however, the character scores a big zero, for certainly there wouldn't be any interaction going on. A character who is "hated" must be a character that one "loves to hate," one that is perhaps mean and ornery but not threatening. This is the kind of character whose meanness is not pointed maliciously at the guest. It is admittedly a fine line to draw sometimes, but some of the greatest fun for guests is created by the ornery characters who deserve torment.

Vulnerable

The main underpinning of approachability is vulnerability. We are really talking here about control or perceived control. The guest always wants to remain in control, or at least to feel as though he or she is. The character that has a built-in vulnerability will help to make it approachable, because that vulnerability bestows control upon the guest. Actually, the actor is always in control. By exposing a vulnerability, the actor disarms any—for lack of a better word—aggressive reaction. This places the actor in the driver's seat.

Interactive characters have no private lives. They live a totally exposed existence. Actors who are open and vulnerable must, therefore, be prepared to be rejected, because they will be taken advantage of. One of the reasons we do not show our vulnerability in real life is because people tend to take advantage of it. This can happen to a character as easily as to a human being. Part of the guest's fun will be to take advantage of or, at least, to point out the character's vulnerabilities. This is not so much maliciousness as it is a normal part of playing out life with the character.

However, for the sake of the actors' psyches, this vulnerability that they play must be carefully removed from their actor self, or else they will take the actions of the guest personally. For this reason the actor should create a strong and deliberate emotional separation from the character and then let it be vulnerable. There are devices that we will discuss in the next chapter that will help create these vulnerabilities in the form of character foibles.

Likable

Likability is yet another quality that an interactive character must possess. Although this quality is somewhat difficult to define, we will be content with the notion that likable people *like* people. Interactive characters must love people and love to be with them. They are generally outgoing and gregarious in nature. Even a "mean" character must love people, even if it is a love of abusing them.

One dimension of remaining likable as a character is not to pass judgment on the guests—on other characters perhaps, but not on the guests. Characters must behave without judgment in the way that children do. This prevents a character from presenting itself in an adversarial manner by way of its opinions or attitude. Judgment is a block that serves to prevent interaction with the guests rather than encourage it. Therefore, we must delete all judgment from interactive characterizations.

Elements of Characterization 7

*U*nlike the stage actor, the interactive actor is asked to create the scene spontaneously and at the same time both stimulate guest responses and adapt them to the scene. This requires actors to think and react as the character because spontaneous responses must be immediate and automatic. There is no time for an actor consciously to process a response "appropriate" to the character, and if the actor is not to betray his or her own personality, the character must live inside the actor as a whole and active psyche. This requires reprogramming an essential part of the actor with a new set of personality factors. Thus, developing an interactive character is the closest an actor will ever get to building a whole new personality.

I often challenge actors who are developing their characters in stage work to think beyond the reality of the play. It is interesting to see how many actors who have trained only for the stage have a hard time imagining, or reacting as, their character outside the context of the script.

While directing a production of *The Taming of the Shrew*, I once asked the actor playing Petruchio to tell me Petruchio's true feelings for Kate. He proceeded to tell me in his own words what he thought Petruchio felt toward Kate. I then asked him to let Petruchio speak for himself and tell me what *his* feelings were for Kate. The actor, in a valiant effort to humor his director, spoke as Petruchio, but as he spoke he seemed to be relating his own ideas through the physicality and characterization of Petruchio. Despite my further prompting, it was obvious that it was the actor speaking, and the characterization was a thinly veiled attempt to disguise his own actor-self.

A stage actor has only the information provided by the text from which to create. A good text, of course, will provide ample information for the specific action of the play, but if that information can be forged into a "personality engine," the actor can create his or her character beyond the text in a truthful and consistent way.

An interactive character, when built properly and developed fully, has its own ego, value systems, opinions, memories, feelings, and vulnerabilities set apart from the actor's, which truly give it a life of its own. The creative power that fuels that character is engendered, of course, by the unique, creative genius of the individual actor, but it is possible to build a characterization with "filters" for those impulses that give it its own living sentience, one removed from that of the actor. Through such filters the power of one personality can be channeled into the power of another, even artificial, one.

Consider our best model for such a character: a real person. I am a person, for instance, who at this writing is thirty-eight years old and who has a complete *character* able to think, act, and react in a particular manner, based on my personality, background, experience, thoughts, values, and desires. My personality has been in development throughout my lifetime. I, like any other real person, am a unique, interesting, and occasionally fascinating personality, but I have been working on that for thirty-eight years! Obviously, no one is willing to put that kind of time into developing a character, nor could they preplan every possible reaction a character could have to life's situations. So a valid shortcut needs to be found.

Have you ever looked closely at a mosaic? I like to step right up to the wall and look at a single tile, then include the tiles that surround it, examining the different colors and textures. Then, keeping my focus on that one spot, I step backward, slowly expanding my field of vision to see more and more colored tiles come into view. At some point, I suddenly see the image on the wall "happen"; the surface of the colored tiles acquires depth and form. Like pixels on a computer screen, or dots in an impressionist painting, colored blocks placed together in the right way create the illusion of a real scene.

We can use this digital concept when building a character. We take the tiles or *elements* of personality that make up a human being and develop them fully. The combined view of carefully chosen individual elements gives the illusion of a whole person. Here we are working with only a finite and manageable number of choices for our character, but when used consistently, they will allow us to present a whole thinking, acting, and *reacting* human being.

This will be our approach in building an interactive character because it is with such elements that actors must assemble a new personality and then use these elements as filters for their own impulse. When they believe in their character, the character will be believed by the guest. Thus, we achieve interactive characterization through a series of choices, and the process for building a character is identifying and fleshing out those choices.

It is the *type* of choices we make for a character that truly makes the difference between a character that works in interactive theatre and one that does not. The actor must draw the character toward interaction, while at the same time developing its theme. The most important thing to remember as we begin this process is the word inter*action*, because the only thing that becomes real for the audience is what is *done* by the character. Interactive characters are purely actional. Whatever needs to be revealed of the character is revealed through its immediate activity, not through mental context. The actor's mental or emotional picture of the character may have value for the actor, but not for the guests—they never see it. They at all times take the character only at face value; therefore, the character must wear all its secrets on its sleeve. This simple fact can be an enormous stumbling block for would-be interactive actors because they must relearn character development within the realm of the immediate and the evident.

Occupation

The occupation of the character is the first and most basic element that must be chosen to create an interactive persona. Most often the occupation is used to name the actor's role. In the example of our Wild West show, the "gunfighter" or the "school-marm" or the "dance hall girl" would be occupations. Simply put, an occupation is a collection of related activities.

What we refer to as the occupation in interactive theatre is not always what a person does for money. One doesn't normally get paid for gunfighting, yet we describe the character's occupation as "gunfighter" because this character engages in gunfighting more than anything else. It is the single, outstanding, active quality of that character and, therefore, its occupation.

The occupation of a gunfighter extends beyond dueling with a pistol; we also associate activities such as stealing, bullying, meanness, gambling, drinking, and womanizing with this occupation. Thus, an interactive character's occupational activities are more than a job description; they are its quintessential actions, duties, and behaviors.

Naturally, we would like to pick the most exciting and captivating occupations for our show, so choosing such occupations as banker or carpenter may not be quite as appropriate as marshal, gunfighter, or drunkard. Let me suggest some occupations for our Wild West event.

Trapper	Indian	Sheriff
Deputy	Gambler	Outlaws
Mail-order bride	Saloon owner	Bartender
Dance hall girl	Barber	Doctor
Schoolmarm	Preacher	Prospector
Immigrant	Cowboy	Rancher
Farmer	Undertaker	Rich widow
Mayor's daughter	Foreign royalty	Explorers
Scout	Gentleman gunslinger	Trail guide
Newspaper editor	Dime-novel writer	Desperadoes
Politician	Traveling actors	Merchant
Judge	Mountain man	Sheepherder

There will be some in this list that will make better interactive characters than others and some that will be passed over as we now examine what makes an occupation workable for interactive theatre.

THE OCCUPATION REQUIRES INTERACTION WITH OTHER PEOPLE

Each occupation must require interaction with other people. This is what brings the character into contact with the guest. Without this dynamic the actor can flounder in a character that is turned inward and that will become invisible to the guest. What are the occupations of the Wild West that require interaction with other people? Take a look again at the list above. Dance hall girls certainly do; barkeeps certainly do; outlaws require someone to rob and abuse; lawmen require interaction with other citizens in keeping the peace and fighting criminals; the politician, merchant, preacher, schoolmarm, doctor, barber, and traveling actors all need contact with people in order to perform their occupations. Thus, these choices pass the first test for good interactive characters.

Some of the occupations in the list fall into a middle ground in terms of their need for interaction. It is not immediately clear, for example, what the occupation of a mayor's daughter entails, until one remembers that women were quite scarce in frontier towns, especially young, eligible women. Being the mayor's daughter does heighten her importance and raises the stakes. If we were to cast the mayor's daughter as the femme fatale of the town, her interactive activity widens considerably. As a lover, object of competition, source of honesty and integrity, or abductee in need of rescue, she creates a great need for interaction. The love angle alone is an endless font of interactive activity.

Likewise, even though the trapper does his "job" in relative solitude, he still has to sell or trade his fur, which brings him into contact with people in the town. An Indian, as an occupation, not as a race, has many possibilities for interaction with the white man. While marginal, these characters can be made to work.

Which characters are not particularly needful of other people? The mountain man, sheepherder, explorer, foreign royalty, rancher, cowboy, prospector, and farmer are occupations that have far less need for other people. These, then, are poorer choices in terms of inclusive action. Does this mean that we don't have the central figures of cowboy or prospector in a Wild West show about the Gold Rush days? It's possible; it actually depends on how they hold up to some of the following requirements.

OCCUPATIONS MUST BE RECOGNIZABLE ARCHETYPES

As we have said, we work within the audience's collective impressions, what is recognizable and automatic in the audience's mind. Therefore, the most obvious and clichéd occupations are perhaps the most valuable. Interactive theatre is the one place where clichés are not to be shunned because there must be *archetypal* characters. The more recognizable they are, the more valuable they will be as interactive characters.

Let us reconsider the cowboy in this light. Historically speaking, it is a solitary occupation. Real cowboys herded cattle out on the prairie and dealt mostly with livestock, the weather, other cowboys, and not much else. However, so much myth surrounds the cowboy that his occupational activity is much broader in the mind of the audience. These include singing, falling in love, battling bad guys, coming to the rescue, and otherwise having a good deal of contact with others. We are not talking about a *real* cowboy, but the archetypal cowboy as perceived by our audience.

This is similarly true for the prospector. This character, too, is extremely recognizable and important to the subject. If strong enough ties to guest-inclusive action are made, this character can be successful as well, but it must be very carefully done.

THE OCCUPATIONAL ACTIVITY MUST BE PLAYABLE WITHIN THE ENVIRONMENT

The occupation's relationship to the environment must also be considered. Which of the occupations in the list can be performed on Main Street in view of the guest, and which ones are limited by this environment? Clearly *any* character can find *something* to do on Main Street, but we are looking for those characters who have the widest range of activity possible. The rancher and farmer seem to have fewer, weaker choices on Main Street, as do the explorer, scout, and trail guide. For this reason we may choose to exclude them.

Unfortunately our prospector character performs his mining duties in a remote part of the hills. As a director, should I forgo this occupation for an environment built on the Gold Rush? Probably not. I may instead gear the character's action to the rising and falling fortunes of the '49ers, revealed when they come into contact with the town. Sometimes we have to push things a bit to fit more activities into the environment, but not so much so that it becomes implausible for the audience. It seems there is enough engrossing activity for a prospector to make a viable character in town without having to see him at the mine. He does have to trade his gold, get supplies, tell tall tales, and make his way through the town.

Some of the other occupations have many possibilities, but only within a small part of the environment. The bartender has a great deal of activity while he is behind his bar, but as he walks down Main Street he may be hardly recognizable. The same is true for the barber or the doctor. Yet some location-specific occupations are more transportable than others. The preacher can preach anywhere and still be as recognizable to the guest as he would be in his church. Likewise, I think the undertaker is portable. Perhaps even the schoolmarm can work if she is played as regarding everyone in town as an ignorant student in need of schooling.

Although any of the occupations we have discarded may be fertile ground for fascinating characters in themselves, their playable action within the environment, their recognizability, and their options for inclusive action with the guest are still weak. I have seen many brilliant characterizations that simply go nowhere in performance because of a poor choice in occupation.

The Occupation Must Support the Subject and Its Themes

Last, and perhaps most important, the occupations chosen for the cast must support the themes to be explored within the subject. Each occupation is best concerned with one theme, and all themes devised for the production should be represented in the cast of characters. It is arguable that in our list thus far most if not all of the occupations do reveal some aspect of our subject.

A Good Example of a Bad Choice

Let me give you now a real example of a character occupation that did not work. In the initial lineup of characters for the Streetmosphere show, we took some guesses and we made some poor choices. My favorite, or rather least favorite, was the character of the street sweep. Imagine Hollywood Boulevard and Vine Street as I have described it previously, with its agents, starlets, has-beens, and other characters of Hollywood in the 1940s. Somehow, since the playing area consisted mainly of a street, the idea of a street sweep—a lower-class, strange sort of character—came about. But there was nothing in the character to support the Golden Age of Hollywood. What is it that a street sweeper reveals about Hollywood? Not much, we thought at first blush. So we decided to make him a street sweeper to the stars.

This street sweep would be one that collects garbage only from the stars: Bette Davis' cigarette butts, Charles Laughton's pipe stems, and tear-stained love letters from Gloria Swanson. Of course, a story was to be told by the street sweeper as he proudly displayed each of his items of fame. Unfortunately, despite our careful planning, we were fooled into thinking that this character might actually work.

The problem was that the custodial departments at Disney theme parks are among the finest in the world. Street sweeps abound throughout the parks and keep the streets impeccably clean. From the guest's point of view, seeing a man sweeping the streets is not immediately distinguishable from what they expect to see in the normal operations of the theme park. So our first problem was that often our street sweeper was mistaken for a theme park custodial person. He had a large push broom, a large trash can on wheels, and he was dressed in what we thought was clearly a 1940s outfit that would set him apart from the white shirt and white pants of the Disney custodial personnel. Our mistake was that from the audience's point of view everyone was dressed up. So how were they to know that the Disney street sweepers were not dressed in forties costumes as well? Not surprisingly, this gave the actor a tremendous problem in not being thought of as a character.

Our second insurmountable problem was how to make it self-evident to any passerby that this street sweep was a "street sweep to the stars." We were stumped. Short of the tacky device of slapping a sticker on him that said "Trashman to the Stars," we could think of nothing to make his character clear. So we slapped the tacky stickers all over his *trash can,* saying "Trashman to the Stars," "valuable items discarded by the stars," and so on. This was another poor assumption on our part because most guests do not read trash cans! To get an audience's attention, more is needed than that. Indeed, any interactive character that must depend on something as contrived as putting a label on that character is not identifiable enough to begin with. We really should have known better.

In addition, the choice of the street sweeper to the stars did not create any guest interaction. Nothing that the character did actively engaged the guest in here-and-now activities. If the character could manage to reveal enough so that he could gather a crowd of guests, his show was still only telling a story about a prop. The prop was the central focus of his theatrical action, and there was very little action involved other than talking. The character bits usually consisted of the guest staring at a prop, with the actor trying to convince the guest that it had actually belonged to Errol Flynn, and that there was a fascinating story about it. This was made all the more difficult because down the street was a shop where guests could buy *real* items belonging to the stars. Eventually we gave up and gave the very patient actor another character. That one worked fine.

This is a telling example of an occupation that is supported by the environment (a street) but that does not support the subject (Hollywood). In like manner, we can have the reverse: an occupation that supports the subject while not being supported by the environment. This too can create great problems. For example, a screenwriter character could support the subject of 1940s Hollywood, but it would have a limited range of activities walking around Hollywood Boulevard. The director of any interactive event must look to these relationships very carefully; otherwise, actors will find it difficult to make their roles work.

MODEL CHARACTERS

From the list of occupations on page 74, I have chosen seven to act as model characters throughout this book, and have wed them to themes we devised earlier. I have made these choices in the same way I would if I were choosing them for an actual show. I have tried to choose occupations of varying social station for balanced scene work, and I have made the cast male-heavy to reflect the times. I have also chosen some that perhaps do not fit our criteria as well as others so that we may experiment with strengthening a potentially weak occupation. The seven occupations are as follows:

Prospector (*Theme: Determination*) This occupation's best environment is not in the town and does not seem to be overly needful of interaction, but we will try to find enough strong activity to make it work.

Schoolmarm (*Theme: Foolishness*) This occupation is somewhat location specific (the schoolhouse); however, I think it may be movable.

Sheriff (*Theme: Self-reliance*) This is a good, solid occupation.

Mail-order bride (*Theme: Hope*) This offbeat choice is a young girl just off the stagecoach. I happen to know that this one is strong.

Gentleman gunslinger (*Theme: Greed*) A foil for the sheriff, his occupation is well suited to Main Street.

Dance hall girl (*Theme: Immorality*) This is a location-specific occupation, but costuming should make her readable. She's a good foil for male characters.

Outlaw (*Theme: Lawlessness*) The roughriding type, he may help raise some hell and put the "Wild" in our Wild West.

The purpose of these characters is to develop and elucidate their themes in the context of the subject. For example, the outlaw is to expose an aspect of lawlessness in a Gold Rush boomtown. Which aspect of that theme is developed depends on the choice of *passion,* which we will discuss later in this chapter. Of the themes discussed earlier, I left out courage. A good occupation to develop this theme would be a cowardly deputy sheriff, because I think it would be more interesting to view courage in the Wild West from the uncourageous side. Yet I left the deputy out for reasons of space and manageability.

This cast size of seven characters would in reality be too small for the show we have designed, but these will give us enough variety to explore the different aspects of character development.

Summary

We can now define a well-chosen occupation as one that requires interaction with others, is immediately recognizable to the average guest, can be performed within the environment, and reveals in a useful and meaningful way the subject and its themes.

Occupational Activities

We are now at the point where the actor's work begins in developing his or her character. With subject, environment, themes, and occupation defined, the writer and director hand the actor an occupational *role* for the show and an explanation of how the character's theme contributes to the overall play or event. An interactive play will include a more detailed account of the character's expected contribution to the story—up to and including a full-blown scenario of its action. An interactive event leaves more for the actor to develop in rehearsal, but it may include historical research; a description of how the subject, environment, and themes are expected to interrelate; and even a written mythology.

There is no set formula for defining an interactive production. The looser structure of the interactive event and the more rigid form of the interactive play may even be mixed. The character development process is the same for both, although interactive plays tend to utilize more "givens." A balance must always be struck between the specific requirements of the production and the creative input of the actor. A genre built on spontaneity, by its very nature, relies on the creative power of the individual actor. If this organic process is to be successful, it must be supported from the very beginning. As far as I am concerned, the actor creates the character, not the writer.

Occupational activities are the collection of related activities that make up the occupation. The actor begins by listing all of the occupational activities he or she can possibly think of. I will usually ask an actor to list no fewer than fifty; most actors can get a hundred or more in a day or two. I tell them to exhaust their store of collective impressions of that particular occupation as it relates to the subject. They are to list any and all quintessential actions, duties, or behaviors that would be typically assumed by the audience for, say, a prospector in a Gold Rush boomtown. It is also fair to ask fellow cast members, friends, family, or strangers to help them add to their list. This exercise is not something that requires vast knowledge of the period in history or of the subject. In fact, I like to do this exercise *before* any substantial historical research is done by the actor, in order to get at the kind of activities audience members might look for and recognize.

Every activity, no matter how small, is to be added to the list. The actors are not to discriminate in their choices *at all*, not even with regard to whether the activity is playable in the environment or what their own preconceptions about the character might be. The completed list should contain much more than is useful or relevant to the finished character. It is intended to provide a painter's palette from which the actors will later choose appropriate colors for their character. In this sense, creativity should always proceed from a position of choice. The abundance of the list gives the whole view of an occupation so that the actors are as informed as possible as they begin to narrow their choices.

Below is a list of occupational activities for each of our model characters. I did the exercise myself, as I described it earlier, although for our purposes I have listed only fifty or so activities each. In order to make these models as little contrived as possible, I have approached each one with a particular actor in mind. These are actors I have worked with, whose talents and personalities I am familiar with. They are people I would likely cast in these roles, so they give me a more organic source from which to create realistically.

OCCUPATIONAL ACTIVITIES OF MODEL CHARACTERS

Prospector

Panning for gold
Arguing claims
Backbreaking work
Living outdoors
Chewing/spitting tobacco
Smelling bad
Living in the wilderness
Using outdoor survival skills
Fighting off Indians and claim robbers
Befriending the ladies
Looking for new strikes
Being mauled by grizzlies
Saving his life in the wilderness
Spilling gold dust
Performing great deeds of fortitude and tenacity
Cashing in gold dust at bank
Making plans for retirement
Talking to his shovel
Naming his tools
Talking to himself
Studying the ways of "proper" folk
Socializing (poorly)
Brawling
Drinking
Being generous
Tracking people
Telling stories of his experiences
Boasting about his claim

Singing songs he made up
Doing a good luck ceremony
Dancing
Making new tools
Drawing a map to his claim
Making poems about gold
Demonstrating mining techniques
Belching
Starting a black book of ladies' names
Making claim sign
Looking for places to hide gold safely
Reciting his bear stew recipe
Searching for containers for gold dust
Foretelling the weather
Examining newest fashions he will buy
Scratching himself
Demonstrating an Indian ceremony
Picking lice out of his hair
Looking for his mule to carry his stuff
Shopping for supplies
Examining anything gold colored
Catching claim thieves
Examining ground for mining possibilities

Schoolmarm

Teaching school
Teaching manners
Being bossy
Being self-righteous
Being prudish

Working too hard
Buying school supplies
Recruiting adults to the class
Chasing kids who should be in school

Being secretly in love
Correcting people's knowledge/grammar
Always being right
Soliciting for funds to keep school open
Scolding children
Complimenting children
Treating adults like children
Being enraptured by the classics and art
Teaching social dance
Conducting a school outing
Supervising school play yard
Walking with a cane for quick reprimands
Reciting poetry
Conducting rehearsal for recital
Teaching a song

Whacking things with stick to make a point
Ringing school bell
Writing speeches for leading citizens
Fidgeting with her clothes
Walking briskly through town
Reciting Aristotle
Welcoming newcomers
Writing love letters
Quoting the Bible
Being critical
Gossiping
Putting her hair in a bun
Having a belt of whiskey
Trying to close the saloon
Being curious about the saloon girls
Helping in a crisis

Sheriff

Policing the town
Breaking up brawls
Settling disputes
Putting drunks in jail
Throwing people out of town
Arresting outlaws
Organizing a posse
Helping good citizens
Having shoot-outs with gunslingers
Defending the unfortunate
Chasing bank robbers
Being shy in front of women
Cleaning the jail
Befriending kids
Practicing with his pistol
Standing up to great odds
Being an excellent shot
Presiding over hangings
Chastising deputy for no good reason

Foiling vigilantes
Attending social functions
Attending church
Escorting ladies around town
Cleaning his guns and rifles
Scrutinizing newcomers
Selecting a deputy
Briefing criminals in town
Building a scaffold
Sending telegram to U.S. marshal
Polishing his badge
Being diplomatic to town leaders
Disbanding mobs
Perusing saloon for troublemakers
Singing to himself
Protecting ladies from troublemakers
Being in love

Telling stories of famous shoot-outs/arrests
Putting up wanted posters
Trying to learn how to social dance
Searching for an outlaw
Playing solitaire in the jail-house
Surviving ambushes
Taking walk with his sweet-heart

Befriending local Indians
Collecting weapons from troublemakers
Breaking in a new horse
Reciting laws to troublemakers
Giving advice to young boys
Jawing with the boys at the general store
Giving speeches on justice
Hiding from the schoolmarm

Mail-Order Bride

Dusting herself off
Controlling motion sickness
Looking for a place to freshen up
Looking for her husband
Carrying a suitcase
Looking for the preacher
Making wedding plans
Meeting her neighbors
Exploring the town
Looking for a place to stay
Telling about her trip from Boston
Falling in love for real
Learning about the West
Looking for work
Getting lost
Breaking down and crying
Raffling herself off to a new husband
Searching for a new husband
Beating up cowboys who tease her
Demonstrating her best abilities (singing, dancing, cooking)
Reading the town paper
Having her palm read
Shopping for prettier/more practical clothes

Reading her dime novel
Searching for a "hero"
Whistling when lonely
Sewing wedding dress or accessories
Writing in her journal
Gathering flowers (for wedding or hair)
Attending church
Sending telegram home/writing home
Mending her clothes
Looking at photographs of Boston
Attending social functions
Being homesick
Praying
Playing a part from her dime novel
Stargazing
Looking for a way home or farther West
Playing with children
Stealing food (has no money)
Begging for food/money
Learning how to seduce
Learning how to knit/sew
Pretending to care for an imaginary child
Learning to ride a horse

Searching for mail-order company manager
Learning the ways of the West (cursing, spitting, smoking,
    drinking, gambling, shooting)

Gentleman Gunslinger

Shooting people
Shooting things (for fun)
Gambling at cards
Drinking
Whoring
Smoking
Bullying and intimidating
    people
Cheating at cards
Robbing stagecoaches, trains
Picking fights
Getting arrested
Romancing the ladies
Having shoot-outs with the law
Organizing a gang
Making sure he looks good
Planning robberies
Plotting revenge
Practicing his fast draw
Trying to best the sheriff
Trying to take over the town
Making amends for past
    wrongs
Patting children on the head
Keeping up with who is in
    town
Upsetting normal life
Pulling down/altering his
    wanted posters
Doing gun tricks
Buying fancy clothes
Stalking "victims"

Riding horseback (doing
    tricks)
Watching his reflection in
    glass
Organizing jailbreaks
Getting a shave
Bragging about his accom-
    plishments
Dining well
Harnessing his horse
Buying better guns
Buying drinks in saloon for
    his gang
Sending telegram
Being possessive of saloon girl
Threatening gang members
Making demands on saloon
    owner
Kissing ladies' hands
Reading newspaper for useful
    information
Scrutinizing newcomers
Performing coin/card tricks
    (sleight of hand)
Strutting with polished cane
Blackmailing town officials
Running for public office
Reading dime novel about
    himself
Telling stories of his accom-
    plishments in a grandiose
    manner

Dance Hall Girl

Dancing with fellas
Drinking
Wearing scanty clothing
Staying inside all day

Getting slapped on the rear
Complimenting the men
Going upstairs with men
Singing

Arguing with the saloon owner

Competing with the other girls

Fighting with other girls

Sticking up for the other girls

Turning down marriage proposals

Being secretly in love with someone

Being envious of upstanding ladies

Showing contempt for "ladies"

Making a nuisance of herself

Being catty

Setting one man against another

Being concerned with her looks

Being big-hearted in a pinch

Being ambitious

Spying for hire

Playing at cards (and cheating)

Washing her clothes

Putting on perfume

Taking a hot bath

Writing a letter

Mending her clothes

Buying fashionable clothes

Breaking up bar fights

Brushing her hair

Admiring herself in mirror

Teaching other girls dance routines

Flirting with handsome men

Practicing dagger throwing

Looking for a husband (wealthy)

Attending social functions

Bragging about her conquests

Helping innocents

Admiring the sheriff

Scrutinizing newcomers

Seducing young men

Practicing seduction

Smoking cigars

Walking sexily through town

Secretly giving money to church

Writing new ballads and torch songs

Telling good jokes

Putting on makeup

Gossiping

Outlaw

Shoots and misses people with gun

Steals "fancy" things

Demonstrates "fancy" gun slinging

Shops for fancy clothes

Practices stern and fear-inducing faces

Shops for better guns

Draws his own wanted posters

Plays at cards

Cajoles people into washing his clothes

Tells stories of his robberies

Examines fashions for his proper look

Boozes

Tries out other men for his gang

Sings his own ballads

Flirts with pretty girls

Looks for hideouts

Tells of his famous gun battle with the law

Tries to impress the ladies

Rides horse (and falls)

Tries to walk with new spurs

Demonstrates ways for kids to look tough

Shops for a better horse

Creates a poetic ballad of himself

Draws map to hideout

Draws map of his travels

Hides from the law

Demonstrates disguises he sometimes uses

Buys supplies

Examines banks for his robberies

Dances with saloon girls

Practices confrontation with the sheriff

Practices his quick-draw

"Scares" people into working for him

Gets his spurs tangled

Whoops and hollers

"Threatens" people who laugh at him

Copies mannerisms of fancy-dressed men

Trips over spurs

Looks for his mom

Stages his own gunfight

Tries on hats for the right look

Robs stagecoaches

Emulates others' cunning plans poorly

Practices jumping into saddle

Stalks miners with gold bags on them

Ambushes strangers

Tells jokes and then won't let people laugh

Asks directions to his hideout

Eats only food tough guys would eat

REFINING THE OCCUPATIONAL ACTIVITIES LIST

Once the actors have completed the occupational activities list exercise, they must begin to narrow their list to usable choices. They do so based on these criteria: they must find activities that reveal *any aspect* of the theme of the character, that require interaction with others for their accomplishment, and that can actually be performed in the performance environment. Activities that do not meet these criteria are cast off, but the actors are still left with a sufficiently large subset of useful occupational activities.

Passion

The occupational activities devised for the character provide it with its audience-inclusive activity. It remains for the actor to devise how to play that activity in performance and how to develop its theme. However, this play needs some internal guidance from the character in order to make it real and believable. If actors proceed with only a menu of inclusive activities for the character, with nothing to motivate their activity, they will be led to choose action arbitrarily. They will find themselves moving from one activity to another, from one character shtick to another, guided only by their own preferences and performance instinct. If this is the case, no clear theme will be developed. It will also become apparent to the audience that the actor is leading the choices of the character. The seams of the character will show, and the audience's belief in it will suffer. Consequently, interaction will be less effective.

We cannot preplan every motive and activity of a character in performance. Things in interactive theatre happen too spontaneously for this to be even remotely feasible. The immediacy of interactive theatre and the tremendous demand for instant recognition make even a small number of general motivations for activities unfeasible. What works, and indeed all that is required, is *one* choice that connects the character to its theme and to *all* aspects of its action.

Acting is behavior, and all behavior is motivated by desire. Thus, each character must have a passionate desire that motivates the character's occupational activities. This is a crucial choice in the character's development, the very core of the character. It is the emotional motivation that impels the character forward into all its necessary activity. It gives purpose to the activity. The activity itself then reveals what it needs to about the character's theme and the subject.

This passion determines what aspect of the theme will be explored by a character—its *slant*, if you will. A dozen characters may have the same theme, but each choice of passion uncovers a view of that theme from a different angle.

THE PASSION IS A SINGULAR CHOICE

The passion must be singular, *one* passionate desire. There is no room for an actor to make a wishy-washy, I-can't-decide-which-one-I-want-to-do-so-I'll-try-both choice. Interactive theatre requires precision and identifiability in order to work. Vagueness of any kind can spell disaster for a character.

I say this because I often have a difficult time keeping actors to one choice because they feel that a single choice is limiting. Their sense is that "the more options I have as an actor, the better off I'll be." This is true enough, but it is *not* true that a singular well-chosen passion will provide fewer performance options than several uncommitted choices. In fact, it works just the opposite. Again, the idea of freedom through structure is very much at work here.

THE PASSION BRINGS FINAL HAPPINESS TO THE CHARACTER

The occupation and its activities are vehicles for the attainment of the character's passion. For indeed, the attainment of the passion is what will bring final happiness to the character. I must emphasize "happiness" here, because it would not be constructive to choose a passion that would make the character unhappy.

THE PASSION CREATES THE CHARACTER'S NEEDS

The passion creates needs. The needs are met by performing the occupational activities. The passion is the *reason* for the character's urgent and intense need to perform those activities. The fulfillment of the character's needs brings it closer to attaining its deep overriding passion. We will discuss later how these needs and occupational activities are further refined to fit the character.

THE PASSION IS AN EMOTIONAL STATE OF BEING

Character passion is a personal want, the character's deepest and most crucial desire, and not an occupational need. For instance, to be intelligent, adored, obeyed, accepted, in control, and respected are all acceptable as a passion. It is an emotional state of being and not an action. This is important to note, because the passion motivates all the occupational activities, but it must not be an activity in and of itself. Otherwise, it will lock the character into a limited set of actions.

An actor will ask, "How do I know I have a good passion chosen for this character?" Although the final test lies only in playing the character for the guest, one may start by asking, "Is it a state of *being*?" Does it answer the question, "What do you desire to *be*?" For the passion is not what action a character needs to take, but what condition must be met for that character's final happiness. I might ask, "You need to be a prospector because you desire passionately, what?" The actor answers, perhaps, "to be accepted" (i.e., as a fine and wealthy gentleman). If he had said, "to be the richest man in town," that would be an occupational goal and would tend to limit the character's actions to just acquiring wealth. "To be accepted" is an emotional state of being and engenders a much broader range of activity. Indeed, if the passion immediately calls to mind *many* occupational activities that could lead to its fulfillment, it may be a strong choice. Thus, it is useful to describe the passion as something you put after the words "to be," because that makes it impossible to describe anything other than a state of being.

Passions for our western characters might be as follows:

Prospector: To be accepted as a fine gentleman
Schoolmarm: To be revered as a great dispeller of ignorance
Sheriff: To be vindicated of his family's bad reputation
Mail-Order Bride: To be a romantic western heroine
Gentleman Gunslinger: To be respected
Dance Hall Girl: To be worthy of true love
Outlaw: To be notorious

THE CHARACTER CHOOSES ITS OCCUPATION OUT OF PASSION

The character always chooses its occupation, and the passion is the reason why. Actors must never allow their character to perform its occupation under duress or until something better comes along. This would deny motive for their actions. For instance an actress might say, "My character is a schoolmarm who really wants to be a dance hall girl." But if the character needs the occupation of a dance hall girl in order to attain her passion, then she *is* a dance hall girl, whether she is employed as one or not. Playing this kind of duality in an interactive character is too confusing for the guest. The character's occupation must always be the best possible choice that character could have made to achieve its passion.

PASSION IS A POSITIVE CHOICE

The alignment of passion must be positive, but as I have noted above, positive does not necessarily mean hearts and flowers. A passion may be based on self-centeredness or self-involvement, for example, but it cannot be based on an outward malevolence toward others. Greed and manipulation for power can be extensions of self-centeredness and self-involvement, but violence, racial discrimination, and other such negative impulses will never encourage interaction. So the passion itself may be a virtuous one, or one of folly, but never a malevolent one.

THE PASSION IS A BROAD AND OBVIOUS CHOICE

It should be apparent at this point that the choices for passion mentioned above are rather obvious ones. If I were to be an outlaw of the Wild West, the passion of being notorious may seem to be painfully uncreative. But there is nothing wrong with an obvious choice of passion. Actors often feel that each of their character choices must be such a unique and creative choice that no one has ever thought of it before. The real uniqueness and creativity lies not in the passion itself, but in how that passion is utilized and how it is justified for the character.

THE GUEST NEVER SEES THE PASSION FULFILLED

Another aspect of the passion is that the audience will never actually see it fulfilled within the scope of the performance. The character's individual needs may be fulfilled, but never its one passion. If this state of being were attained, then the behavioral motivations of the character must change and, therefore, the character must change. It would be like the crew of the S.S. *Minnow* actually getting off Gilligan's Island; the show would be pointless from then on.

A PASSION MAY MAINTAIN A DELUSION

Most characters work directly toward the attainment of their passion. But it is possible for an actor to make a choice that is not so outward and direct, and still make it work. Some characters can behave as though they have already attained their passion. A Hollywood has-been character, for example, with a passion to be popular again, may behave as if he is still a big-timer even though everything else about him screams to the contrary. Our dirty, dusty, lowbrow prospector, whose passion is to be accepted as a fine gentleman, could be played as though he believed he were a fine gentleman, with good results. Such characters live in a state of desperate denial that can be very comic. In effect, they are playing out a need to maintain their delusion.

It may seem that this method of characterization is reversed, from a creative standpoint: going from choices of activity to those of motivating passion. However, this reversal is necessary for building an interactive production. One cannot build from an actor's choice of passion to a production choice of occupation or environment easily, because unlike other forms of theatre, interactive choices must connect.

However, it is appropriate for an actor to think both ways, to try the process on from either direction to see which one generates useful, creative answers. I have known actors to start from a flash of inspiration and then fit a passion and occupational activities to it with great success. But this is the exception rather than the rule. Most often, the actor's creative inspiration and the process meet somewhere in the middle.

ORIGIN OF PASSION

Once the actor has chosen a passion, the origin of the passion must be chosen, the why or how the passion came into being for the character. At this point an actor can begin to have a little fun and feel more creative and unique. The origin is the circumstance or event that activated the passion for the character. Whether this moment occurred during childhood or adult life, it is the point of origin for the character's central purpose in life. It justifies the passion.

The passion and its origin are choices that are primarily for the actor and do not often (although they can) come out in performance. Many, in fact, are secret passions. The audience doesn't need to understand them in order to understand the character. The audience still sees the character played out in a natural and consistent manner. The passion and its origin are nonetheless crucial choices for the actor. They act as an internal guidance system to direct the reactions and behavior of the character.

At the end of this chapter is a listing of character elements for each of the model characters, along with a conceptual sketch of the character's look. Check ahead to see whether my choices for the passion and origin of our western characters have breathed a little more life into them.

Foible

The essence of what makes a comic character is a flaw or foible. Aristotle wrote in his *Poetics* that comedy is an imitation of characters of a lower type, that it consists of some defect or ugliness that is not painful or destructive. In comedy there is a benign flaw in the character that is held up to ridicule. This is what comic characters should do for us. They should hold up a particular human foible in a good-natured, humorous way for us to view for entertainment and insight.

There is something that we, as the audience, recognize or relate to in these flaws. We see them either in ourselves or in other people. Humor, in its own healing way, says, "Look, this is what we as people do wrong sometimes. We should be aware of it, and perhaps forgive it, and change for the better." In this way, each character makes its own dramatic statement to the audience. Like a message in a bottle, each character carries a particular human failing for us to examine. An interactive show filled with characters built in this way gives us the opportunity to examine the whole ludicrous and wonderful parade of human failings. The effect is a sort of feast of recognition and a comic absolution of our shortcomings as human beings.

I think each actor must make the choice of foible for him- or herself. It may flow from choices already made or from the individuals themselves. Don Knotts has made a career of playing nerveless and cowardly wimps such as Mayberry's Barney Fife on "The Andy Griffith Show." Sometimes actors are good at representing one particular flaw. Often they will gravitate to their best choice whether they are consciously aware of it or not. The psyche of the actor, in conjunction with the choices already made at this point, tends to suggest creative ideas to the actor. This should be supported in rehearsal as much as possible. It is important for the foible to be a natural, comfortable, fertile choice for the actor, because much depends on it.

THE FOIBLE WORKS AGAINST ATTAINMENT OF THE PASSION

In an interactive character, the purpose of the foible is to work against the attainment of the passion. This is how the foible fits into our character mosaic. The occupational activity is the vehicle for the character's attainment of the passion, and it is made difficult by the character's own personal flaw, or foible. This makes the character's struggle ultimately with itself and not with the world around it; again, the elements of drama are carried on the character's back. This choice provides the conflict to the drama. But, you may wonder, what makes the character interesting, what makes it real, what makes it fun? The foible does. There is a built-in polarity between the action to attain the passion and the action against it provided by the foible. Therein lies the comedy.

If you examine comic characters that seem to have a life of their own, you will see this structure in effect. Archie Bunker's passion is to sit quietly at home in his favorite chair, watch his TV, and have everything always be the same. But the foible that works against him is his prejudice. Rodney Dangerfield, as his stand-up character, "wants respect." However, everything about him comes off as low class; even his trademark gesture of tightening his tie gives you the feeling that he is uncomfortable and that he is wearing clothes that are just not right for his personality. He has a passion to be respected, but his foible is that he is really low class. If Don Quixote's passion is to be a knight-errant and to vanquish unbeatable foes, right wrongs, and defend the defenseless, then his foible is that he is so wrapped up in a fantastical view of reality that he doesn't see true evils and dangers, and therefore he can't fight them.

THE CHARACTER IS BLIND TO THE FOIBLE

Another important aspect of the foible is that the character must always be blind to it. It cannot be aware that it has this human failing. Once the character is aware of its foible, the character is no longer as interesting to the audience. Those dynamics we spoke of earlier tend to break down because the fault can't trip the character up as easily if the character is aware of it.

In addition, the audience should always know something about the character that the character does not know. This element gives the character the quality of vulnerability we spoke of earlier. It also creates a fascination with the character. Guests are one up on the character, as though they are peeking into the character's self and can see something that the character cannot. It gives them a feeling of power and control over the character and frees them from fears and inhibitions. Thus, the foible must always be a blind spot in the character's awareness.

THE FOIBLE IS ALWAYS APPARENT TO THE GUEST

In performance, the foible must always be apparent to the audience. It cannot be something that comes into play only under certain circumstances. For instance, if the outlaw were to have narcolepsy as a foible, he might suddenly fall asleep at the height of his robbery. This could be played to great effect, but it would not always be apparent. It would be noticeable only when he falls asleep. In the ever-changing flow of the audience, a given guest sees the character for the first time and must take that character at face value. So if a foible is to read to the guest, it must read all the time. This can sometimes be a difficult thing to achieve but it must be done. The actor must find a way in the character's physicality, look, and/or speech to make that foible always apparent.

Take, for instance, the foible of vanity for our dance hall girl. How can vanity be displayed so that it is always apparent? The actress must build vanity into those aspects of character that are always visible: the character's look, physicality, gestures, mannerisms, attitude, and walk. As the dance hall girl approaches guests from across the saloon, she telegraphs vanity so that the guests are sensitive to it before their encounter with her begins. Then, when her vanity comes into play, the guests are aware of its possible influence on the situation. They will want to see how the character reacts.

HOW GUESTS USE THE CHARACTER'S FOIBLE

Consider this encounter: The dance hall girl makes eye contact with two couples sitting at a table in the saloon. She smooths her gown and checks herself in the mirror behind the bar. She focuses on the men at the table and saunters over with a walk and a smirk that says, "I know I am too beautiful for words." When she arrives she regards her own appearance with a look of approval and gives a "So sorry for you, dearie" look to the women at the table, before drawing a bead on the men. The message is clear; this girl thinks she is God's gift to men. She opens the encounter with a comment to one of the men that she could tell he was admiring her new gown, and says it was a very expensive gift from the owner of the saloon, who is a very important man in town. She says she doesn't blame him for staring.

The guest's response will be in one of two directions. He might indulge her foible by saying something like, "You're the most beautiful woman I have ever seen," which may lead to her singing a song for him, inviting him to dance, or doing other things intended to "steal him away" from his girl. On the other hand, he may decide it would be fun to use her foible against her and say something like, "I love your gown, my wife has one just like it." At this point, the character's confidence may collapse, and the scene might revolve around her begging or bribing the wife to leave town before the saloon owner sees her wearing the dress and fires her because she told him it was one of a kind.

Notice in the second example that the actress took the guest's cue to play her vulnerability, and her compliance gave the table of guests the upper hand in the scene, while the true control of the scene remained with the actress. The employment of the foible brings vulnerability to the character. In the first scene the foible was indulged, and the path toward passion fulfillment—in this case "to be worthy of true love"—was open, while in the second the foible blocked that path. Both encounters are interesting, but neither would have happened as easily if the foible were not constantly apparent in the characterization. It is a way of telegraphing to the guests what kinds of things *could* happen and of giving them time to think about how they might react. Guests are rarely good at being spontaneous on their own; they need an advantage.

DEFINE THE ORIGIN OF THE FOIBLE

It is also useful for a character to design the origin of the foible. It is important for the same reasons that choosing the origin of the passion is important. It gives the actor the background and dimension needed to understand the foible fully. Check the list of character elements at the end of this chapter again and notice the foibles and their origins. If human beings are defined by their faults, then these characters should be coming more into focus.

WORLDVIEW

The actor's search for the origin of the foible can lead to the discovery of the character's worldview, its point of view on life and its place in it. In some cases this is the cause of the character's blindness to the foible. The way it sees the world blocks its awareness of its shortcomings. Knowing how that character views the world can be valuable information for the actor who plays it. For instance, for Annie Trueheart, the mail-order bride's worldview might be "anything is possible," since her parents so lovingly supported her every fancy, while this makes her unaware of her naïveté and gullibility.

SOCIAL STATION AND THE FOIBLE

Each character's occupation carries with it an implied social station. The schoolmarm has a higher social station than the dance hall girl; the sheriff has a higher social station than the prospector. This social station gives them a social dominance, which remains the same for every scene they perform. It is a reflection of their position in society and determines the level of respect they are accorded by other characters.

The foible provides a personal dominance that overrides the implied social dominance. It is a function of personality and will change with the changing circumstances of the scene. However, since the foible is always apparent to the guest, it will give the character a dominance tendency, wherein that character will always *tend* to begin at a certain level of personal dominance. There are high-dominance foibles, such as pride or snobbery, and low-dominance foibles, such as naïveté, clumsiness, and nervousness. A sheriff whose foible is abject cowardice may not inspire a dominant position in an encounter, despite his higher social station. Our choice of a proud Katie Fondler (dance hall girl) would come off more nondominant if we were to choose shyness as her foible. Notice that our choice for Sheriff Weston to be shy with women causes him to tend to be nondominant only with women.

A character will tend to start out in encounters with either a high or low personal dominance, depending on the choice of his or her foible. This personal dominance may contrast with the character's social dominance. The fun of character dominance is watching it change. One of two things can take place. A character with a high-dominance foible can take an embarrassing tumble in social status, or the character with a low-dominance foible can accidentally stumble to victory. These personal dominance transactions happen against the backdrop of a fixed social dominance.

With the choices we have made thus far, we now have the basic structure of an interactive character. The occupation and its activities place the character in a dimension of inclusive activity, the motivating passion propels the character forward, and the foible creates the fun and comic twists along the way.

Virtue

At this point, our characters have been built on Aristotle's premise that comedy is essentially the ridicule of human folly; thus far, the foible provides this comic dimension. In my work over the years, the closure for any given encounter has been in some way a comeuppance for a character's fault. However, during the long run of Streetmosphere, my cast and I made an interesting discovery. We began to realize that not all of the encounters were closed due to a retribution of some sort. Every once in a while some redeeming quality of a character would bubble forth and settle the conflict, not with a comic examination of human frailty, but with a display of virtue. These encounters would end, not with a giant guffaw, but with a more endearing ". . . aawww isn't that sweet" quality.

What we had discovered was that each character possessed virtues, whether or not the actor had consciously chosen them. To us it was as though the element of virtue were an undiscovered planet, circling out in the dark of the character's solar system, its influences having always been at work but only recently discovered. I have always found it fascinating how an interactive characterization inevitably takes on a life of its own, particularly when it develops its own virtue without the conscious intervention of the actor. It seems only fair, then, that if we are going to imbue the character with foibles, we must give it virtues as well.

The Virtue Redeems the Fault of the Foible

If the foible, unseen, trips up the character from its pursuit of its passion, then we must define the virtue as that which redeems the fault of the foible and places the character back on the path to passion attainment. The foible gets you into trouble; the virtue gets you out. All character scene work uses either virtue or folly in the struggle for passion attainment.

Our definitions of foible and virtue are relative to the character's passion, and are not societal mores. For instance, if a character's passion were to be a deceiver, then honesty would be a foible, not a virtue. Keep this in mind when choosing foibles and virtues, and don't confuse them with what the audience sees as moral or just behavior.

If an actor cannot find a virtue that fits the character during the development process, I suggest he or she play the character a while longer to see if one surfaces on its own. Look again to the list of virtues for our model characters at the end of this chapter.

Primary Needs

The character's primary needs are those that most directly serve the attainment of the passion. Like the passion, they are urgent and intense needs—high-stakes needs. The primary needs of the character should be few—only two or three—and should indicate the types of activities the character will be engaged in most often. The character spends most of its time trying to fulfill these few primary needs and achieves them in performance through its occupational activities and the immediate involvement of the guest.

The passion is the core desire that connects and motivates all the character's primary needs. It is its parent desire, so to speak. The actor's choice of passion is usually invisible to the guests, but the character's needs must be *very* obvious to the guest. They are the more immediate motivations of the character's occupational activity.

Eustus Panfreed, our poor and simple prospector, has a passion "to be accepted as a fine gentleman." What does a person in his position *need* in order to accomplish this? First, he'll need money. This need connects him with all activities related to the acquiring of gold. Second, he needs to learn manners and gentlemanly ways. This connects him with others he feels are his betters, gives him a vulnerability, and provides a comic contrast. I can picture this dusty old prospector trying his best to look dapper and polite to the upscale folk of the town. Third, he would need to make friends in society. I have listed this element as "sharing what he has and what he knows." I think this gives him a better quality of generosity and humility, as opposed to being a social climber. I don't believe Eustus would be clever enough for that.

What makes a good choice of primary need? If it immediately calls to mind many occupational activities that could lead to its fulfillment, if it is a need that requires interaction with people for its fulfillment, if its employment can be used to reveal the character's foible, and if it excites and inspires the actor, it is a very good choice for a primary need. When in a quandary about what needs to choose, I refer actors to their occupational activities list. Therein lie the activities whose fulfillment will be required by their yet undiscovered needs.

Each primary need should suggest a number of occupational activities. The generous Eustus Panfreed has a primary need of sharing what he has and what he knows. This primary need is culled from several occupational activities: boasting, telling stories, giving advice, and befriending the ladies. Some of gunslinger Ben Creel's occupational activities involve cheating, plotting against the sheriff, and ingratiating himself with the townspeople, but they all boil down to a more general primary need of plotting for control.

The guest does not fulfill the character's passion directly. Rather, guests fulfill the character's needs by their interaction with the character and thus fulfill its passion indirectly. For example, if guests successfully recite their catechism at the schoolmarm's prompting, they fulfill her need of seeing the results of her teaching. They do not bring her to a state of being revered as a great dispeller of ignorance, but they do fill an immediate need that leads in that direction.

Admittedly, when we talk about *activities* and *needs* we are using a bit of semantics. An activity is an action, but a character's desire for its accomplishment is a need. Primary needs for all the model characters are listed in the character elements lists at the end of this chapter.

Primary Activities

Once the primary needs are chosen, the actor should work through his or her refined occupational activities list and narrow the list further to primary activities. It should now be apparent which of those activities best develop the character's particular slant on its theme, answer the primary needs, and provide the most expansive range of action. Certain activities will seem to float to the surface and make the actor feel as though he or she will have far more opportunities with them. These best activities become the character's primary activities. This is the final edition of the character's menu of occupational activity. Usually eight to ten primary activities—several for each primary need—is a sufficient number for an actor to focus upon.

An actor should never make the choice that his or her character does not *want* to do the activity, or else he or she will naturally tend not to do it—which reveals nothing—or be forced to do actions that are designed to prevent him or her from doing it. This creates a kind of action once removed, and it is very hard for an audience to follow. The character should never set itself up *not* to do its occupation. The character not only should passionately want to do its occupational activities, but also should enjoy them. This is a positive choice, and positive choices are attractive to the audience. All of the character's actions should be affirmative ones.

To illustrate, if I were to play a gambler in Vulture Gulch, it would be a weak and limiting choice to despise gambling. Certainly gambling is a terrible vice, and a person afflicted with it *should* struggle not to gamble. But placing the desire not to gamble in a gambler character would block the audience's view of the absorption in, and consequence of, the vice. The character would always be preoccupied with an *internal* struggle and searching for ways not to gamble. That would not read to an interactive audience. If I play a gambler, I must love gambling. I must gamble at every opportunity and immerse myself in every aspect of gambling. Only in this way can I reveal actively and in great detail all the nuances of the Wild West gambler.

Often a primary activity will be a generalization for a number of similar occupational activities. For example, the schoolmarm's list includes teaching school, teaching manners, teaching dances, and teaching songs. These might be combined to create a primary activity of "teaching anyone anything." In this way, the list is boiled down to the broadest, most playable action.

Primary activities should relate better to the character's foibles and virtues, in terms of revealing those elements to the audience, and should allow for playable action. They should also be the most fun for the actor to play, and easier to play in the environment as well.

The primary activities list should give one a comprehensive view of the type of performance that will be seen from that character and what it will contribute thematically to the whole production. This is not to say that the actor discards the other workable activities on his or her refined list. Often actors who have worked their primary activities for a long run will go back through their original list and find fresh, untried ideas. Check the character elements lists that follow and notice how the primary activities are generalized versions of the more playable occupational activities.

At this point the actor should have a well-motivated set of activities that will bring him or her into close interaction with the guest and will reveal the themes and subject of the production—all of which will be accomplished through character action, not conventional plot. Thus a scene created through spontaneity behaves as though it were deliberately designed to enhance the production. Here we have completed the conceptual design of the interactive character. It is now time to actualize these elements.

CHARACTER ELEMENTS LIST

ROLE: Prospector   **ACTOR'S NAME:** Pat

OCCUPATION: Prospector

CHARACTER'S NAME: Eustus Panfreed

THEME: Determination

PASSION: To be accepted as a fine gentleman

ORIGIN OF PASSION: He was born in the Sangre de Cristo mountains. His parents were backward and ignorant. As a child, he was fascinated by all the "perdy and fine" people he saw in the city. His parents told him he would never be like them, that he was poor, and that there was no getting around it. Years later, all three were badly mauled by a grizzly bear in the mountains. His "Maw and Paw" died, but somehow he survived. He figured that this was proof he was worth something after all and that all he lacked was money.

FOIBLE: He doesn't see his own worth. He believes that gold will so change his life that he will become the person he believes he ought to be. Gold will make him rich, respected, desired, intelligent, accepted, and loved.

ORIGIN OF FOIBLE: The fine people he so wants to be like are all rich. He figures that gold mining is his ticket to wealth.

VIRTUE: Polite, generous

PRIMARY NEEDS: (In order of importance to the character)
1. Learning gentlemanly ways
2. Sharing what he has and what he knows
3. A new, rich strike

PRIMARY ACTIVITIES: (The activities that address needs and are key to passion fulfillment)
1. Boasting about his claim, showing his gold dust
2. Attempting to be fine
3. Befriending the ladies
4. Telling tales
5. Observing the actions of finer people and emulating them
6. Giving good advice (from a mountain man's point of view)
7. Learning and misusing new words and manners
8. Spontaneously experiencing recurrences of old injuries
9. Searching for news of a new strike (his claim is not panning out)
10. Forgetting things

CHARACTER ELEMENTS LIST

ROLE: Schoolmarm   **ACTOR'S NAME:** Karel

OCCUPATION: Schoolmarm

CHARACTER'S NAME: Oratia Buggle

THEME: Foolishness

PASSION: To be revered as a great dispeller of ignorance

ORIGIN OF PASSION: She is a lonely librarian from a small New England town. While she was working late in the library one night, a shelf of books collapsed and struck her unconscious. She believed she had a vision; in it she was bathed in the fountain of knowledge and given the task of bringing knowledge to the world. When she awoke, she found herself sprawled on the floor with her face pressed against a periodical on the expansion westward, and she took it as a sign that she should teach. New towns in the West had a desperate need for teachers and were not picky about credentials. Having no formal schooling as a teacher, she figured the West was the best (only) means to accomplish her divine task.

FOIBLE: Narrow-minded, old-fashioned, prudish, pedantic— overly enthusiastic

ORIGIN OF FOIBLE: She was raised by her maiden aunt whom she emulates and admires.

VIRTUE: Diligent

PRIMARY NEEDS: (In order of importance to the character)
1. To know everything, and tell everyone
2. To inspire others to seek the fruits of knowledge
3. To instill discipline

PRIMARY ACTIVITIES: (The activities that address needs and are key to passion fulfillment)
1. Correcting people
2. Being enraptured by literature and art
3. Soliciting funds for the school and school events
4. Being truant officer to kids and adults
5. Teaching anything to anyone
6. Treating adults like children
7. Being secretly in love
8. Being a prude
9. Giving lectures
10. Consulting her muse

CHARACTER ELEMENTS LIST

ROLE: Sheriff   **ACTOR'S NAME:** Rob

OCCUPATION: Sheriff

CHARACTER'S NAME: Sheriff Weston

THEME: Self-reliance

PASSION: To be vindicated of his family's bad reputation.

ORIGIN OF PASSION: He grew up on the prairie with his parents and five brothers. His father was killed by outlaws, and his other brothers left to seek vengeance and ended up as notorious outlaws themselves. He was left to care for their mother, who died of shame.

FOIBLE: Nervous and shy of women, overly polite, and blinded by his chivalry

ORIGIN OF FOIBLE: He grew up with five brothers and no sisters on the prairie. The only woman he had seen before the age of twelve was his mother. She taught him only grand, chivalric notions of how to treat a lady.

VIRTUE: Loyal

PRIMARY NEEDS: (In order of importance to the character)
1. To see justice and honor served
2. To defend the wronged and the unfortunate
3. To be fearless

PRIMARY ACTIVITIES: (The activities that address needs and are key to passion fulfillment)
1. Policing the town
2. Settling disputes
3. Arresting drunks and outlaws
4. Defending the unfortunate and the wronged
5. Being shy in front of women
6. Being polite and chivalrous
7. Standing up to great odds
8. Staying clean
9. Organizing a posse and chasing criminals
10. Helping good citizens

CHARACTER ELEMENTS LIST

ROLE: Mail-order bride   **ACTOR'S NAME:** Molly

OCCUPATION: Mail-order bride

CHARACTER'S NAME: Annie Trueheart

THEME: Hope

PASSION: To be a romantic western heroine

ORIGIN OF PASSION: She was raised in Boston by rich and overly protective parents. Her life in Boston was very dull, and her upbringing gave her too much time to read dime novels about the West and dream girlish dreams. When she read an ad in the newspaper promising able-bodied women a life of adventure and romance through a mail-order bride company, she signed up and ran away to meet her destiny.

FOIBLE: She clings to her unrealistic belief in the romantic myth of the West. She is naive, gullible, impressionable, and prone to infatuations.

ORIGIN OF FOIBLE: She has an overly encouraged imagination, the result of her parents indulging her every whim and fancy.

VIRTUE: Kindness

PRIMARY NEEDS: (In order of importance to the character)
1. To experience the romance and adventure of the West
2. To find her husband
3. To find her way around town

PRIMARY ACTIVITIES: (The activities that address needs and are key to passion fulfillment)
1. Searching for her husband
2. Learning the ways of the West
3. Looking for work
4. Looking for lodging
5. Getting lost
6. Meeting her neighbors (the townsfolk)
7. Looking for a place to freshen up, freshening up
8. Looking for a preacher, planning the wedding
9. Falling in love for real
10. Indulging in new experiences

CHARACTER ELEMENTS LIST

ROLE: Gentleman gunslinger   **ACTOR'S NAME:** Michael

OCCUPATION: Gunslinger

CHARACTER'S NAME: Benjamin Creel

THEME: Greed

PASSION: To be respected

ORIGIN OF PASSION: He never had parents, at least none that he knew, and he never had anything of his own. Feeling unwanted, he was always mean-spirited and violent. He spent his youth bouncing from one orphanage to another, always rebelling against the strict control they invariably exerted upon him. He finally fled to the West, where no one could tell him what to do, and quickly began a life of crime.

FOIBLE: Selfish and self-involved

ORIGIN OF FOIBLE: He realized that the only way to get what he wants is to look out for himself. No one cared for him, so he cares only for himself.

VIRTUE: None discernible

PRIMARY NEEDS: (In order of importance to the character)
1. To plot for control of the town
2. To manipulate others
3. To acquire money and power

PRIMARY ACTIVITIES: (The activities that address needs and are key to passion fulfillment)
1. Plotting against the sheriff
2. Ingratiating himself with the townspeople
3. Plotting and executing crimes and holdups
4. Keeping his gang together, looking for good (bad) men to join
5. Indulging himself in every way
6. Taking advantage of others' misfortune
7. Gambling for anything
8. Romancing the ladies
9. Cheating at anything
10. Looking dapper

CHARACTER ELEMENTS LIST

ROLE: Dance hall girl   **ACTOR'S NAME:** Maria

OCCUPATION: Dance hall girl

CHARACTER'S NAME: Katie Fondler

THEME: Immorality

PASSION: To be worthy of true love

ORIGIN OF PASSION: She never attained the love of her father, whose standards were impossibly high. She finally rebelled against him by becoming a dance hall girl. The love of her life was a married man, but she lost in the battle for his love.

FOIBLE: Vain, selfish, and proud

ORIGIN OF FOIBLE: The only worthwhile things she has gotten in life were due to her good looks.

VIRTUE: Good sense of humor, sympathetic

PRIMARY NEEDS: (In order of importance to the character)
1. To look her best
2. To defeat the competition
3. To find a man whose heart she cannot break

PRIMARY ACTIVITIES: (The activities that address needs and are key to passion fulfillment)
1. Flirting with married men
2. Building men up, then turning them down
3. Dancing/dancing with men
4. Singing to men
5. Primping
6. Giving girls bad advice on what men like
7. Setting suitors against each other
8. Being occasionally bighearted
9. Getting what she wants
10. Acquiring wealth and security

CHARACTER ELEMENTS LIST

ROLE: Outlaw   **ACTOR'S NAME:** David

OCCUPATION: Outlaw

CHARACTER'S NAME: Ned Beazzle, aka "Notorious Ned"

THEME: Lawlessness

PASSION: To be notorious

ORIGIN OF PASSION: He was born with a low IQ, "just a touch slow." His ill-bred family told him he was a stupid, no-account nobody all his life. He was mistreated, overworked, and laughed at for his disadvantages, particularly by his "Paw." He stole his father's pistol and ran off to prove the world wrong. He hates being laughed at and refuses to perform menial tasks even for himself; he will get others to do them for him with his pistol.

FOIBLE: Dim-witted, dense, and gullible

ORIGIN OF FOIBLE: He has no education and knew nothing but negative reinforcement as a child. Abuse has given him an "attitude." The phrase "If he were smart he'd be dangerous" applies.

VIRTUE: Sympathetic toward children

PRIMARY NEEDS: (In order of importance to the character)
1. Acquire a notorious gang
2. Build his reputation
3. Behave as badly as he can

PRIMARY ACTIVITIES: (The activities that address needs and are key to passion fulfillment)
1. Practices fear-inducing faces and looking tough
2. Steals fancy-looking things
3. Looks for new hideouts
4. Coerces people into joining his gang
5. Makes up and sings his own ballads about himself
6. Threatens people who laugh at him
7. Tells tall tales about his exploits
8. Plans "cunning" robberies that don't work
9. Tries to impress the ladies
10. Practices his fast draw and "fancy" gunslinging

Semblance 8

A character's semblance is the sum of the character's physicality, vocal quality, use of language, and appearance. The process of creating the character's semblance is one of personifying the character elements of occupation, passion, foible, virtue, and needs, with an eye toward providing the essential qualities of interactive characterization: that the character be extraordinary, fascinating, identifiable, approachable, vulnerable, and likable.

Physicality

The process of giving the character physicality is the search for the physical details that inform and convince the audience of who the character is. These physical details include the way a character stands, walks, and moves—its rhythms, mannerisms, and idiosyncratic gestures. All of these details combine to make the character physically evident. The actor must show, physically, the occupation and foible of the character. The aim is to personify these elements, to give the guest a sense of what the character *does* (occupation) and the uniqueness of its personality (foible).

117

The physicality of the character should make it stand out in a crowd of guests. It is the quality of being a person you cannot take your eyes off, by revealing the essential qualities we spoke of earlier. Developing these details involves active, creative exploration; they can't be designed sitting down with pen and paper. They must be experienced by the actor, who needs to be on his or her feet experimenting and exploring. This phase is a visceral journey rather than the cerebral one we have been involved with so far.

A character, like a suit of clothes, is first conceived, designed, cut, and sewn. Once the garment is ready, it must be tried on so that the wearer can feel what it is like, and adjust the fit so that it is comfortable and right. This sensory exploration of character should be conducted by the actor without mental constraint. Actors should allow their character choices to run in the background and not consciously select or limit their choices of physicality. Here the actor needs to be encouraged to play and explore. It is the natural result of ensemble improvisation, which we will explore in Part III.

I remind actors that there are no accidents in their characterizations, that they are in complete control of what is revealed to the guest. They must use fully every element to support their creation. Sometimes actors get off track by their own choices that lead them to a dead end. Yet they are reluctant to backtrack because they are afraid of invalidating their past effort. The path of creativity is strewn with discarded notions; it is all part of the process. It amazes me how a person's own thought process can lead away from the intended goal. When an actor is afraid to discard a choice that really doesn't work, I tell him or her, "If thy choice offendeth thee, throw it away." Who cares? You can always pick it up again later if you change your mind.

Many see giving physicality to a character as simply adding physical traits that suit the character. But this treats physicality like putting ornaments on a Christmas tree. It does not complete the task. Actors must completely transform their physicality into a whole new one in order to convince the audience, as well as themselves, that the resulting character is a real person. Actors must eliminate the mannerisms that reveal themselves and replace them with those of the character. In order to do this actors must first determine what their physical mannerisms are. (For a fuller discussion of this, please see Physicality Parade in *Acting Interactive Theatre*.)

When actors eliminate all their own personal mannerisms from the characterization, they no longer feel like themselves. This helps free the actor from the self-conscious anxiety that comes from spontaneity. The words now sound right, because it is no longer your voice. Your movements feel right, because it is no longer your body. Once the creative impulse is channeled through another personality, the actor becomes more *observer* than *owner*.

Characters, as we have said, must be slightly larger than life. Part of this largeness is a character's field of influence, or presence. A character's field of influence is made up of its energy, both vocal and physical, and something less definable than that—a kind of awareness or *resonance* that goes beyond normal personal space. Interactive characters must possess this aura and must extend it beyond the proximity of the guest to fill the whole performance space.

This requires more than a physical change. It is a mental change, even an emotional and spiritual change. If actors can master it, they can imbue their character with a powerful and unmistakable charisma, which is an invaluable tool for interactive performance. (See Magnify Presence in *Acting Interactive Theatre*.)

One must build a physicality that can be sustained throughout the given performance time. Having a truly outrageous and fascinating physicality is a wonderful asset, but not if it throws your back out, blows your voice, or alters your body in a harmful way. It is sometimes difficult to tell whether a certain physicality will cause you problems until you play the character for a while, but there are some commonsense measures you can take. I have seen physicality that looked wonderful with an off-balance stoop or a swayed back, which fit marvelously into the characterization but prevented the actor from getting out of bed the next morning. I don't advocate making small choices, however. I have also seen surprisingly unusual physical distortions that could be played for a long period of time without negative physical effects.

The actor who played the chief of police in the Streetmosphere show walked in a stumble that was created by his actually walking on the sides of his feet, then pounding his feet flat as he walked. It created a stagger that looked great, but it appeared as though he would break his ankles any minute. Yet he did this daily for three years and never had a problem with it. However, this same character also had a protruded lower lip that was achieved by curling his lower lip under, in a pout. Again, this was a wonderfully effective character physicality. But over time the actor sensed changes in his chin and lower lip that led him to believe he was changing how he held his normal face, because those muscles were being used so differently. "Chiefy" eventually had to find another pout.

I use a series of exercises to begin this physicalization process, and I do them as a continuous string that can last over an hour and a half. This workshop has never failed to give actors a true feel for their characters' physicality, vocal quality, and other areas that need rethinking. (See Body Centers, Mill and Seethe Greeting, Mill and Seethe Gifts, Voice from Body, Mill and Seethe Emotions, and Mill and Seethe Tasks in *Acting Interactive Theatre*.)

Vocal Quality

Vocal quality is the way the character's voice sounds—its tonal quality, cadence, and dialect. The sound of the character's speaking voice is a very effective conveyor of personality. The vocal quality should be a natural extension of the character's physicality, which provides a much more open and natural sound. I suggest starting with the vocal quality that the physicality suggests and working with it from there, adding any inflection or style that further clarifies the character.

Many actors spend relatively little time working on their vocal quality. I caution them to temper their choices with good judgment and to create a voice that is sustainable for whatever performance demands may be made on them. Character voices in particular are apt to cause vocal problems when overused or used improperly. Whatever the vocal quality, it must be produced in an open and relaxed throat, and it must provide the actor with the power to project over a large performance space.

A common pitfall is to attempt an outrageous voice to enhance the character's extraordinariness. But often you end up with a unique voice that wreaks havoc on the throat and is difficult for the guest to understand. Subtle but purposeful choices tend to work much better. They make the character seem more believable and less cartoonish. At the same time, they may have a unique tone, inflection, or cadence that *does* make the character seem extraordinary.

Approach to Language

How characters use the spoken language has a profound effect on how they are perceived by the guest. Any necessary regionalisms or dialects need to be worked out by a qualified coach, and instruction should be provided so that the whole company executes the dialect consistently and accurately. Some shows represent a cross section of a particular society. For these I usually offer three basic dialects: an upper class, middle class, and lower class.

Apart from its dialect, each character should have its own distinct way of using the language. There are many ways a character can be revealed through its approach to language. Even its grasp of language can be revealing. The character's vocabulary and grammar also reveals quite a lot. Whether it is apt to speak metaphorically or anecdotally is significant. The way the character curses, evades certain parts of speech, misuses parts of speech, and uses slang, together with the speed with which it speaks, its diction, its volume, its impediments to speech, its level of confidence in speaking, and its enjoyment of the language—all contribute to how the character is perceived. Initial choices should be made in character development, but, as with any of our choices, they should be allowed to develop in performance.

Language can be as strong an indicator of setting to the guest as costuming or environment. A character speaking Shakespearese quickly places the setting as Renaissance England, but even less remote periods can be enhanced through language. For instance, Streetmosphere's 1940s setting was basically contemporary American. To sound as "forties" as possible, I had the ensemble study the cadence and characteristics in 1940s movies and radio shows. Both men and women had their own distinct vocal patterns. We analyzed and reproduced their cadence for every character in the show and gained a distinctive 1940s feel.

We also did extensive research into the vernacular of the 1940s. The English language is rich in slang; it is brimming with it. I created a slang dictionary, with a surprising number of terms just from the 1940s. Some were familiar, and some were amusingly obscure, but all smacked of the forties. When the characters spoke in the vernacular, the forties came alive! (See Character Letters in *Acting Interactive Theatre*.)

Noise

The noise the actor makes when moving through a space can also reveal character. An actor may choose noise-making props that clang or jingle as they are carried. This is very useful in a large, open environment for attracting attention. A clever actor can make good use of sound. I once had an actor who played a "gumshoe" detective wear a device that made his shoe squeak. Characters should be eye catching, but they should not ignore being ear catching too.

History

In addition to how the character sounds and how it uses language, what the character says and what it knows is of great importance. Historical research is a necessary part of learning any period role. An interactive character will often be tested in its knowledge of its period in history. However, general scholarship alone does not fit the bill for this type of application. Knowing the events of the period and their relevance to history is not as important as knowing what the people of the time knew about their everyday lives, and what they thought and felt about it.

KNOW ONLY WHAT THE CHARACTER KNOWS

An interactive character reveals as much about its historical period by what it *doesn't* know as what it *does*. Being well versed in the times is certainly no disadvantage, but a beggar in the sixteenth century, for instance, would know next to nothing about the workings of the court of Elizabeth I. He may even show the period's lack of public communication, by today's standards, by *not* knowing the outcome of something as big as a military campaign, or even that there had been one. A 1940s Hollywood girl off the bus may know little of the motion picture business, yet her unrealistic assumptions about it may reveal a great deal about star-struck common folk. The trick is to know what the character would know and what it would not.

KNOW EVERYDAY FACTS

The show will concern itself with here-and-now activity within the environment. Therefore, the most important type of knowledge is the everyday variety. What kind of money was used? How much did things cost? How did people get to work? How did they cook, decorate, party, dance, fight, court, and so on? Often the small and mundane things have the greatest impact. We relate best to our own everyday activities, and when we see the same activities translated into the character's period, it makes that character seem more realistic. Focus on what the character needs to know to get through its day.

KNOW ACTIONAL FACTS

The best historical knowledge is the kind you can use in performance, those historical references that can be turned into action. All occupational activities fall into this category. In addition, any ritual or behavior common to the time is useful in revealing the period. These actions may be recognizable to the guest, or not. The former reinforces the setting, the latter presents a mystery to be solved or something to be learned.

KNOW AND REFLECT THE VALUES AND MORES OF THE TIME

In addition to action, the values and morality of the period must be exhibited. What were the cultural suppositions about love, marriage, sex, religion, society, money, gender, superstition, government, and so forth? Here the differences from our time are most important. Issues like the role of women, the obedience of children to their parents, respect for elders, the mobility of social station, customs, and manners often differ greatly and provide excellent opportunities to explore contrast.

MAKE AN HISTORIC REFERENCE BIBLE

To prepare for historical research during rehearsals, I create an historic reference "bible." I gather a host of reference books and glean from them bite-sized, actional, everyday references. Anything that is significantly different from, or significantly the same as, the present is snatched up in small easy pieces. I then categorize them into a single tome. The result is a book that provides many useful specifics for the production, anything that everyone in the cast is likely to need to know.

My bible for 1940s Hollywood contains everything from the studio system to popular nightclubs to how much a car costs. My bible for Renaissance festivals contains everything from genealogies to science and medicine to currency denominations and Peddlers' French (the secret language of thieves). These books are the nuts and bolts of usable history for the interactive actor. In addition to their use of the bible, actors may also indulge themselves in any other research specific to their character occupation.

Know What Is Anachronistic and What Is Not

It is important for the actor to know where anachronisms lie. My bibles often contain lists of what was invented in the time, and lists of what was not. There are many good reference books available for this kind of information.

These lists are always tempered by what the average guest might assume to be correct or incorrect. If the guest *thinks* something is a modern reference, it is. It is never advisable to argue a point or even to be in a position of having to justify a point of history to a guest. The goal is to present as many images of the period as possible, while avoiding as many images of the present as possible. The motive is always the suspension of disbelief. (See Guided Dream in Character and Character Letters—Variation II in *Acting Interactive Theatre*.)

Costuming

Costuming for interactive characters has always been, and probably always will be, problematic. In a perfect world, actors would have extensive input into the design of their costumes at the *end* of the rehearsal process, when they are clearest about what their characters need to reveal. But this is often difficult to achieve for a number of reasons. From a practical standpoint, beginning a costume's design at the end of a rehearsal process creates too much delay between the start of the performance and completion of the costume. On the other hand, character elements that seem important at the beginning of the development process may give way to better ideas later on, but there may be no time left to make changes to the costume.

From the costume designer's standpoint, the idea of an actor's input into the design often strikes terror into his or her heart. Very few costume designers are prepared for the demands of designing for an interactive show. It is very different from the way they are taught in graduate school. A good designer is taught to support the director's concept. While this is still true in interactive theatre, designers also need to be able to give up *their* ideas for the sake of the *actor's* ideas, which doesn't come easily to many. The tendency is to say, "I have designed this costume with the whole intent of the show in mind; you the actor must simply wear it and make it work." This doesn't hold true for interactive characterization, however, because it is more like the process of costume design in clowning, in which the look of the character is developed along with the characterization. The two go hand in hand because each must intimately support the other. The worst possible situation is to have an actor succeeding in developing a unique and fascinating characterization, and then being forced to wear a costume that is completely incongruous with that creation.

This is not as rare a problem as you might think. In my experience it happens all the time. I think the director has to take complete control over the process of costume design and mediate between the actors' ideas and the designer's ideas. The relationship is then quite simple. The actor, with direction, knows what needs to be revealed in the costume, and the designer knows how to reveal what is needed.

In looking for a costume designer for an interactive show, the director needs to make this relationship clear at the outset in order to give the designer time to adjust to this different mode of thinking. In addition, a good costume designer for an interactive show must figuratively live in the actor's shoes and thus know how the costume will meet the practical needs of performance. Often interactive costumes need to be more durable than stage costuming, and they must be more sensitive to the climate the actor is performing in. Since many interactive shows are outdoors, costumes may need to be warmer, cooler, or layered. In costuming for ballet, for instance, comfort and flexibility are key factors in the design elements. Interactive costuming has similar needs.

These needs can provide some unique challenges to a costume designer. One actress, playing a Hollywood gossip columnist, was wigged and wore a large-brimmed hat. It was an outrageous style and visually striking; however, in any moderate breeze, the hat would give the actress a stiff neck. Her neck muscles were strained in a way that caused tension in her throat, and this caused the actress to lose her voice. (It took a chiropractor and a voice specialist before the costume department would believe her.) When the hat was changed, the problem disappeared.

The designer's choice of materials should also consider breathability, durability, and washability. For characters that may be caught in the rain, materials such as feathers, crepe, and so on do not work at all.

I have found some effective compromises to this problem of

costuming for interactive characters. The designer should always be prepared for an actor's input, including some last-minute changes. Meetings should be scheduled between the designers and actors early on in rehearsals, and "best-guess" concepts should be devised. As rehearsals progress, the director approves design sketches and has the designer make the basic garments, but without the trim and the accessories. These add-on items are then reviewed with the actor and added at the latest reasonable point in the rehearsal process.

In this way I cut out design elements that might be too specific or irretrievable if incorporated into the basic costume, and I am able to leave room for adjustment later in the process. What a character wears in terms of hats, shoes, trim, belts, jewelry, carried items, capes, watches, glasses, hairstyles, and so on can greatly alter the basic look of a costume. Each actor is thus allowed enough room to fine-tune the character's appearance once the development process is concluded. This process can prove to be a bit difficult for costumers, particularly in the latter days of production, but it is by far the best compromise for providing the show with consistent, identifiable, and fascinating characters. This is why I look for designers who love to work with actors.

The designer must understand that the intent of the costume's design for interactive theatre is to reveal occupation. When a guest glances at a character, what it wears must indicate to the guest immediately what its occupation is—whether plumber, movie star, or gravedigger. In addition, the costume must catch the eye. It must be magnified, be interesting, and have colors and textures that will not fade into the background of a crowd of guests.

An important additional consideration is how the costume reveals the particular personality of the character. However, it is important for the designer not to put the cart before the horse and design a costume that reveals personality at the cost of occupation. The first thing the guest must know is whether that character is a talent agent or a gunslinger or a farmer. If in addition to making the occupation clear, it can be revealed that it is a *slovenly* talent agent, or a *stupid* gunslinger, or a *bookish* farmer, then that is all the better.

Most costume designers are trained to design a whole look based on the subject and theme of the play as defined by the director. The best designer for an interactive show is one who will design for the subject but will not ignore the actor's needs. He or she must remember that, in interactive theatre, the weight of the performance is carried by the actor, not the playwright.

Props

Along with costumes and accessories, an actor's choice of properties can have a significant impact. I believe it is important for the director to leave actors completely free to choose whatever props they feel will enhance their characters' performance, meeting a few simple criteria.

PROPS SHOULD ACTIVELY REVEAL CHARACTER

The chief criterion is that a prop must actively reveal the character. Props can be invaluable aids in helping the guest recognize the character's occupation. A girl just off the bus carrying a suitcase in Hollywood would identify that character's occupation to the guest quite well. Likewise, a Hollywood director carrying a megaphone would be quite revealing of occupation.

ACTORS SHOULD PREPARE PROPS FOR A SPECIFIC USE

When a character requests a particular prop, I usually ask what the actor intends to *do* with it. If the answers are supportive of his or her character choices, then it is a good prop. If the answers are "I'd feel better with it" or "I'll find something to do with it," then I encourage the actor to leave that choice aside until something specific is known about its benefit. A tendency for those new to this genre is to rely upon props as crutches. The feeling is, "The more props on me, the more options I'll have when I'm suddenly at a loss." The result can be a show that is populated with characters encumbered with props that do and say nothing for the show. Although I leave actors free in their choices, I do insist that they choose only props they absolutely need, and that they have *specific* uses for them.

PROPS CAN BE USED AS BUFFERS TO INTERACTION

A prop that is unique in itself may attract the attention of a guest. His or her interest in that prop itself may give the actor an opportunity to create an interactive experience. An actor who played a Renaissance pirate for me (in fact, the one I modeled the prospector character after) was quite an awesome sight in his full beard, eye patch, leather doublet, and hook on one arm. He looked fearsome, and frightened children. This was a concern until the actor found a jester stick that one of the festival artisans had made in his character's likeness. This was a stick with a decorative jester's head on one end, made to look like his pirate. The actor bought the odd-looking thing and stuck it into his character's belt. From that moment on, the sight of this gruesome character with a cute little jester stick of himself in his belt made him appealing and quite popular with children, who were interested in stopping and asking him about his jester.

An actor must be ready to use a good prop. The actor playing the pirate quickly capitalized on his new jester stick. He soon had a ready store of stories as to what the prop was, where it came from, how he used it, and why he carried it. Each story led in the end to an interaction that involved the guest who inquired about it.

PROPS SHOULD INSPIRE THE ACTOR

One of the best ways for an actor to be inspired by a prop is to create a flea market of sorts. It is difficult for an actor to sit down and dream up what props his or her character might carry. With a flea market, all the available props from the warehouse are brought out for the actors to peruse. They are allowed to rummage until something strikes them as useful. It is satisfying how actors can stumble across unexpected treasures in this way.

It should be clear to directors that making choices of properties *for* the actor is a useless endeavor because it works against the creative process. Only what inspires an actor toward characterization will be useful. If the prop fills my criteria of revealing character and providing the actor with specific active choices, then I am well disposed to approve it. But I do encourage actors not to weigh themselves down with too many props because they will eventually discard most of them.

Background 9

Once major character choices are made, as outlined in this part of the book, the actor should create a more detailed background that justifies those choices. These are what I call *actor's* choices, because they are choices the audience will usually not be aware of, but they serve to help the actor feel the character better so that a consistent characterization will be evident in moments of spontaneity.

Actors may need to predetermine some background information in an interactive play, but this should be done as little as possible. Only information that needs to be established to justify a plot line or a necessary story action should be preordained for the character. Actors need as much leeway in this regard as possible. However, they must still be guided by the director.

The reason I present this process so late in character development is the overwhelming tendency for actors to make these choices too abundantly and too soon. This limits the actor. For instance, if an actor conceives early on that his character was born and raised by a wealthy New York family, then later realizes that the character works best as a "tough guy," he might say to himself, "But I can't be a tough guy, because a rich kid would never have grown up that way." After building such a background choice into other established notions about the character, it may be impossible for the actor to think of changing the character's background to something workable—like being raised in an orphanage.

Throughout most of the character development process, I strongly caution actors whenever they make these choices. But once the key choices are made, the actor can—and must—flesh out his or her own perceptions of the character.

Using personal scripts, that is, using aspects of your own life in the character, should never be done. It can spell disaster not only for the character, but also for the actor's personal well-being. There will be enough of the actor's self in the character as it is. That's not altogether bad, but I caution actors not to look for therapy through characterization. An interactive character is no place to work out personal issues.

ESTABLISHED BACKGROUND SHOULD YIELD TO THE SCENE

Once background development is begun, there is another caution I make plain: These choices are not written in stone. The actor should always yield to what is created in the moment, and established in performance. Background choices should support and enhance the characterization, but never limit it.

For instance, the sheriff was initially conceived as the youngest son in a family of seven brothers. If performance circumstances conspired to establish the sheriff as an orphan, and that choice was the expedient one for that encounter, then the actor should go with it without hesitation. Otherwise, the advancement of the scene may be blocked. Likewise, if the mail-order bride character made a background choice of being extremely fond of chocolate, it may work well in many circumstances. But if a scene involves her in which she *hates* chocolate, and her background preference has not been established, then the actress should not hesitate to go with that choice, because good improvisation technique dictates that she accept the assumption without question. If the audience doesn't know she loves chocolate, the notion doesn't exist.

The obvious exception to this rule is an interactive play in which information is required for a plot line that cannot be altered. Whenever improvisation is the medium, it is always best to keep background information as *mutable* as possible. As you will see in Part III, improvising with an established character has its own brand of challenges. The characterizations we have created thus far are immutable, yet the background *justifications* for them may change when—and if—called upon to do so in performance. A character's occupation, passion, foibles, virtue, needs, and activities remain constant. But background histories and anecdotal references may be altered to serve the scene.

THREE ASPECTS OF BACKGROUND

I group background detail into three basic areas: the character's innate *personality* (what it is born with), its *childhood development* (what it learns by experience), and the nature of its current *professional life*. Frequently, I develop notesheets for these choices, with questions and plenty of trial adjectives. Most actors seem to find them useful in focusing their thoughts, although any guidesheet I hand out comes with my insistence that the recipient have a pencil with a big eraser. (See Background Sheets in *Acting Interactive Theatre*.)

Part III

Improvisation

*I*f the character development process outlined in Part II is the *noun*, then improvisation is the *verb*. Improvisation activates the interactive character; it activates the temenos. Were we rehearsing a show, the character development workshop outlined in Part II and the techniques discussed in Part III would happen simultaneously. As actors discover their character elements, they connect to their creative power in a workshop I call "Freeing the Imagination." Then as they develop their character choices, they learn the skills of good improv scene work. As they advance their characters, they hone their narrative skills in improv. Finally, as the characters take shape, and an improv ensemble is formed, the two workshops merge into a "scene work in character" workshop (Part IV), in which the actual performance elements of the production are created.

Ensemble Improvisation 10

There is nothing new about improvisation. Not since the first Greek comedians got together to create a comic routine or the first commedia dell'arte troupe was formed in fourteenth-century Italy has there been anything new to talk about in improv. It has been around for centuries, and the ideas and techniques that make it work have always been there. Only our application of them and our method of explaining them change. Moreover, there is nothing magical about learning improvisation. Like learning to play the piano or ride a bicycle, it is a skill anyone can learn simply by understanding how it works and by applying one's self to it. In these chapters we will explore improvisation from a traditional perspective: what I call ensemble improvisation.

I distinguish ensemble improv from the more loquacious modern forms that have cropped up in recent times. Today, when you say "improv," people think of improv comedy clubs where "improv comics" perform (they used to called them "stand-up comics"), or one thinks of ComedySports™ and TheaterSports™ clubs where improv "teams" quite literally compete for your laughter and approval. The chief purpose of these formats is to make people laugh. But too often these formats lose the story line to a comic trick or a clever put-down. This "laugh factory" style too easily forgoes the ancient tenets of good scene work, characterization, relationship, focus, and ensemble playing that enhance the comedy. It is as though the craft of the stand-up comic and that of the improviser have become confused. I meet many people who "do improv" these days but too few who do it well. It seems they have forgotten (or perhaps have never learned) the basics. As a result, good technique is being popularized out of the genre.

Comedy is certainly a priority in ensemble improvisation, but it is not its sole purpose. There are alternatives to just being funny. These include evoking amusement, wonder, endearment, fascination, and delight at the exposure of the human character and its culture. There is no competition in ensemble improvisation. There is no playing for oneself, playing for control, or compromising technique for the sake of a laugh. For the audience, it is not merely a realm of cleverness and wit, as in modern improv comedy, but rather one of relationship, character, insight, and, yes, mirth. For the player, it is a realm of harmony and creative support, not a realm of reaction-hungry, antic comedians grappling for the punch line. There is nothing in the theatre so astounding and side-splitting as good ensemble improvisation.

What is an ensemble? Here is another abused word of our modern theatre. An ensemble is a group that shares three things mutually and in abundance: trust, play, and joy. Trust, because trust is required of true play. Play, because playing is the ensemble's purpose. Joy in each other and in the work, because joy is the result of true play. The audience is the beneficiary through its contact with the ensemble. Guests see the unusual and inspiring sight of a group working together in harmony and precision—each one focused in support of the other. They are delighted by the intricacy, complexity, and whimsy of the play, and are moved by the apparent joy being generated among the performers. We will see later on how closely the rules of improv match the tenets of play and the creation of a temenos.

Ensemble improvisation is the *engine* that drives the action of the interactive ensemble. In the chapters that follow, I will break down ensemble improv into its component parts so that each part may be understood singularly, and then as they relate to the whole. Together we will build this engine. There is nothing new about the techniques that I will present here. What *is* new, as we will see later, is how these techniques are used to include the guest in an interactive drama.

Improv Exercises

These chapters outline the theory and process of improvisation, yet the best way to understand and build skill in the technique is through the use of exercises. These theatre games, as they are called, are often used as performance vehicles, or "structures," in most staged improv formats. They are not generally used in interactive performance, but are a great means for training the actor in improvisation in order to apply it subsequently to interactive scene work.

I prefer the term *exercises* to "games." I think it is more appropriate because we literally isolate a particular aspect of the technique and *exercise* it. Just as a weight trainer uses an exercise to develop a particular muscle, I use improv exercises to develop a particular mental process or technique. I use a precise set of exercises in a specific order in my workshops to achieve ensemble and free individual creativity. These exercises are contained in the rehearsal supplement to this book, *Acting Interactive Theatre*.

Teaching and the Rules of Improv

In the art of improvisation, we create ideas through inspiration, and manipulate them through what we unfortunately call a set of rules. The problem with rules is that they set up criteria and create comparison. For an art form that depends on creative spontaneity, this is a bad precedent to set. The most difficult task for a teacher of improv is to get students to understand and master the rules, while at the same time not allowing the rules to limit their spontaneity.

I can point to a rule and say, "The rule says this must be so, and this must not be so." I may then compare my own performance or the performance of my fellow player and say, "You followed the rule," or "You did not follow the rule." The peril is that this kind of comparison and judgment erodes the foundation of mutual trust and creative play that gives rise to the unique, original, and creative thoughts that the rules exist to manipulate in the first place. Of improvisation, we say there are no right or wrong answers, yet we add that the rules must be followed or the process won't work.

It is a symptom of our empirical, Western way of thinking that when we are given a set of rules or criteria, we adhere so tightly to them that we forget the intent of the process. We are great manipulators of rights and wrongs, dos and don'ts, but not many of us are true creators. Improvisation, of all the arts, demands flexible thinking, accommodation, and nonjudgment. Still, it is difficult to teach an art as complex and fluid as improvisation without boiling it down into these smaller, more definable aspects of the greater process—"the rules."

The task is not impossible if the student keeps in mind one important thought: Improvisation is not a science, but an art. The student of improv must not say, "If I follow these rules, then I will be a brilliant improviser," for that is not true. Rather, the student needs to say, "When I am a brilliant improviser, these rules apply." These so-called rules are *aspects* of good improvisation, and nothing more. The price of this lesson is that the student must reprogram his or her pattern of empirical thinking and learn to think in a new way, using a mode of thinking not based on criteria but on a mood of trust, joy, and play.

Freeing the Imagination 11

The Actor's Relationship with Self

*I*n order to improvise, actors must come to terms with their own creative power. They must be able to tap, at will, the limitless resources of their imagination in order to fuel the improvisational process. Few are born with this ability, and most must achieve it in the same way that any other talent is refined—through hard work, patience, and practice. Many people believe that a brilliant imagination is a gift that some have and some do not. I strongly disagree. The first step for an actor, or anyone else for that matter, to take in freeing the imagination is to believe in his or her creative power. Actors may not have seen or used it, or have known how to access it, but it is there nonetheless, lying beneath the surface. Each person's imagination is as deep and rich and powerful as another's. It is simply a matter of one's connection to it. To begin to build that connection one must first believe that it is there.

I have a proof that I perform for students who need this sort of verification. I ask them to lie down on the floor, breathe deeply, and clear their minds. I then relate a brief narration that, unannounced to them, includes no adjectives or descriptive language whatsoever. I may say, for example, "A man walked down the street. The wind blew. He approached the church steps and knocked. A woman answered the door, took the letter from him, and smiled."

At the end of the narrative I will choose one actor and ask a series of questions, requesting that each of the other actors present answer them for themselves, based on their own experience. I ask for specific detail. The chosen actor will instantly describe details down to the color and texture of objects, as well as what purpose the events in the narrative had. I will then point out that no descriptive language was used in the narrative; every detail was filled in by the actor, automatically and effortlessly, using his or her imagination. If I then ask what the other actors saw, each describes an entirely different scene, unique to his or her own imagination.

Removing Blocks

Clearly each actor's imagination yields its own unique creation. If imaginative power exists in each of us, what then is the process by which we access that power? Certainly, it is not one of *building* an imagination, for imagination is already there. It is, instead, a process of removing the blocks and constraints that stand between us and our natural imaginative power. Each one of us has a lifetime store of fears and mental conditioning that block, or at least constrict, our access to this creative force. This section describes many of the common blocks we have, and provides a method to remove them or, at least, a path around them.

Many teachers of improv start with the rules and go on from there, expecting their students to be able to think creatively from the outset—and on cue, too. But improv technique only manipulates ideas. Where, then, do the ideas come from? In building an improv ensemble, it is vitally important begin with each individual's relationship to his or her own imagination. For only with an imagination free of constraints can one successfully apply the technique of improvisation.

Trust

The first step is to build mutual trust within a new ensemble. Without a trusting and supportive environment, a temenos cannot be formed, and the creativity we seek to open in the individual cannot flourish. It makes no difference how clever, quick-witted, or funny the individuals of the company are; if there is no mutual trust among them, the ensemble's work will be chaotic and uninspired.

True genius in improvisation lies in the players' achieving a creative *harmony*. When the players eventually reach a state of collective imagination, their ideas extend beyond the reach of any one individual, and the scene itself loses any appearance of randomness and resembles truth. A well-improvised scene appears as something impossible to have been thought up on the spur of the moment. Each player seems to read the minds of the other players, and each new idea is so supported and knitted into the fabric of the scene that it appears to have been the only possible choice. It has a magical quality, and it is a truly inspiring thing to watch. To achieve this, the players must work their invention without obstruction, resistance, protection, or control. In short, they must share trust.

WHAT IS TRUST?

Trust is a firm belief or confidence in the honesty, integrity, reliability, or justice of another person; it is a faith or reliance on another. But trust is a quality that is difficult to come by. Therefore, one of my primary criteria in casting an ensemble is the very qualities of honesty, integrity, reliability, and justice. In other words, I like to cast *trustworthy* people because it is simply easier to build trust with a group of individuals that can understand the concept.

BUILDING TRUST

How does one build trust in a group? Many say that trust is something you cannot build, that it is something that just happens over time between certain individuals and cannot be predicted or created. But nothing could be further from the truth.

Trust *can* be nurtured—and *must* be—in order for the ensemble to be successful. Respect is earned, but trust is *given*. The first thing a player must realize is that trust is a gift, indeed, a deliberate gift. You cannot barter trust. Either it is singularly bestowed upon one by another, or it is not. From an early age on most of our parents taught us not to trust strangers. That rule is based on the notion that anyone we don't know could potentially harm us. It's a good rule for life, but, as we will continue to see, rules that are good for life are not the best rules for creativity.

We are conditioned almost from birth to mistrust one another. I'll often ask a new ensemble to define *mistrust* for me. They will usually say, "not trusting someone." I will refuse that answer and ask them to define what "not trusting someone" is.

They will usually have trouble with it until I say the word *fear*. Mistrust is fear, and fear is our natural reaction to the unknown. Open a door to a dark room and you experience fear: fear of the dark, fear that someone is there to harm you, or perhaps fear of tripping over a piece of furniture that you cannot see. Turn on the light, however, and the same room may become a warm and comfortable place. When we don't know how a person will react, what he or she will say or do, we pull back. But, when we get to know how another thinks, feels, and reacts to a variety of things, the door is open for a trusting relationship with that individual.

Giving trust always represents risk. Perhaps this is why it is so difficult to come by. What we risk when we trust people is betrayal. The fear of betrayal, not betrayal itself, is chiefly what prevents us from trusting one another. "I do not trust you because I am afraid that you will betray me. You may betray me, or you may not, but I don't know which, so I'll not risk it."

Fear in any form stifles action, but in improvisation fear stifles the creative process. Most fear is fear of the unknown, and, like lighting up a dark room, knowledge dispels fear. So the more we *know* about the person we are being asked to trust, the easier it will be for us to give trust. From the first moment a new ensemble is together in one place, I begin the process of building a knowledge of one another within the group. In doing so, I lay the foundation for trust.

BUILDING FAMILIARITY WITHIN A NEW ENSEMBLE

It is a tricky business to build a positive and supportive familiarity within a group in a relatively short period of time without triggering egos, comparisons, and defensiveness. But I have learned a few tricks of my own. I believe in *imprinting*. First impressions are a real and lasting thing. I use this to my advantage with a new group by having the first meeting of the ensemble be in a social setting. I will usually hold some sort of reception in a bar separate from the place where the production or rehearsals will take place. In this way players meet each other in a social setting in which professional comparisons and judgments are less likely to occur.

I especially like a setting in which adult beverages are served, there are nice conversation areas, and there is a good pool table. It is important that all staff and instructors be present as well, in casual dress, to show first that they are human beings too. Another important experience that this provides for the group is, of course, a sense of play. A good opening reception can go a long way toward beginning the temenos for the ensemble.

Obviously, one of the important ways of gaining knowledge of others is hearing about their backgrounds, their beliefs, their likes, dislikes, values, and so forth. One of the worst ways of presenting this information is for everyone to sit around and talk about themselves. Thus, in one exercise, I have the group partner up, interview one another, and then present their findings about their partners to the group. This device eliminates ego games and adds the pleasure of hearing one's self being talked about by another.

One of the most effective and, surprisingly, easy ways of breaking barriers and building familiarity within the group is through physical contact and eye contact. I use a number of exercises that provide a fun and playful context for simple contact. One of my personal favorites is what I call my "ensemble warm-up," which consists of a series of hugs, shoulder rubs, and compliments.

Building Trust Through Positive Affirmation

Another good technique is positive affirmation, which is an incredibly powerful tool for bringing people together. Life seems to provide so little affirmation of the good in us. It makes me sad to see a person so bowled over by a genuine, unbidden compliment. Our work lives and, in many cases, our home lives are so geared to the awareness and eradication of faults that too few of us have a full awareness of our own worth.

My "first good impressions" exercise is a joy to watch and even more fun to take part in. It can be scary, but it is effective. In a "reception line" format, each player is asked to give each of the other players his or her first *good* impression of them—professionally, personally, whatever. Genuine affirmation and recognition of what is good about another person is a rare and empowering thing. Such positive affirmation not only gives lift and security to players; it also gives them an accurate picture of how they are perceived by other people, which is crucial information!

Watching someone receive a genuine, unsolicited compliment is fascinating. Some people are uncomfortable with being complimented. I have seen some visibly shaken by it, even panicked. Most people will usually react with surprise and fumble their thank you. Often their uncomfortable feeling stems from the fear that they do not *deserve* the compliment. For some reason, people find it difficult. They may call it modesty, but if modesty prevents people from accepting an aspect of good in themselves reflected by another, then they are misunderstanding true modesty.

Likewise, some people find it difficult to *give* a compliment. Deep down they may feel that giving someone a compliment is really saying that that person is better than they are. But here again it is yet another symptom of a lack of acceptance of self-worth.

SELF-TRUST

Mutual trust in an ensemble helps tie it together and allows it to work as a whole. But there is a deeper, more fundamental kind of trust needed for an ensemble and, indeed, for any artist seeking creative potential, and that is self-trust. Self-trust is self-bestowed. Just as mutual trust is a gift, so too is self-trust. Likewise, self-trust also represents risk. Self-trust is harder to achieve, but it is easier to trust one's self if one shares trust with another. Building mutual trust in an ensemble, then, lets one know that *someone else* is willing to trust him or her. So developing group trust can go a long way toward laying the foundation for inspiring self-trust.

When I say self-trust, I mean a person's firm belief in his or her own creative power. If knowledge is the road to trust, then the player must gain a better knowledge of the creative process and of the fears that limit it. We will now uncover this process and its stumbling blocks. (See Biographies, HRC Warm-Up, Falling, Harmony, and First Good Impressions in *Acting Interactive Theatre*.)

Spontaneity

An actor who fancied himself an improvisationist once said, "I'm a good improviser, I just like to plan out what I am going to say ahead of time."

Many people's perception of imagination is that of an empty room that must be painstakingly stored with ideas for later use. But in reality, imagination is an endless warehouse full of ideas, the door to which we have locked and misplaced the key. Freeing the imagination is not a process of storing up ideas, but one of opening doors.

Spontaneity is the ability to summon an immediate, raw, unaltered creative impulse. It is like flinging open the door to that infinite warehouse. Actually, it's more like opening the door to Fibber McGee's closet than to a well-ordered storehouse. Ideas of all shapes and colors rush out pell-mell with a sort of hapless joy.

Unfortunately, few of us are in tune with our spontaneity. Our access to it is hampered by our fears that compel us to brace the door and allow only one idea at a time to squeeze through the cracks. We then scrutinize it and worry whether it is the correct or appropriate idea, asking, "Is it right? Is it good? How will it make me look?" These are emotional blocks to the natural abundance of our creative selves. To dissolve them, we must first face them, accept that they are ours, forgive them, and then release them. These fears have names, and I would like to introduce them to you now.

Emotional Blocks

THE FEAR OF JUDGMENT

The first, and worst, is the fear of judgment. We all fear the judgment of others, particularly in matters of creativity. We are afraid that we will be judged as dull, uninteresting, unfunny, and unintelligent. As a protection against it, we struggle to present to the world the self-image that we perceive others will find acceptable. However, we need to realize that this self-image is our perception of other people's perception of us, and our perceptions of how people view us are so often badly distorted because we rarely receive accurate and cogent information on the subject. Thus this self-image that we create and project to others is ultimately based on unsupported assumptions on our part. Yet, we *screen* our creative impulses until we think they fit our self-image. We need to realize that the self-image we project is usually not the one people see anyway. Therefore, our safest bet is to be ourselves and to let our image take care of itself. If we are to be judged, let us be judged for who we *are*. There is no shame in that.

APPROVAL SEEKING

Approval seeking is a primary motivator of human behavior. We all share a lifetime of seeking the approval of others. When we are children, we seek the approval of our parents; we want to be a "good boy" or "good girl." When we are in school, we seek the approval of our teachers; we want to be an "A student," perhaps even a "teacher's pet." When we grow up, we seek the approval of our bosses, or our friends. We want to be known as the "right person to go to" to get the job done, or a "great girl" or a "great guy."

This is not to say that seeking approval is wrong, but approval seeking is a block to creativity. You cannot be worried about what someone is thinking about you and be creative at the same time. We need to see that approval seeking is a personal choice and not a necessity. The irony is that you should worry about what other people think about you in the first place. They don't really care about you; they are too busy worrying about what you think of them. The truth is that people who crave approval rarely get it. It is sad but true. Free your imagination, and you will have all the raw materials you need for approval later on. Self-judgment is caused by the approval-seeking trap. We prejudge our ideas in order to fit them to the image that we perceive will gain us approval, and that is why approval seeking can't help you in creative thinking.

THE FEAR OF FAILURE

In the fear-of-failure trap, we place the burden of success upon spontaneity before a single thought is conceived. We question ourselves, "Will it work? Will these ideas of mine be useful? Will they be successful?" But spontaneity is a condition of abundance. You must have an abundance of ideas first, and *then* be selective. A creative mind can be successful only when working from a position of choice. An abundance of ideas is necessary in order for us to select with advantage.

In our development, we are told that we must succeed. But too often we end up asking ourselves not only to succeed, but to *succeed without ever failing*. Where in our development do we get the notion that to err is wrong? Our educational system teaches us that 90 percent of the answers correct equals an A and less than 50 percent of the answers correct equals *failure*. But the success rate of a single creative thought is far lower than 50 percent. It is no wonder that our creativity is stymied by our insistence that only successful ideas surface.

THE FEAR OF EXPOSURE

Last in this list of fears is the fear of exposure, that is, the fear of revealing *oneself*. Open yourself to spontaneity, and you will be surprised at what comes forth. As an artist you will reveal truth, including your own personal truth. The fear of exposure stems from the idea that you will be held responsible for your creative impulses, that they are *who you are*. This betrays a typically ego-centric Western way of thinking, that we ourselves are wholly responsible for every thought in our heads. It may surprise you to know that many cultures think quite differently.

Many cultures believe, for instance, that creative inspiration comes from other spirits, or from some sort of divinity. The Greeks believed in the Muses. Down through the ages, artists have been revered because of their special connection with the divine. Michelangelo believed that each of his sculptures existed whole and complete within the stone and that, once he became fully aware of them, all that remained was for him simply to remove the rest of the stone. The same belief was held by ancient Eskimo scrimshanders. Even in our own lexicon, we refer to an artist as being "gifted," which implies the presence of someone or something as giver. Likewise, the word *inspire* means to "cause, guide, or motivate as by divine or supernatural influence."

Unfortunately, once we believe we are the sole authors of our creative thought, we think we can then be judged not only for the success or failure of those thoughts, but also for *who we are*. This belief leaves us terribly alone; perhaps, it is the seed of the "suffering artist." How much better it is to see ourselves as channels for the inspirations of an infinitely creative and abundant universe. If so, our inspirations may be colored by the uniqueness of who we are, but they are also part of a larger whole.

Cognitive Constraints

What is your model of the mind? Is it a computer, with functions of input, output, and processing? Is it a playground, where new ideas can be manipulated or toyed with? Is it an opponent, something which you are always working against? Beyond the emotional blocks that inhibit us, the way we think, our cognition, affects our access to creative thought as well.

We are so conditioned from our early development with certain patterns of thinking that most of us are completely unaware of any other way to think. Many people believe that they are not creative thinkers because they simply do not have the ability. I disagree. Many people are not creative thinkers because they've not been taught how to think creatively.

Our schools, on the whole, do not teach creativity. A course on artistic or intellectual inventiveness is rare in college and, sadly, absent in grade school, where most of our thought processes for life are formed. Let's take a look at the four basic functions of the mind, and see how they are supported by our educational system.

The first is *concentration*, simply focusing the mind and paying attention. From our earliest school days we are well taught to pay attention in class. When we don't, we usually get a severe tongue-lashing, or even a set of sore knuckles to remind us of its importance.

Memorization and recalling is the second basic mental function. We all have had ample opportunity to develop these skills because most of our formalized schooling involves the memorization of facts and the recalling of them later on. We jot down facts from lectures and textbooks and study them until we memorize them and can recall them without the aid of notes in what we call a test.

The third basic function is *analyzing and criticizing*. If we have had a good education, we learned to dissect an idea, system, or structure into its component parts, and learned to identify how those components interrelate. We learned to relate new ideas or systems to preexisting ones in order to measure or evaluate them. This function, though necessary, so often crowds out the fourth function altogether.

The fourth basic function is that of *generating new ideas and visualizing the nonexistent*. Our educational system is based on analyzing and manipulating that which already exists around us, but it hardly ever asks us to see or create that which has not yet been seen or done. Little wonder that the stereotype of the artistic or the intellectual innovator down through history has always involved some sort of aberrant personality. One would almost have to be, in order to break out of our strongly reinforced educational patterns.

Education doesn't teach us creative thinking. In fact, it is geared toward eliminating it. Most of our formal notions of intelligence are based on logic and analysis. Our so-called IQ tests are based almost entirely on logic and analysis. This type of thinking requires recognizing, memorizing, and manipulating patterns. It is useful, to be sure, but is this all that we are measuring to describe what we call our intelligence? According to the IQ test, it is.

Our educational system does a good job of covering three of the four mental functions. The tragedy is that it doesn't cover all four. We are led to assume that critical thinking is the only way to think. As a result, we have been brought up not only to be unaware of our creative potential, but also to undervalue it. My grade school treated creative thinking as nonessential, even frivolous! But freeing the imagination means reprogramming our minds to accept a creative-thinking process. This process often conflicts with critical-thinking patterns. Perhaps this is why our educational system chooses to ignore it.

We begin reprogramming by identifying our existing patterns so that we may then learn to set them aside. This is not a process of abolishing those patterns (because they are important for obvious reasons), but rather of learning to *disengage* those rules and take on a different set of rules whenever the time for creative thought arises.

FOLLOWING THE RULES

Following the rules is one of the first things we were taught in school. Thousands of rules were heaped on us in our first ten years of schooling: "Don't color outside the lines," "Wait for the bell," "Be on time," and on and on. Often we learned the rules for their own sake, without understanding the essence of what they exist to protect. Students were usually better rewarded for following the rules than for questioning them. There are many good reasons for following rules, but we become so comfortable with them we overlook the times when we must question the rules, break new ground, and innovate.

THINKING WITHOUT CRITERIA

The educational game we are taught to play from kindergarten through graduate school is to fill the predetermined criteria for approval. We learn to concentrate, memorize, and recall facts, analyze and criticize them, prove to our teachers through tests that we have accomplished those tasks, and then we graduate, perhaps without ever having to have thought one new thought.

To improvise, you need to acquire the ability to *think without criteria*. Truth is all around you; what matters is where you place your focus. If I were to hand you a wooden stick and ask you to measure it, you would very likely pull out a ruler and tell me how many inches long the stick is. You would give me only a measure of its length. If you accurately measured the stick as twelve inches long, then you would give me the *correct* answer. But you might have also measured its weight, or its volume. You could also measure its color, its beauty, its shape, its chemical composition, the memories associated with it, or its orientation in space. Only preconditioned criteria led you to reach for your ruler.

In creative thinking, as in improvisation, you can choose your own criteria. You don't have to wait for the ghost of your grade school teacher to give them to you. When we have a choice, most of us will choose the first, most common, accepted, and safest criteria for our thoughts—usually the ones that we perceive others will approve of. But we need to think without criteria. For once we become comfortable with the feeling of thinking without criteria, we are then freer to choose our criteria differently.

THE ONE RIGHT ANSWER

One of our strongest mental patterns is to look for the *one right answer*. This notion of "right answer/wrong answer" is good for practical things, obviously. Some things have only one right answer. The idea is fine for math, for instance. The wrong answer in our physics calculations may make our buildings fall over; but this type of thinking greatly undermines creativity. As with measuring the stick, there are *many* right answers.

Somewhere during our grade school education, when most of us lost our power of imagination, we learned to look for only one right answer. It was as though our teachers reduced the wide and mysterious pageant of existence down to a sort of binary code, where everything was yes or no, on or off. Perhaps this stems from our culture's desire to quantify, rather than qualify the world around us. Our modern age is a place where a thought or impression has less value than a fact, because it is less easily measured and put to use in the physical world around us.

AVOIDING AMBIGUITY

We are conditioned to avoid ambiguity, but ambiguity is all around us. Life is ambiguous. We must therefore learn to embrace ambiguity when using our creativity and to open ourselves to the *many* answers to our questions.

Assume an ambiguous attitude and you will see things in more than one way. Much of humor is ambiguity. We are led to think one way; then suddenly a different point of view is revealed that had been there all along, and we are made aware that there is more than one way of seeing things.

SEEKING ORIGINALITY

Many improvisers hold themselves back by struggling to be unique or original. Deliberately striving for originality is a lot like not thinking of a white elephant. When you try to have an original thought, you place a constraint on your ideas based on what you believe is *original*, or what you believe others perceive originality to be.

The only way for us to be original is to be *genuine*. You are the only *you* in existence. No one thinks the way you do or has the same opinions, values, or experiences you do. Therefore, when you are being true to yourself, you are being original. If you crave originality, your only hope is to stop trying and be yourself. It is the only way you can be assured of being unique. Learning to let go and to value your own creative nature are the only paths to originality. (See Stream of Consciousness, Automatic Reading, Automatic Writing, and Black Box in *Acting Interactive Theatre*.)

Free Association

The human brain is built to associate ideas. The associative powers of the mind are nearly miraculous; faster than any supercomputer, they automatically, instantaneously, and effortlessly link one idea to another. An improviser in touch with this incredible power need never want for an idea.

In free association, one idea is "flashed" to another. Offer the mind a thought, and it will immediately connect it to another. It does so without conscious effort on the individual's part, and it *needs no criteria*. Present it with the thought of an *apple*, and it may give you *tree*, then tree to *woods*, woods to *man with an ax*, man with an ax to *Paul Bunyan*, and so on. Yet, when you tell yourself, "I will *think of* what goes with apple," you impose a hidden host of subjective criteria.

An inexperienced improviser will struggle to "think up" his or her next brilliant idea. But what happens is that no idea at all comes, much less a brilliant one, because the improviser is not searching for the *idea*, but for the *correct criteria*—criteria he or she doesn't have or need. Where the improviser needs to place the focus is on the immediate action of the scene. There he or she can use free association to *flash* on the new idea. The encouragement here is "Don't think, be." Absorb the scene, and let your mind work for you. If the improviser is too busy worrying about how the idea might fit, he or she can't be absorbing the information in the scene to use as a flash resource for an abundance of new ideas.

OVERVALUING AN IDEA

Ideas come from ideas. Every new idea is either an extension, synthesis, inversion, or duplication of previous ideas. But what we often do is overvalue an idea. Sometimes we just wait for that bolt of inspiration to strike us from the blue. We want to find that special, brilliant idea that will make everything right. But in improvisation one idea is as good as another. The improviser must come to understand that an idea of itself has no value; it is only the *context* in which we place it that gives it value. In an improvised scene, the idea comes first, and *then* the context makes the idea clear. How can you value one idea over another before you even know how that idea will be used in the scene? You can't and you shouldn't. Get in touch, instead, with the technique of free association. (See Word Ball, Image Association, and Metaphor Description in *Acting Interactive Theatre*.)

Incorporation

Incorporation is the process that gives a useful form to our free association. The mind loves wholeness, and it will seek to place disparate thoughts into context. This is what happens when we dream. Odd bits of information, desire, and anxiety are discharged during sleep to make way for the next day's mental business. As they are released, this process of incorporation takes over and gives them shape. They seem unusual to us because they are unimpeded by conscious constraint, allowing our own unique view of wholeness to be revealed.

As in free association, the mind incorporates instantly and effortlessly if unobstructed. In improv, free association takes place first; then incorporation takes the stream of linked thoughts and synthesizes them into new thoughts that create context or wholeness. Free association links single thoughts, and incorporation merges groups of thoughts. Incorporation may take the string of free-associated thoughts introduced above—*apple, tree, woods, man with an ax, Paul Bunyan*—and synthesize them into a thought such as, "*Paul Bunyan* was hungry, so he took his *ax, went into the woods,* and chopped himself an *apple tree.*" These two operations of the mind work in tandem, with lightning-fast complexity, yet they may also be isolated and work separately. (See Half-Wit, Unrelated Phrases, and Expert in *Acting Interactive Theatre*.)

Summary

These elements of creative thought—trust, spontaneity, free association, and incorporation—can be isolated, practiced, and conditioned to respond to the actor's will. This is how they are rehearsed—separately—and then they are brought together in a unified technique. It is akin to the idea of reducing the artistry of the pianist to the practice of scales, arpeggios, and chords. Once mastered individually, they are combined in a playing technique that gives us a fine sonata or, in our case perhaps, a great jazz riff.

There is no attempt here to explain the complex mystery of the human mind. However, this mystery need not be solved in order to use its definable operations to our benefit. Our task is to free the emotional blocks to our spontaneity by dissolving fear into trust and to unlock the cognitive constraints on our associative powers by reprogramming previous conditioning. With this accomplished, we are now prepared to tackle the "rules of improv" and apply them to the improvised scene.

Scene Work 12

The Actor's Relationship to the Actor

An actor who fancied himself an improvisationist once said, "I don't like to improv with other people. They throw me off."

I mprovised scene work requires more than one's personal spontaneity. The individual's process of spontaneity must now be applied to a collective process of spontaneity, shared among the players in the scene. If one's imagination can be likened to a sandbox, then a single person may use pail and shovel to build any type of sand castle he or she likes, in any way that is pleasing. However, scene work adds a new playmate to the sandbox, and the players must now learn to *share their toys*. A bigger and better sand castle may be achieved, but only if they agree to play together.

Improv Pitfalls

SELECTIVITY

Selectivity is one of the worst things that can happen in scene work. Selectivity happens because of creative blocks. It can be overvaluing your ideas, seeking originality, fear of judgment, or fear of failure. All of these things can induce a person to be particular about his or her ideas in an improv.

Selectivity is *screening* your thoughts for either the *best* idea or the *safest* idea. It is analyzing and discriminating your ideas, in essence, before they are allowed to happen and before they are shared with the ensemble. In the moment when you call upon your imagination for a new idea, your conscious mind denies all but the one idea it perceives to be immediately successful, never knowing what that idea is. Instead of enjoying an unconstrained flow of ideas, you are stymied by the tyranny of the "best" idea. As a result you hold up the scene.

To conquer selectivity we must come to understand that *any* idea is safe, and *every* idea is the best possible. We must, of course, analyze, discriminate, and manipulate our ideas, but we can do that only when we have ideas to work with. Selectivity puts the cart before the horse, if you will. It is like mining for gold and looking only for the pure metal, rather than pulling up tons of ore to refine later; a vein of pure gold is very rare. Accomplishing this means learning to trust our imaginations and the imaginations of our partners.

INFLEXIBILITY

Inflexibility is another serious pitfall in improv scene work. One form of inflexibility is hanging on to an idea past its usefulness, or *waffling*. It may come from the feeling that it is the only idea that you have, or simply from a reluctance to go back out into the void and take another chance on spontaneity.

Inflexibility also manifests itself in a player's negation of another player's ideas. A player will resist the invention of his or her partner by saying *no* or otherwise blocking the forward action of the scene. This results from a lack of trust in the partner's ability, or in a lack of willingness to support his or her ideas. The fear is that the other player's ideas may turn the scene in a new direction, forcing the player once again to go out into the void to test new ideas.

So inflexibility in one's thinking is a result of a lack of trust either in oneself, as evidenced by waffling, or in the other player, which manifests itself in the negation of that player's ideas. We will examine these common problems in more detail later, but the solution to inflexibility is, again, the realization of self-trust and ensemble trust.

CONTROL SEEKING

Control seeking happens when a player forces his or her ideas into the scene, or stalls the scene while playing for time to come up with an idea of his or her own. Frightened improvisers seek control, and they do it in a number of ways.

First, a player seeks control by not listening or by using only his or her own ideas, usually in a nonstop stream so that the other improviser cannot get a word in edgewise. I call this *steamrolling* because one player is figuratively flattening the other in the scene. Another way improvisers play for control is by *stalling* the scene until they are able to come up with their own idea that is satisfactory to their way of thinking. They will do this by repeating themselves or by negating their partner's premise. They may also map out the entire scene in their minds and try to make the scene go that way. They are not actually creating spontaneously; they are prethinking everything they do. I call this *scriptwriting* because they are literally scripting their improvisation. Finally, the least noticeable (but just as deadly) form of control seeking is when one player improvises his or her way into a position of power and *dominates* the scene so that he or she can dictate to other players what happens next. This improviser always casts him- or herself as the character "in charge." The character is always the boss giving orders, the coach rallying the team, or the expert there to solve the problem.

Improvisers such as these are uncomfortable with the process of improvisation, with the feeling of not knowing what happens next, or with being put in a position by another player to have to summon forth a new bit of information. They don't like to be put on the spot or they feel out of control, so they place themselves in a controlling position. Along the way, they make the scene dull and uninspired.

HAVE AN ATTITUDE OF PLAY

Creativity is easier with an attitude of play. When we are at play, we are seeking only to have fun, to experience joy. Creativity is easy during play because our defenses are down. There is no feeling of risk in play. Mental blocks and fears are removed, and there is little concern for filling perceived criteria. There is no need for practicality or critical thinking. There is no need to be right, because in play there is no right or wrong. There is only fun, or not fun.

The play of make-believe is never a win or lose proposition. It is, instead, either a win or *nonwin* thing. When you win at play, you win. When you lose at play, you *learn something*. So instead of being paralyzed by our mistakes, we learn from them—we grow. A good ensemble learns to enjoy its mistakes for the gifts they bring. Plato said, "Life must be lived as play." If you are play-ing, you are still living and learning.

Positive Assumption

My partner and I want to improvise a scene. We begin with noth-ing: no character, no plot, no setting—nothing. We are creating from a void. We need an idea to begin and, knowing that one idea is as good as another, I simply open my mouth and speak:

"Hi, Mom, I'm home."

I have just created the universe within which my partner and I will build a scene. I have just made an *assumption*—several assumptions, in fact. If I delivered my line to my partner (which I hope I did because my partner is the only other person onstage with me), I've laid the assumption that my partner is my mother and I, her son. I have also made the assumption that I just arrived home. I may also have added other information by virtue of the attitude or emotion with which I delivered my line. My partner must now respond and build the scene by adding an assumption of her own, and so on. My partner turns to me and replies:

"Dr. Anderson, the rocket is ready for launch."

To which I say:

"'To be or not to be.' That's what I said, and they roared with laughter."

Are you following the scene? I hope not, because each assumption has no obvious connection to the preceding assump-tions; therefore, there is no continuity. In order for a scene to make sense, each assumption must in some way build upon the previous assumption(s).

Think of an assumption as a building block and your task in the scene is to build a tower with such blocks. Each block must be laid upon the previous blocks. Each block rests upon the blocks beneath it, and each block is a support to the blocks above it. In the example above, no tower was built. We simply laid the building blocks out on the floor, each one separated from the other. Nothing progressed because new assumptions failed to extend the previous assumption.

In order for our "idea tower" to be successfully constructed, two things must be accomplished by each additional assumption. First, the previous assumption must be *affirmed*. Remember that any assumption we make in improv, once made, cannot be denied; ideas are indelible in improv. Once we present an idea, the audience will not forget it, even if we do. Ignoring or discarding ideas is not an option in improv. So how might we affirm my original assumption? Let's try this:

"Hi, Mom, I'm home."

"Hello, Son, you're home."

My partner has just affirmed to the audience that, indeed, she plays the mother in this scene, I play the son, and I have just arrived home. Let's continue in this vein of making positive or affirming assumptions and see what happens.

"Yes, Mom, you are my mother, and I have arrived home."

"Yes, my son, I am your mother, and you have just arrived at our home."

We are still affirming, but our scene is going nowhere because there is no new information being added. This is the second thing every assumption must do. It must affirm the previous assumption, then *add* new information.

"Hi, Mom, I'm home."

"Hello, Son, you're home early."

"Yeah. The volume of water increases as it goes from a liquid to a solid."

"It sure does; your dog died today."

"I know; I really like science class."

This one is not quite right either. Although it may be amusingly absurd, there still is no scene being developed. As we have said, each assumption must somehow be an extension of the previous assumption. I can affirm, and I can add, but I must also *extend*. Here is where all those automatic creative processes come into play. We need to unleash the associative power of our mind on the assumptions previously established in the scene, and allow our minds to suggest possible progressions. Let's try it and see what happens.

"Hi, Mom, I'm home."

"Billy, you're late! . . . And your sister has told me all about what happened at school today. You are in big trouble, young man."

My partner's response to my initial assumption has just filled in an enormous amount of new information. We now know the following: My name is Billy; I have just arrived home late from school; something unusual happened at school that day; my sister informed my mother all about it, and I am probably implicated in it; I'm in trouble with my mother; and she is not happy. Not only do I have this new information, but my assumption has also been affirmed.

What free associations did my partner make on my initial assumption? Obviously, the phrase "Hi, Mom, I'm home" conjured up for her the image of a schoolboy returning home from school. It could just as easily have been a GI returning home from the war or a middle-aged man returning home to his elderly mother. The important thing is that the previous assumption was used as a flash for the new thought, and that this thought was used without screening.

The key here is to remain open and to immerse yourself in the ideas of the scene rather than becoming involved in your own thoughts. Your imagination takes care of the rest. If, however, your prominent thoughts are about how to make the scene successful, then you are only cluttering the corridors of your imagination and ideas can't get through.

Imagining should be as effortless as perceiving. It should not feel like work. Everything that happens correctly in improv happens effortlessly. Your job as improviser is simply to facilitate the use of the ideas that come automatically. If I am making improvisation sound easy, it is. The difficult part is releasing yourself from the fears and judgments that impede you.

Let's finally pursue this scene in a way good improv might lead it.

Actor 1: "Hi, Mom, I'm home."
Actor 2: "Billy, you are late, and your sister has told me all about what happened at school today. You are in big trouble, young man."
Actor 1: "Aw, Mom, it was just a simple stock purchase arrangement. Can't I have any fun?"
Actor 2: "Good boys don't go around buying their schools and firing their principals."

Many people assume that their first thought will be their most mundane thought, and so discard it. They'll say, "Why can't I take my second or third thought? It might be better." But once you bypass your first notion, you're subjecting yourself to the judgment game, which you usually lose. Besides, the more immediate response seems more natural. In addition, it simply isn't true that your first thought is automatically the most mundane or commonplace. It depends on your mental attitude. If you assume an ambiguous mental attitude, as we talked about earlier, the wildest things will occur to you without even trying.

I typed out the scene example above, spontaneously, before I began this section. The idea of a grade school kid masterminding a corporate takeover of his school is not a commonplace idea. It leapt out as a result of my mental attitude at the time. The fact that I was then arranging investors for a new company may also have had something to do with it. Your mind will toss out some genuinely crazy things if you let it. Think of it as one of those lottery machines with the floating Ping-Pong balls. Just open the little gate and suck out an idea, and be assured that it is random and fresh.

When you free-associate, or flash, from previous assumptions, you place your mental focus on the whole picture, on the entire collection of previously laid assumptions, not merely on the previous assumption alone. There would be no consistency in a scene in which each new assumption is flashed only from the previous one. You let your mind use its natural powers of incorporation to give your thought context. Don't think about the process; just allow it to happen. Free-associate, then incorporate!

To summarize, positive assumption is an organic process by which one premise is extended by another. Each successive assumption affirms the previous one as true and present, and adds a new assumption flashed from all previous assumptions. As a scene progresses, each new assumption is like a piece of a jigsaw puzzle; each little bit adds to the whole picture. It is a beautiful process, but there are three basic ways to disrupt it.

YES, BUT . . .

Most actors easily understand affirming their partner's assumption, and they usually have no problem with the idea of adding new information in their responding assumption. Where they often fall down is to fail to connect their new assumptions with what has gone before. Where they should say, "Yes, and . . . ," they actually say, "Yes, but. . . ." This happens when one improviser is inflexible in his or her ideas or plays for control.

DENIAL AND NEGATION

When improvisers fail to affirm the previous assumption, they either *deny* or *negate* that assumption. It's as if one improviser pulls out an "assumption eraser" and decides, "Well, I really didn't like my partner's assumption, so I'm just going to erase it and write my own on top of it." Here is an example of a denied assumption.

Actor 1: "Honey, you'd better take a look at the car. There is something wrong with it."

Actor 2: "Trudy, I've got good news. My mother is going to stay with us for a month."
Actor 1: "What? I hate your mother. She can't stay, and that's final."
Actor 2: "Either she stays or I go."
Actor 1: "Fine! You can go live with your mother!"

With this example the audience is left wondering what happened to the car. Here's an example of a negated assumption.

Actor 1: "Say, this is some hot car you've got here. Let's go cruise the neighborhood."
Actor 2: "It's not a car, it's a golf cart, and get off the fairway you're blocking my shot!"
Actor 1: "Wow, I've been a mechanic all my life, and I've never seen a golf cart with an eight-cylinder 487 in it."
Actor 2: "It's battery driven, you moron; now either hand me my club, or I'll get a new caddie."

Despite Actor 1's attempts to patch the negation, Actor 2 twice negated his premise. To the audience this scene would appear as two improvisers who can't seem to agree on what their scene is about. Remember that once an idea is established, it is indelible; the audience never forgets.

WIMPING AND WAFFLING

The third basic mistake in positive assumption technique is for one improviser to affirm all assumptions but to add no new information. The following is an example of no new information:

Actor 1: "Well, Mr. Curator, you have broken a priceless Grecian urn."
Actor 2: "Yes, I am afraid I have broken it all to pieces."
Actor 1: "Now you are going to have to put it back together again, and hope that the board of directors doesn't notice when they have their reception here tomorrow."
Actor 2: "You are right, I will have to repair it before the reception."
Actor 1: "If Allister finds out, we'll find your remains in the medieval torture exhibit."
Actor 2: "Well, Allister better not find out then."

Here the scene is carried entirely by Actor 1. Actor 2 has offered nothing new to the scene, even though Actor 1 offered some very detailed assumptions from which Actor 2 could flash.

Actor 2 basically wimped out on adding any new information of his own to the scene. Thus I call this *wimping*.

When both actors wimp together, we get a *waffle*. A waffle sounds like this:

Actor 1: "Hey Jake, nice motorcycle."
Actor 2: "Yeah, it's brand new."
Actor 1: "It's really cool, that you got wheels. We can cruise now, man!"
Actor 2: "Thanks, this baby will go three hundred miles on a gallon of gas."
Actor 1: "We should go for a ride."
Actor 2: "Yeah, we should."
Actor 1: "We could go to the beach with it."
Actor 2: "Yeah, that sounds like fun, the beach sounds great!"

Little or no new information is offered by either actor in this scene, and it goes nowhere. Waffling occurs when something should clearly be happening in a scene but it is not. The two dudes in the scene should just get on the bike and cruise to the beach! (See Think Tank, "Yes, and . . ." Scene, and This Is You in *Acting Interactive Theatre*.)

Concentration

When asked to describe the act of mental concentration, most people will say it is a narrow focusing of one's attention. I ask this question all the time, and most of the descriptions I hear paint a picture of *squeezing* mental awareness, as in focusing a laser, or *distilling* it like condensed milk or orange juice concentrate. All of them have the feel of great mental exertion.

This view is unfortunate, because concentration is not a squeezing or condensing of thoughts, but a relaxing and releasing of them. Concentration is letting go of every thought other than the one you are centered on. People see concentration as a strenuous mental effort; no wonder they avoid it whenever possible. Concentration is really just selective perception. The effort it takes to concentrate is not unlike the effort it takes to relax.

If I play a piece of symphonic music for you, and ask that you listen only to the oboe, you would be "concentrating" on that sound. You would let all the other instruments fall away from your conscious awareness, and hear only the one instrument. After a while, you would become absorbed in that one sound. It would fill your awareness and take on a significance that it previously did not possess. You would hear more detail and variation in the sound. You might even hear things you never noticed before, like the breath of the musician on the mouthpiece. When you concentrate completely on the oboe, you do not hear the rest of the orchestra. Concentration, then, should be thought of not as mental focus, but mental listening.

Concentration is of paramount importance to the improviser. Without it he or she cannot tune out the blocks to spontaneity, be present in the scene and fully aware of its action, or be open to the creative process of free association and incorporation.

ANXIETY

The most common block to concentration is simple anxiety. This is the mental clutter that interrupts your concentration and whispers messages of dismay to you, such as: "I'm not creative." "I can't think of anything." "This won't be any good." These little voices of doubt can do much to disrupt your creative flow. My favorite is the little game the mind plays when it says things such as the following:

> *You won't be able to think of the next thought . . . You know you are not going to come up with an idea, because you are spending all of your time listening to me say that you are not going to come up with an idea . . . How can you come up with an idea when you keep listening to me? . . . See, you are wasting time . . . The time for coming up with an idea is past; you've already blown it.*

This self-defeating loop used to catch me all the time until I finally learned not to fight it, but to embrace it and then let it fall away. Building concentration means getting better at negating distractions by relaxing and releasing thoughts. (See Concentration in *Acting Interactive Theatre*.)

Listening

Your imagination will naturally spring to new thoughts from the thoughts that are presented to it. Listening to what is being established in the scene will provide your imagination with the imagery it needs to grant you new assumptions appropriate for the situation.

The skill of paying attention is one mental ability that can always stand improvement. Many people learn to hear, but not listen—really listen. A rudimentary level of mental attention is enough for one to hear and understand what is being said or done, but it takes an emotional attention in order to listen. Listening involves not only what is heard and understood, but what is felt.

In improv there are always two things to listen to: what is going on in your mind, and what is going on in the scene. It is difficult but necessary to ignore what is going on in your mind and to immerse yourself in the here and now of the scene. When you are listening to your mind, you are listening to the fears and anticipation that bring you away from the action of the scene. Therefore, you must get your emotional involvement away from your self and into the scene. (See Listening to Environment, Double Conversation, and Listening While Telling in *Acting Interactive Theatre*.)

Focus—Give and Take

The mind has difficulty in absorbing two sources of information at the same time. The same is true as an audience watches a scene. If more than one thing is happening at once, guests will have difficulty absorbing and understanding both. For this reason, all scene work must present a single focus to the audience, one thing to look at and understand at a time. Unless the focus is to be static, which is dull, improvisers must learn to move the focus from one place to the next without creating a split focus. Focus must move freely and seamlessly about the scene. If it does not, the scene will appear contrived or unrealistic. It takes a fair amount of "sixth sensing" and teamwork to promote good focus. The more rapport and experience improvisers have with each other, the better able they are to pass focus well.

Being the actor with the focus onstage can, of course, be a lot of fun. But the tendency for the unwary improviser is to hold on to the focus or to take the focus from someone else. Both cause problems for allowing the scene to progress in a clear and natural way. The simple solution to both problems is to learn to give focus.

When focus isn't shared among players, the problem tends to perpetuate itself. When a player has the focus, but is conditioned to expect other players to take that focus from him or her, the player will habitually struggle to keep it. When an improviser doesn't have the focus, and is conditioned to expect that focus will never be given, he or she will likewise learn to take focus away from others.

I've heard many directors try to teach improvisers when to give and when to take the focus. After years of directing, my considered opinion is that focus should never be taken. I allow that focus only be given. It is the only way that a truly seamless transition can be achieved.

That which takes place in the focus of a scene must always be allowed to fulfill an intent and arrive at some moment of relinquishment before transfer of focus takes place. In this sense, the focus must always be given, as in given to an individual, or given up, as in given up to the company at large. A partner must then accept the focus passed to him or her or pick up the focus given at large. An actor who takes focus before the moment of relinquishment only steals it. This usually leaves the partner's phrase incomplete and contributes to the dysfunctions of stealing and holding focus.

Watching a scene in which the focus is constantly being grabbed by one player from another is uncomfortable. There is something disturbing about it that makes it difficult to maintain interest in the scene. Except in the case of tandem action, such as two players singing a song together, the focus is simply a matter of who is speaking or who is performing a key action. If more than one person is talking at the same time, there is a split focus. Moreover, when both are talking, they can't be listening and, therefore, cannot be engaged in positive assumption.

The best way to ensure that the focus in a scene will always be given and shared among the players is for the players themselves to agree to play the game before the scene starts. The game is, "You give me the focus, and I'll give you the focus." In my "pass the balloon" exercise, the focus is personified as a balloon that is passed back and forth among the players as the scene progresses. The holder of the balloon must also hold the focus; the one without the balloon lends focus. In this game many bad focus habits are immediately exposed. It also effectively displays the simple power of agreeing to be playful. Good focus work can transform scene work from a veritable war of ideas to a delightful game of mutual support.

Good focus habits are not a hallmark of the experienced improviser; even the most experienced can fall into bad habits. In fact, the more experienced improvisers are, the more susceptible they are to this bad habit. I've seen the work of expert improvisers transformed to new heights by attention to their focus habits. (See Pick Up an Object, Absolute Focus, and Pass the Balloon in *Acting Interactive Theatre*.)

Interrogatives

Interrogative statements, more commonly known as questions, can be deceptively harmful in improvisation. If I ask a question in an improv, I have probably added no new information to the scene. I have essentially passed up my turn at the idea tower and have asked my partner to add new information for me.

Since we are both improvising, neither of us knows where the scene is going. My partner doesn't know the answer to the question any more than I do. So why should I ask the question? I should do for myself what I am asking my partner to do: make an assumption.

An inexperienced improviser is not yet comfortable with the feeling of mental uncertainty that is always present when one improvises. The mind's natural response to a condition of uncertainty is a question, and this is what usually comes out of the mouth. The way to break the habit of asking questions is to learn to stop yourself before you ask the question. Ask the question in your mind, answer it, and present that information as a statement (assumption). If the question habit is not broken, it can lead to scenes that sound like this:

Actor 1: "Hi Fergie, what are you doing?"
Actor 2: "Oh, cleaning my cab. I had a busy day yesterday."
Actor 1: "Oh, yeah? What did you do?"
Actor 2: "Well, there was a convention of lieutenant governors, and I had to ferry them all around the city."
Actor 1: "Wow, where did they go?"
Actor 2: "Well, we were supposed to go to city hall, but there was a big demonstration there, so we ended up in the parking lot of the A&P."
Actor 1: "Wow, were they mad?"
Actor 2: "Sure, they were mad. One of them beat up a cop."

There is really only one actor improvising in this scene. Also, even though Actor 2 was providing assumptions, the scene still did not go anywhere because question asking leads to story-telling, not scene work. This does not mean, however, that you should never ask a question in any improvised scene. In practice, a full and detailed assumption can be embedded in an interrogative statement, such as this:

Actor 1: "Cleaning the cab again, eh Fergie?"
Actor 2: "Yeah, ferrying a bunch of lieutenant governors around sure can trash your cab. What slobs!"
Actor 1: "Is that your wallet there on the seat?"
Actor 2: "Nope. Hey, look! It's one of the lieutenant governors', and there's money in it. Looks like my state tax refund came through after all."

Here each question asked contains new information for the scene. Now you may tell yourself that you will remember to add information with your questions, but that won't work unless you first learn to discard the dependency on asking questions. If not, your questions will sound like the first example rather than the second. I force new improvisers to ask no questions at all until they have first proved they are comfortable in making statements (assumptions). (See Question Scenes and No Questions for One Day in *Acting Interactive Theatre.*)

Second Support

To this point we have considered scene work with only two part-ners. When an additional character enters the scene after it has begun, it offers second support. The *second* refers to the sec-ondary addition of a character or characters to the scene. The *support* refers to the objective of that secondary addition, that is, advancing the established action of the scene. Second support is possible only when the second supporter is in a position to observe and understand the scene before becoming a part of it. There is no way, after all, that one can lend support to a scene that one doesn't understand. The second supporter always enters the scene with a strong new assumption related to the scene, which develops the action in a constructive way.

Blundering into a scene because you would like to be a part

of it is not second support. The second supporter must decide whether or not it will be beneficial to the scene to make an entrance. A scene may not need second support. No matter how brilliant an idea the second supporter may have, its addition may spin the scene off in a less successful direction. It is not a decision to be taken lightly by the potential supporter.

It is also true that a scene may be progressing quite nicely on its own, yet the idea and the timing might be so auspicious that the second supporter may decide to enter and bring it to an even higher level. An example of this is a scene that involves an important, but offstage, character. If at the right moment that character were suddenly to appear with an assumption perfectly suited to the situation, a wonderful result may be achieved. It is always a judgment call on the second supporter's part, and he or she often carries the responsibility for the future success or failure of the scene.

However, if a scene is going poorly, second support of any kind may be appreciated by those in the scene. If there is little to lose, the risk may be worth it. Awareness, sensitivity, and selflessness are the keys to good second support. (See Second Support Conversation in *Acting Interactive Theatre*.)

Dominance Transactions

In any theatrical scene, at any given moment, one character has dominance. That dominance may be great, as in a scene with a burglar pulling his gun on a hapless victim, or very small, as in a scene in which executives at a meeting vie for the head seat at the conference table. On the stage, as in life, dominance always changes. Scenes in which dominance is small will change hands more rapidly and subtly. In scenes in which dominance is great, it will change more slowly and more obviously. Awareness of how dominance in a scene is transacted can be a valuable tool for improvisers as they try to craft a realistic and truthful scene.

As with most social animals, the dynamics of dominance and submission are always at play in our interactions. They are imbedded in our psyche perhaps from the earliest stages of evolution, and are part of who we are. They drive our social behavior. Dominance is preferred to submission simply because dominance is the safer choice, and safety is a key to self-preservation; it is our strongest and most basic instinct. Playing for dominance in an improv comes naturally because it feels safe, and safe feels right. But the improviser has to reverse this instinct in order to create situations that are interesting to an audience.

When a character is dominant, it reveals only that which it chooses to reveal. When a character goes from a state of dominance to a state of *indominance* (a word I have made up to replace the word *submission* because, when I call it that, actors get the impression that it is something to be avoided), involuntary information about that character is released. In real life, this change is seen as failure, something to be avoided at all costs. But, when it happens in the theatre, a character arriving at indominance acquires the powerful theatrical tool of vulnerability.

When a character is vulnerable, it is open to inspection by the audience. The deep truths that we love to hide in real life are revealed in that character. The fascinating and compelling insights into the human condition, for which we go to the theatre, are revealed for us in this way. Thus, the lowering of dominance reveals truth in a character, and rising from indominance celebrates the truth in a character. The transition from indominance to dominance is a scene that we love to watch as an audience—and love to play as actors. It is the scene in which the downtrodden tramp finds the winning lottery ticket or the underdog prevails.

In life, we play to maintain dominance. In the theatre, we play to change, or transact, dominance. It is sometimes difficult to convince an improviser to release his or her personal connection to the idea of dominance. The tendency is to fall into the control-seeking trap, play for dominance, and seek to maintain dominance. The resulting scene is usually static and uninteresting.

Improv is not safe for its characters. The theatre itself is not a safe place—it was never intended to be. The theatre is a place for us to see and experience vicariously through its characters all the things we would not want to experience in our real lives. Who would want to be tied to a railroad track, leap from a cliff, or even lose at canasta? The audience loves to experience these things for its own amusement or insight, but from the safety of its chairs. The improviser, however, must take the leap!

It is not being dominant or being indominant that makes a character interesting; interest is created when dominance changes. Comedy lives in every dominance transaction. Once improvisers realize that the real juicy stuff happens when dominance transacts in a scene, and once they become as comfortable with indominance as they are with dominance, improvisers will begin to use this dynamic with a playful abundance that will fascinate their audience. I have developed exercises that focus on letting improvisers experience the power of the indominant position and making them aware of the value of dominance transactions. (See Dominance Postures, Master-Servant Scene, and Accepting Insults in *Acting Interactive Theatre*.)

Trust, Support, and Cooperation

Most teachers of improv have one ultimate commandment. Mine is "Trust, support, and cooperate." If an improviser understands and uses these three concepts, very little can go wrong.

Trust is relying on the genius of others. It is having the attitude toward your fellow improvisers that they are the best in the world and that they are there to make you look good. It is believing in the creativity of your fellow ensemble members. It is trusting yourself and trusting the process of spontaneity. It is relinquishing control.

Support is making your partners look good. It is caring as much about their success in the scene as your own. It is setting up your partner for the good stuff and bailing him or her out of the bad. It is what I call playing the other's character, that is, placing your mental focus on the needs and desires of your partner's character in the scene rather than your own. Your partner, naturally, will be doing the same for you. This gives you both a deeper connection with the subtext of the scene and makes for insightful playing.

Cooperation is relinquishing your own ideas in favor of the ideas at hand. It is playing for the betterment of the scene rather than for the betterment of yourself or your character. It is conducting yourself with a true spirit of give-and-take, and approaching the work in a spirit of play.

Narrative Skills 13

The Actor's Relationship to the Story

Without attention to the narrative of the scene, the sum of the process I have outlined from freeing the imagination through scene work may still result in a meandering of ideas. Through narrative skills the improviser can manipulate the assumptions of the scene to give the scene meaning, structure, and closure.

Assumptions

There is no such thing as a bad assumption. There is no such thing as a wrong assumption. The context we build around our assumptions is what gives them value and meaning. We cannot qualify the assumptions we make with how good or bad the idea is. We can, however, talk about how well that idea was expressed. Was it expressed clearly or vaguely? Did we paint a full picture of our idea, or did we merely sketch in the outline? Consider the following scene.

Actor 1: "You have it in your hand!"
Actor 2: "Yes, it is the Morning Star Diamond, Juno. Sacred stone of the Incas, the most precious gem in all the world and it is finally ours!"

Actor 1: "Yes, but how do we get out of here again?"
Actor 2: "The tombs of Macumba are full of deadly snares, but not to
one who knows their secrets. Trust me, Juno, we shall prevail."
Actor 1: "Oh my God, there is something coming out of the dark! It
is heading toward us!"
Actor 2: "Great Scott, giant spiders! They were thought to be extinct
millions of years ago. I have taken no precautions for this deadly
peril. Juno, you must help me!"
Actor 1: "Anything, Master!"
Actor 2: "I want you to sacrifice yourself so that I may escape!"

Actor 2's assumptions are more detailed. He gives us specific information: names, places, historical references, and so on. He paints a more vivid picture than does Actor 1.

Think for a moment how much easier it is for Actor 1 to flash on his partner's assumptions than it is for Actor 2. Actor 2's more substantive assumptions present more points of association to Actor 1's imagination, giving him more to work with. Actor 1's assumptions are vague, causing Actor 2 to have to work harder. Actor 1's assumptions are also missing adjectives, and adjectives add color to assumptions.

Also notice Actor 1's use of pronouns. Pronouns are vague and should be avoided in improv. A good rule of thumb for improv is to replace a pronoun with the genuine article. For instance, instead of saying "something" is coming out of the dark and "it" is coming at us, Actor 1 could have defined the threat at that time instead of leaving it for Actor 2 to come up with giant spiders. Actor 1's assumption was not wrong or bad; it was in fact a wonderfully workable idea. He just didn't define it as completely as he could have.

But making full assumptions doesn't mean making them endless. This, again, would be scriptwriting, which happens when an improviser with an abundance of ideas decides to keep going and tell the whole story. This is what it might look like if Actor 1 went overboard with his assumptions:

Actor 1: "You have it in your hand! It is the rare Morning Star
Diamond, the most precious gem of the Incas, Master. We found
it at last! Now all we must do is leave this tomb without trigger-
ing any of the dangerous traps, and without being eaten by any
of the giant spiders thought to have been long extinct. Then once
free of this bug-infested country we will return to civilization
where you will sell this diamond at Sotheby's, buy a villa in the

south of France, and we will live happily for the rest of our days
in a life of leisure."
Actor 2: *"Yup."*

If you were Actor 1, you might be thinking, "Wow, I'm really cookin' today," and may wonder why Actor 2 felt the scene went poorly. As the audience we want to see the story unfold in front of us, not merely be told what's going to happen. In order to keep the scene going, Actor 2 will have to find some sort of new conflict, perhaps something like this:

Actor 2: *"Wait, Juno, there is something inscribed on the side of the diamond. It says, 'Made in Japan.'"*

Improvisers should add one idea at a time, giving the audience and their partner just a piece of the story, then pass the focus to their partner. That way, the scene unfolds to the audience through a creative collaboration, which is often as interesting to view as the scene itself. (See Sentence at a Time; Story, Story; and Image Scene in *Acting Interactive Theatre*.)

Who, What, Where

Any narrative, in order to be a narrative, must contain three basic elements: a person, an action, and a place. As an audience watches a scene unfold, there are three capital questions corresponding to these basic elements that need to be answered. They are the *who, what,* and *where* questions. The audience not only needs them answered, but needs the information up front, as early in the story as possible, so that it understands what the story is about.

Establishing the answers to these questions is the improviser's first priority in a new scene. When one or more of these questions is left unaddressed for too long, the audience may suddenly lose interest in and/or respect for the scene. An audience member may watch a scene with a well-defined action and location, but may still be wondering, "Who the heck are these people?" The preoccupation with that question will distract them from the scene, and the audience will remain uncomfortable until it is made clear. Likewise, the question may be, "Where the heck are they?" or "What the heck are they doing?" and the problem is the same.

When the all-important questions—Who? What? and Where?—are answered, the *when* and *why* questions will naturally fall into place throughout the course of the scene. The *whys* are the relationships between character and action, and cannot be arrived at until the other essentials are established. (See Who, What, Where in a Minute and Screenwriters in *Acting Interactive Theatre*.)

Observation and Memorization

Each new assumption adds to the whole picture—a picture that constantly grows as the scene progresses. Improvisers must keep the full picture in memory in order to move the scene forward effectively. If they fail to retain all of the assumptions played out, they may launch the scene in too many directions at once or lose the information they need to make an effective closure. Improv is like walking backwards. You cannot see where you are going, only where you have been. Each step that you take backwards adds to your field of view. In any given moment of an improvised scene, the future is drawn from the past—not from the previous idea alone, but from the collective assumptions drawn so far.

An improviser's powers of observation and memorization are keys to retaining this ever-growing assembly of ideas. Names, places, and actions must be remembered accurately; otherwise the scene will become confused. Each improviser should be playing from the same deck, so to speak. Improvisers who become good at remembering every detail presented in the scene become more nimble in manipulating that scene in useful ways. Their ability to incorporate previous ideas will improve because those ideas will be readily available to them. When specifics are reincorporated into a scene, it gives the illusion of their existing before the scene. This makes the improvisers appear more skillful and connected with one another. Also a scene that is rich in reincorporated specifics is easier to close. An improviser's power of observation and his or her capacity for memorization can be exercised separately, then applied to scene work. (See The Memory Game in *Acting Interactive Theatre*.)

Keeping the Action Onstage

The action of the scene must unfold to the audience in the here and now. The audience cannot truly witness the action of the scene unless it is played out in the present, at the location in which it appears to the audience. But an unwitting improviser may lay assumptions that place the action offstage. This may be action that has already occurred; present action that is happening elsewhere; or action that will happen, or may happen in the future.

Improvisers can also create offstage characters. I am often surprised at the ingenuity with which some improvisers create characters that are integral to the scene but are nowhere to be found. Sometimes, both the main action and the characters performing that action are only imaginary. This conveniently removes the responsibility of working with one's fellow players. Offstage action is an easy crutch, because no one actually does the action, and no one is actually there to give answer to the assumption. When one player starts it, the other player is often snared into the same trap, and before long both players are playing a scene that the audience never *sees*. This type of scene is very dull to watch. The players become nothing more than bystanders and talking heads, doing more storytelling than scene playing.

PREVENTING OFFSTAGE ACTION

There are a few rules of thumb that can be valuable in preventing this from happening. One is never to create an offstage character, unless it is done as a deliberate invitation to an actor waiting to second support as that character. For instance, I might be improvising a scene in which I have a broken leg, and I may refer to the doctor who set the bone. That reference may be fine if it furthers the action onstage. (Perhaps the cast was placed on the wrong leg.) But if the action is about what the doctor did in his office, or is doing now elsewhere, or what he may do in the future, then I have created an offstage character.

Another rule of thumb is to keep the action in the present tense as well as in the present place. Action that once happened, or may happen in the future, tends to lead one offstage. Consider a scene in which two archeologists muse over a pile of bones at an excavation site. Their attachment to action of the past might result in a scene about what life was like fifty million years ago. On the other hand, action based on the present-tense elements of archeologists extracting a pile of bones from the earth might lead to more here-and-now action and less standing and talking.

If I do assume future-tense action into the scene—what will or may happen—my rule of thumb is to follow that action into the present. Consider a scene in which two juvenile delinquents discuss stealing a car. Instead of talking about how they will do it and what they will do with it once they get it, they should stop waffling and just go do it. Then, instead of listening to them talk about it, the audience can actually see them find the car, watch them hot-wire it, see them driving down the road, and truly feel a part of whatever actions take place. The audience will not only "be there" as they weave through traffic and drag-race people at stoplights, but it will also be there when they are suddenly stopped by police and thrown into jail. In other words, the audience can experience the outcome of those actions, not merely the characters' speculation about them. It will also experience action never guessed at by the characters' suppositions. In improv, if something is going to happen, then make it happen.

Canceling the Action

Canceling the action of a scene is more than just negating an assumption. It happens when the general course of a scene seems to be leading toward a climactic moment but suddenly backs down from that moment and reroutes itself in a different direction—often a less climactic one. The pilot realizes the airplane is out of gas. As the plane begins to plummet to earth any number of exciting things can happen, but suddenly . . . the co-pilot remembers that there is a reserve tank, and the plane continues on its way.

Canceling the action also happens when an assumption renders the previous course of the scene unnecessary or obsolete. A man carries a priceless Ming vase and trips; the vase flies out of his hands, arcs across the room, and is suddenly caught by another man who safely returns the vase to its owner. Canceling the action often happens when improvisers can't quite see what would happen next. (They are thinking instead of reacting.) They need to trust the process and know that the next assumption will make itself clear.

What might have happened to the two men in the plane? They might have bailed out and parachuted behind enemy lines. They might have crash-landed on the mountainside and found Brigadoon. They might have crashed and died, then returned to haunt the maintenance man who failed to fill the tank. *Anything* might have happened and would have been more interesting than continuing on their way.

Breaking the Routine

Breaking the routine is altering the expected course of action in order to create conflict. Consider this story. *"Jack obeyed his mother and took their cow to market to sell. He went to market, sold the cow, and came back home to the delight of his mother."* Now let's break the routine. *"Jack obeyed his mother and took their cow to market to sell. Along the way he met a strange man. Jack sold him the cow for three magic beans . . ."* If the routine were not broken, the story of Jack and the Beanstalk would not be told.

An improviser should regard the character with the same attitude as an author and be willing to create for that character any destiny that will best support the scene. Once again, what we would normally say *no* to in life, the improviser embraces and says *yes!* It is the duty of the improviser to embrace and delight in the extraordinary and the dangerous.

Actors who make the mistake of personally identifying with their characters may resist uncomfortable action in the scene in the same way they would resist it in real life. I sometimes have to remind improvisers that it is, after all, only make-believe and that their characters are not they, so they should go ahead, lose an eye, and see what happens next. As with dominance transactions, I tell them to disconnect their own personal survival instinct from their character, and not to play their character as though it is a friend they must protect. The rule of thumb is, when in doubt, put your character in peril. (See "Ding" Scenes and Extraordinary Assumptions in *Acting Interactive Theatre.*)

Reincorporation

Reincorporation is the repetition of a previously revealed bit of information or situation within a scene. It is a powerful tool for giving form to developing scenes, and it can provide closure. In the course of a scene, there might be one or two points that have gotten a particularly good reaction from the audience. Those are the elements that should stick in the back of the improviser's mind and be reincorporated in the scene to help extend the premise.

A fine example of this was an encounter done in the Streetmosphere show. A Hollywood has-been actor meets a girl off the bus who is bent on becoming a star. The premise begins as the has-been gives the girl sage advice on how to "make it in Hollywood." A successful point of interest develops when the has-been decides to *charge* the girl for a bit of information, making it obvious that he is destitute himself. Reincorporating this idea led to the has-been finding more and more ways to charge the girl more and more money for his "expert" advice. "That's how it's done here in Hollywood," he says.

Now the scene takes on a new dimension, one of exploring the human foibles of desperation in the has-been, and naïveté in the girl. Through simple reincorporation they extend the premise. The repetition provides emphasis, comedy, and an air of suspense as the audience begins to wonder how the game will end.

A number of ways to close the scene also become evident to the two improvisers. In the course of the transactions, the has-been has revealed some of his own problems in Hollywood, such as not currently having an agent. The girl can use the opportunity to close the scene by disclosing that she has just signed with an agent and offering to make an introduction for the has-been. In a final act of reincorporation the girl uses her newfound knowledge to charge the has-been a fee in return for the favor—one equal to or exceeding the amount he has already extorted from her. Through simple reincorporation, a clever ironic twist worthy of applause is found.

This pat encounter was the result of a free improv, one in which the actors paid attention to reincorporation. The tool of reincorporation gives the improvisers the means to create the illusion that they knew where the scene was headed all along, when in fact they did not.

Motivated Exit

Any character entering a scene does so using the rules of good second support and, therefore, motivates its entrance with an assumption. The characters already in the scene then lend proper focus to the entering character. The same idea is true for exits.

When any character exits a scene, it must do so with the focus of all the other characters in the scene. The exit should include an assumption that carries the exiting character offstage and out of the action. This is one way clear action is maintained in a multiple-character scene. (See Motivated Exit in *Acting Interactive Theatre*.)

Closure

A conditioned sensitivity to the use of exposition, conflict, irony, resolution, and even morality comes into play in the development of an improvised scene. I use the term *sensitivity* because it can be no more than just that. If improvisers try too consciously to "write" the scene, it will quickly bog down and fall apart. They would have to think too long, judge too much, and stop listening to their partners in order to give the scene structure. Instead, they must rely on their instinct, and that of their partner, to give form and intent to the progression of ideas that make up their scene. Nowhere is this more crucial than when the players attempt to close the scene.

Closure is more than an ending. Closure ties up all the remaining loose ends into one neat package. It gives final motive and resolution to all the threads of the action. It is the ultimate act of incorporation. Anyone can end a scene, but good closure is probably the most difficult aspect of improvisation. This is why I have saved it until the last.

In truth, there is little else to say about closure here. Everything that is needed for good closure has already been discussed, except perhaps that indefinable element, that sixth sense that improvisers acquire after working together for a while, that extra edge that long-standing trust and knowledge of a partner can bring. If improvisation were a science, you would now know all you need to know. But it is not. Improvisation is an art. I cannot prescribe here a leap of inspiration or a moment of genius. As artists, improvisers are now on their own. (See First Line, Last Line and Title Scenes in *Acting Interactive Theatre*.)

Part IV

Interactive Performance

*I*n these chapters we combine the skills of ensemble improv and interactive character development to create action that reveals the subject and that actively includes the guest. Now we begin to breathe life into the interactive production by improvising in character to form relationships and to create the mythology that gives our story depth and realism. Here too we use the improv process to develop the structured and repeatable performance elements that will form the body of the production.

Scene Work in Character 14

We return here to our Wild West production
and its model characters. By now we would
have established a temenos within the cast
and, by using the techniques of ensemble
improv, cast members would have begun to grasp the art of
play. Our interactive ensemble must now make that play
element inclusive. The ensemble must turn its sacred circle
outward and draw the audience into its activity so that
guests partake of the gifts of play in the same way the
ensemble does, experiencing the joy of creativity and harmony themselves.

The work is not so much a presentation as it is an *invitation*. Rather than putting on a show to entertain its audience, an interactive ensemble entertains by inviting that
audience into its creative sandbox. Here the audience is
coaxed and guided into building a sand castle with the
players, enjoying the actors' creative genius and at the
same time discovering, or rekindling, its own. The resulting
sand castle is achieved through trust, play, and joy.

Improv from here on is a combination of skilled inter-
play *among* the performers and improv *with* audience par-
ticipants. Interactive actors must be skilled in improvising
not only with professionals but with amateurs as well. They
must teach the game of ensemble improvisation to the

unskilled guest. They must play the game with them, and make them look good.

Improv with Established Characters

Improv in its purest form begins with nothing and then attempts to answer the five basic questions of any situation: Who? What? Where? When? and Why? (or at least the three most obvious ones: Who? What? and Where?). In the case of stage (or abstract) improv, this information can be created or changed at the whim of the performer. I can start a scene as the mailman and end it as the tooth fairy if it suits me. This provides great latitude in how the scene progresses, but in improv for interactive performance, character, location, and period are largely established prior to performance. So, the *who*, *where*, and *when* of the scene do not change.

The *where* and *when* are usually absolute facts (i.e., Main Street of the Gold Rush town Vulture Gulch, circa 1865), but it must be said that the *who*, although predesigned by the actor, does represent that complex and changing entity called a human being. It should, therefore, not be resistant to some level of alteration that might be dictated by the context of the scene.

For instance, a scene is played in the Wild West saloon. Seated at the table are a gunslinger and a preacher, gambling. An actress stands nearby preparing choices for furthering the scene and developing interesting action. If this were a scene played at a comedy club, the actress entering could choose any character she wished. She might choose to be a saloon girl, a nun, or a pregnant wife. In an interactive show, the actress would have only one choice, that of her prepared character, in this case, a saloon girl. Her choices here are limitless, within the realm of her interactive character of saloon girl. She may still be pregnant, she may even be a wife, but she is *not* a nun. At a comedy club, she might enter as the director, yell *"Cut!"* and change the reality into the *filming* of a Wild West scene. But in an interactive show, time and place are absolute, and she would not have the choice of altering the reality.

When we apply ensemble improv technique to an interactive show, we refer to it as *interactive improv* and define it as improvisation fed by the established characters and environment, directed toward outward and inclusive action with the guest.

Of the five "W's" mentioned earlier, the two remaining are the *what* (the action) and the *why* (motive). The skill of the interactive actor is the skill with which the picture of *who, when,* and *where* is painted for the guest, and how the actor develops and justifies the *what* and the *why.*

Interactive improv presents challenges to the actor different from the abstract improv of a comedy club. The result can be more impressive to the audience, and more rewarding to the actor. It is akin to the great tradition of Italian comedy, the commedia dell'arte. The characters and situations are stock, leaving the improvisationist to deal more carefully with the fascinating and enlightening realm of human behavior and motive. (See Ben's Chili Bowl, Party Scene in Character, and ABC Scenes in *Acting Interactive Theatre.*)

Active Choices

Active choices are how the primary activities of the character are translated into meaningful, active play with the guest. An actor must take each primary activity and look for ways to make active choices for that activity. An active choice is an outward activity that requires immediate action or involvement from the guest in order to be fulfilled. It is not a contemplative or cerebral activity, but an outward, doing activity.

AN ACTIVE CHOICE IS AN OUTWARD ACTIVITY

Let's imagine Eustus Panfreed having just realized that he misplaced the map to his new strike and can't remember where it is. The activity is Eustus trying to remember how to get to his claim. If Pat played it as Eustus sitting on the porch of the general store with his eyes rolled back in his head in an effort to recall, it would encourage little guest interaction. Indeed, guests would have no idea who he was or what he was doing, regardless of how absorbed Pat was in the character.

If, instead, Pat played Eustus marching into the street begging for help, promising gold shares to anyone who could help jog his memory, he would then be inviting some potentially fascinating interaction.

AN ACTIVE CHOICE IS A HERE-AND-NOW ACTION

An active choice is immediate, in that it is a *here-and-now* action, not storytelling of offstage action or the relating of events from the past or future. If Eustus encountered guests with a *story* about the time he lost his map, how can the guests become actively involved? If he describes how at this very minute half the town is out in the hills looking for his gold claim, how can the guests become actively involved? They can't. The actor must make the here-and-now choice.

AN ACTIVE CHOICE IS INCLUSIVE

An active choice is also inclusive, in that the action requires the involvement of the guest for it to be accomplished. The *active* in active choice refers, of course, to the *guest* being active. It should be assumed that the character is always active. Guests are either verbally active, meaning they are spontaneously creating and sharing their own ideas; physically active, performing a here-and-now task; or engaged in a combination of the two.

Active choices for Eustus' problem may include his getting guests to help him retrace his steps over remembered landmarks in a sort of giant treasure map; his soliciting creative methods from guests for jogging his memory, then doing them; or his getting guests to help him look in town or search other guests for the stolen map.

ACTIVE CHOICES CONNECT THE ACTOR TO THE GUEST THROUGH NEED

Happily, human nature finds it easier to give than to receive, at least as far as interactive theatre is concerned. The word *interaction* means reciprocal action or effect, an exchange of needs and offers, of action and reaction. Guests find it much harder to act than to react. Therefore, the best posture for an interactive character is one of being in need, because one of the nicer things about human nature is that people love to *help*.

Character Relationships

Without relationships, a story is a meaningless collection of facts. Creating relationships with the guests, thereby involving them in the story, is the primary focus of the interactive genre. Yet the relationships between the *characters* form the backbone of the story. Through character relationships, encounters are formed and the scenario of the production is allowed to unfold. Whether the narrative of the production is a linear-plot scenario of an interactive play or the collective themes of an interactive event, character relationships fuel the action and give it meaning. Without them, there is little context for guest interaction.

Predetermined character relationships give actors a starting place, a way of behaving toward one another that gives them a head start in creating interesting action. It also presents the impression that the theatrical reality has a prehistory, thus making it seem more realistic.

FORMING RELATIONSHIPS

What should one interactive character *relate* to in another to form a relationship? What have we defined for these characters that is relatable? Their occupations provide the characters' sphere of action. How do these relate? How do their passion, needs, foibles, and general disposition color their actions, and how do they contrast with those of others?

Look for differences that must be assimilated. The sameness in the characters will show itself. Concentrate, therefore, on the struggle for common ground, especially where there is none. The characters' backgrounds may feed relationships. Their attitudes about themselves and others will have much to do with how they might relate. Pull these items apart and examine them in discussion. Play them out in scene work and explore them as they surface.

ESTABLISHING RELATIONSHIPS IN PERFORMANCE

Relationships *among* characters must be established and re-established in performance each time a new guest becomes involved. There is clearly an element of repetition at work here. But, obviously, the actors are not in a position to build their relationship from the beginning for each new guest that walks by. To do this they would have to meet for the first time every few minutes. Relationships are always in progress for characters (unless they are deliberate strangers). The starting point, then, is usually in the middle of the relationship—having been somewhere, but going somewhere too.

This, however, does not exempt the actors from establishing that relationship continuously. There must be an almost constant stream of information that motivates their existing relationship, even as it develops in new directions through the scene. Actors have a tendency to forget that the audience doesn't know them, or their relationships to each other, as well as they themselves do after weeks or months of performance.

MAKE RELATIONSHIPS POSITIVE

The types of relationships actors should create among their characters should be constructive. Whether the relationship is a harmonious one or one steeped in conflict, it must allow for the growth of interesting action and good improv technique. Relationships that are cruel, negating, or indifferent will not lead to constructive action. Some actors tend to confuse conflict with negation. Conflict complicates action interestingly and leads to a climax. Negation works to prevent action from taking place, whether it is interesting or not.

NEVER PLAY PERSONAL RELATIONSHIPS IN CHARACTER

Character relationships should be separated from personal relationships between actors. It is dangerous to play character relationships too close to actual relationships. Words and events in performance can be taken as personally motivated slights, reproaches, or even approaches. This sort of thing, when intentional, is unprofessional behavior, but it does not have to be intentional to be a threat to ensemble trust. It is often but a mistake on the part of the offended party, having interpreted personally what should have been heard only by the character. Even so, it breaks the trust in the ensemble and hinders the production. (See Roundtable Relationship Discussion and Character Attitude Toward Characters in *Acting Interactive Theatre*.)

Mythology

The mythology is the sum of the facts, histories, and relationships "known" by the ensemble prior to the beginning of the performance. It is the backstory of the production, the collective relationships of characters to each other and to their environment, the body of information that all of the ensemble accepts as given when the show commences.

The intent of a mythology is twofold. First, it gives the illusion of a detailed reality. The richer the background, the more real the illusion seems. Consider, for example, what J. R. R. Tolkien did for his fanciful creation of Middle Earth in his *Lord of the Rings* trilogy. The richness of his myth is what gave his story such power. Second, it gives the actors a starting place for their improvisations. A detailed knowledge of the character, its history and position within the created reality, propels the improvisation forward in a direction appropriate for the production.

MYTHOLOGY IN AN INTERACTIVE PLAY

The mythology in an interactive play establishes common information that has some relevance or importance to the plot. Interactive plays will have a more rigid mythology than an interactive event because of the fixed story line. It is important to be specific in this case. Consistency in the mythology will yield a consistency in the action and relationships improvised in performance, making it easier to support the predetermined story line.

MYTHOLOGY IN AN INTERACTIVE EVENT

A mythology in an interactive event grows as the event grows. It adapts itself without conscious effort on the cast's part to the most successful performance choices. Over time, it becomes a collection of those choices. For instance, two characters originally mythologized as friends find great success in performance as rivals. As their successful routines are repeated, background details are altered to support the routines, and a new mythology of rivalry replaces that of friendship. Likewise, characters who once shared a background of going to the same school may now share a background of attending rival schools.

This exemplifies both the strength and the dangers of the interactive event. The strength lies in the adaptability of the performance, and the danger lies in the drifting of key objectives. The director must take care to keep the changes in line with the dictates of character theme, passion, occupation, and support of the subject. Otherwise, the production will move inexorably toward entropy until it finally loses its vision. The reward for this vigilance, however, is a production with a present and living spirit, quite unlike any form of rehearsed theatre.

CREATE A PERSONAL MYTHOLOGY

Well-prepared characters will know the environment they are performing in. They will know the period in history, the vernacular, and the particulars of their performance space. Having a *personal* mythology—stories, anecdotes, or memories of events that have taken place in the performance environment—can provide material when spontaneity falters and will serve to connect the character to its environment. This is different from the characters' background choices presented in the character development chapters. Personal mythology concerns itself specifically with a character's relationship to its performance environment.

As always, what is developed in front of the guest takes precedence over a preconceived mythology, even if it means temporarily discarding some of that mythology. This happens often. Just remember that it is an advantage to develop a good back-story and memories, *and* it is important not to let it limit your work. (See Town Meetings and Characters Letters—Variation II in *Acting Interactive Theatre*.)

The Performance Elements 15

N ow that we have developed the characters and the technique for improvising them, we can develop and rehearse the action of the show.

Character Action

The least-structured performance element is character action. Character action is a character pursuing its primary needs within the environment. It is the character out among the guests, being that character's self, making active choices, and seeking to fulfill its passion. It is a free-improv state with no preplanned course of action. Its structure lies in giving life to the specific choices that make up that characterization.

Character action may involve the character's relationship with the environment, the character's relationship with another character, or—most important—the character's relationship with the guest(s). All character action strives for guest-inclusive action.

Character action happens *between* the other performance elements; it is the glue that holds the others together. It is also the creative soil from which the other elements spring. The experiences of the character following the active fulfillment of its needs with the guest, its environment, and other characters create many of the ideas from which the other more-structured elements come.

Once the actor has played the character for a while, it attains a life of its own. The actor can then let the *character* lead, as it explores its relationships and the fulfillment of its need. With good character action, the actor flows *with* the character in a state of discovery, spontaneity, and inspiration.

Endowments

An endowment is an invitation to the guest to play along by bestowing upon him or her a role to play in the production or scene. It is the most basic aspect of interactive theatre. It's what makes theatre *interactive*. No matter how detailed and exciting the show, it is meaningless as interactive theatre without a place for the guest to play along too.

In an endowment, an actor relates to the guests in such a way as to define for them their identity and place in the created reality. Assumptions are made that imbue the guest with attributes befitting the action. For example, the schoolmarm passes guests near the saloon: "Jefferson Crawley! Ever since your gold strike, you've been truant from my classroom. Do you think that riches are any substitute for an education?" The prospector frantically searches through his belongings: "Ula May! Thank God, you're here! I jus' cain't find the deed to my claim anywheres! It was in my vest pocket last night at the barn dance. I showed it to yer just before ya most graciously asked me to dance." The gentleman gunslinger approaches a guest on Main Street: "Slick Jamison, as I live and breathe. I haven't seen you since our little disagreement in Mexico. Now, I thought we had decided never to pass company again."

WHAT DO ENDOWMENTS DO?

Endowments give the guest a head start in cocreating with the actor. They allow him or her to start from *somewhere* rather than *nowhere*. Even the professional improviser is given something with which to begin a scene; it is even more important for the amateur.

The endowment is the passport for inclusion in the temenos. It offers guests their "mask" so that they may play without fear of judgment. Being given a character that is not themselves makes it feel safe to be spontaneous. "This isn't me; it's someone else." It is then easier for the guest to access his or her own creative power and play it out behind the mask of an arbitrary character.

Actors sometimes forget the power of endowments and let guests struggle with their identity and self-consciousness. To remind actors, I will sometimes set up a dramatic scene and ask them to play themselves. They readily agree that playing one's self is the most difficult role an actor can play. I then ask them to imagine how much more difficult it would be for someone who is not trained as an actor. Guests need endowments!

Endowments can be offered as openers to newly greeted guests or can create a platform for guest-initiated action. As in the examples above, an endowment alone can be a premise for a new scene, if it carries a tension or conflict to be resolved. Even guests already captured by the spirit of play, who volunteer action and involvement with characters, can benefit by an endowment. By providing them with specifics, the actor can enhance the growth and development of the action.

CREATING AN ENDOWMENT ZOO

Endowments are used constantly in the course of interactive performance, regardless of what type of performance element is used. In rehearsal, actors isolate "targets" for their endowments. A target is a guest type, or demographic, that is encountered often enough in performance to warrant the creation of an endowment character for it. Such targets might include a middle-aged couple, a child, a teenage girl, or a college guy. Endowment characters are created for these targets and added to the actor's personal "endowment zoo." This is a journal of descriptions for each endowment character the actors discover in performance. It is a cast of characters from their personal novel, so to speak—characters whom only they know and use.

WHAT INFORMATION SHOULD AN ENDOWMENT CONTAIN?

A good endowment reveals three things: the guest's identity, his or her relationship to the character, and what the character stands to gain from the guest. The identity endowed upon the guest should include a specific name, or handle, as well as an occupation. This occupation is defined in the same way the character's occupation is defined in character development—what it does for a living or what it does more than anything else. It must connect the endowed guest to the subject and the environment. The schoolmarm's guest, cited above, is a successful prospector of the town.

The character's relationship to the endowed guest must be clear. The character *always* knows the guest. But does it know him or her personally, or by report, or by reputation? Also, what is the history and relevance of that person in the character's life? The gentleman gunslinger's guest has a history of "a little disagreement in Mexico," with the implication that it was not so little. This gives the guest enough information to play along, but not so much that the story is told. It allows the guest to offer the next piece of the puzzle.

What the character stands to gain from him or her speaks to how its contact with the endowed guest may fulfill the character's need. What does the character want from the guest? What action does the guest need to perform to fill that need? Can the guest do it alone, or are others needed? How badly does the character need it, and what is it willing to do to get it? The prospector needs Ula May's help in finding his deed, *or*, if the guest took the intended cue to be the one who romanced it away from his vest pocket, the prospector has an urgent need to resist the advances of the manipulative Ula May.

The character's need in an endowment should always be a high-stakes one. The need's urgency, and its relevance to the character's mission in life, helps the actor reveal the character in the exchange. The prospector's endowment reveals a weakness for the ladies and a gullible innocence, which is dangerous for a gold prospector on the frontier.

Presenting the Endowment

A loud pronouncement is not the best way to present an endowment. It is like putting a spotlight on a member of the audience and asking him or her to dance. A lack of ceremony is best. Making the endowment in an unassuming and matter-of-fact way derails some of the shock of being asked to play because speaking to someone you already "know" is not a big deal. It is much more interesting to create endowments that imply that action has already taken place than to make one a big introduction. The former gives you someplace to start; the latter requires you to start from scratch. In each of the examples given above, the key action has already taken place. Character and guest then deal with the consequences of that action.

Endowments should make guests someone special. This is their chance to live out a heightened reality. Making them mundane serves no purpose. Remember that the positive affirmation of the guest's self is what empowers him or her to cocreate with the character. One must create characters for guests that are the best, the most esteemed, the most notorious. Offer them a role as a winner, and they will readily take it.

Offer as well a higher dominance than your character's. Giving guests the upper hand makes them feel safe. The first assumption guests make whenever a character approaches is that they will soon be embarrassed, outwitted, or taken advantage of. Putting them "in control" lessens that uneasiness and inspires them to use their power. Moreover, the fact that the character needs something from the endowed guest places it in a subordinate role . . . and there is nothing more fun than playing the subordinate role with a well-endowed guest.

CONFLICTING ENDOWMENTS

With each character scattering its own unique endowments throughout a performance, it is almost inevitable that guests, having been endowed in a certain way by one character, may later be endowed differently by another character. Actors will invariably ask what they should do to prevent this, and the answer is not to be concerned about it. It is a readily accepted convention for guests to be endowed differently by different characters. It is all part of playing along.

I do, however, caution actors that if a guest professes a different identity from the one they have just endowed upon that guest, they should not press it. They should immediately assume they made a mistake, and accept the guest's idea of who they are without question. After all, the point is to give guests a character to play with, and if they already have one they like, there is no need to offer another. It would be like negating your improv partner's assumption. Actors should see it as a challenge to be "mistaken" in as interesting a way as they can.

It is not uncommon for guests to retain a previous endowment if they particularly enjoyed the role. Indeed, it is better for the development of the show as a whole if guest characters remain consistent. Many interactive play scripts contain endowment characters that must remain consistent in order to further the plot. These are worked out with the entire ensemble before hand. Some casts make rules for endowing certain types of guests in a certain way, such as all guests with beards are outlaws, or all women wearing glasses are schoolmarms. The guests don't know these rules, so they will be impressed with the cast's apparent attention to their character. This device is most useful for interactive plays, allowing guests to be fit to roles consistently as the plot unfolds. (See You Have, I Want and Endowment Reception Line in *Acting Interactive Theatre*.)

Lazzi

The word *lazzi* is taken from the tradition of the commedia dell'arte, or Italian comedy, of the sixteenth century. The word itself means turn, or trick, or stage business. Italian actors would resort to *lazzi* whenever their scene began to drag or their inspiration gave out on them. For instance, one of Arlequino's better-known *lazzi* was to catch a fly on the wing and devour it with great gusto.

There are many similarities between the technique of interactive theatre and that of commedia dell'arte. Both styles involve the improvisation of quintessential characters of a particular period. The improvisation of these archetypal characters revolves around their idiosyncratic behavior and their reactions to circumstance.

Lazzi Is a Simple Comic Action

For purposes of interactive theatre, I define *lazzi* as a simple action, gesture, or phrase that reveals the extraordinary nature of the character and gives the effect of surprise and laughter.

My favorite *lazzo* (*lazzi* is the plural form, *lazzo* is the singular) is one from an actor at the Disney-MGM studios who portrayed a Hollywood has-been actor. This character, named Roman Holiday, is a sadly untalented eccentric who has not worked in years and is quite vain. Roman sees himself as a young ingenue star, even though he is aging ungracefully. His determined denial of himself as anything but a young, dashing leading man is part of what is endearing and comic about him.

In designing this character, the actor wished to wear a toupee. He was balding himself, and felt this would be a handy visual cue of Roman's vanity and lack of self-awareness. He decided he could make this a strong visual statement through the use of an unusually bad toupee, which the character never admits to wearing. We eventually found him an extraordinarily unflattering rug; the hair coloring didn't even match, let alone the style.

As the actor proposed the idea, I suggested activating it into a *lazzo* by Velcroing the toupee to the front of his head only, so that whenever he bowed to a lady or stooped over, the toupee would flop forward, uncovering his bald head. When this happened in performance, his toupee usually stood straight up like the crest of a cockatoo and, of course, Roman was entirely unaware of the embarrassment.

LAZZI REVEALS THE CHARACTER'S FOIBLES

Roman's *lazzo* never failed to get a reaction from the guests because it was a vivid representation of that character's foibles, which were a lack of self-awareness and vanity. Not only did the guests get a good laugh out of it, but it was immediately clear what that character was all about. Good *lazzi* does this. It reveals in a comic way the foibles of the character. *Lazzi* tells no story; there is no beginning, middle, or end; it is just a simple action, gesture, or phrase.

Our dim-witted outlaw Notorious Ned might find success with a *lazzo* by having his gun rigged so that when he draws it, only the handle comes out of the holster. In situations in which he needs to show off or bully people, this accident would elicit surprise and laughter as well as inform the guests about how unprepared he is to be a notorious outlaw. More could be revealed if he would then fumble with the gun, trying to put it together again, having only more and more pieces fall off of it until his gun lies in a pile on the ground. He might then scoop it up and run away in frustration and embarrassment. This would make good *lazzi* because not only is it comic, it also reveals the "If he had a brain, he'd be dangerous" quality of the character.

LAZZI IS PERFORMED DIRECTLY TO THE GUEST

Interactive characters constantly work to build their storehouse of these *lazzi*, which can be called upon at any moment in performance when things begin to drag. *Lazzi* is properly performed by a single character directly to the guest, not to another character. As actors move through their character actions, they search for appropriate moments when the right *lazzi* might enhance their total performance. *(*See Walk Through a Day in *Acting Interactive Theatre.*)

Conceitti

Conceitti is another term taken from the commedia dell'arte and literally means conceits. *Conceitti* are short, prewritten mono-logues designed to display a character's particular brand of pre-tension or hubris. They are tirades of boastful self-importance or righteous passion. The Dottore in the commedia, for exam-ple, would often go off on a barely intelligible stream of philo-sophical dogma or scientific jargon. The Lovers were wont to lose themselves in a lavish description of their love for each other. These were totally premeditated, highly emotional, comic jags and were used, like *lazzi*, when invention failed or oppor-tunity knocked.

The fact that they are scripted is excused by the fact that they are short tricks used only to embellish the scene. They require no dialogue or interaction. They are of minor importance as perfor-mance elements go, but they are handy tools for actors to carry in their bag of tricks to bring to bear when the time is right.

Encounters

Whenever one character engages another character in perfor-mance, that is an encounter. Encounters open up a new perfor-mance dimension in that, when one character engages another in improvisation, the characters create action as a team and work together to use that action to incorporate one or more guests. The action is thus more complex. The characters create a greater con-text in which to involve the guest. More than merely meeting the sheriff in a Wild West town, one might meet an outlaw and the sheriff engaged in a confrontation. The guest's involvement in that action would then take on a whole new complexity and importance.

An encounter is sometimes more casually referred to as a *bit*, as in a "bit of stage business." It is defined as a complete action devised by two or more characters that requires resolution or clo-sure. *Lazzi* tells no story, but an encounter *must* tell a story.

Although more complex than *lazzi*, encounters are still one-action problems—one clear conflict, one problem to be solved. Encounters include actions such as a boy asking a girl out on a date, a man borrowing money from a friend, and a fired employee trying to get his job back. Encounters make up the majority of the performance experience for the guest, so it is important to understand them.

ACTION MUST BE SELF-EVIDENT

The action presented in an encounter must be self-evident; that is, anyone walking up in the middle of the event must be able to tell at a glance what is going on. The sheriff and outlaw may be playing to any number of guests, but there is no unity of audience in interactive theatre. At the beginning of the encounter there may be six or eight people watching, but at the end there may be more than a hundred people who have been interested enough to stop at some point during the scene. Therefore, the guest must never be required to see the encounter from beginning to end in order to understand what is happening. An encounter is a scene for a free-roaming audience.

If our sheriff's action remains the one-action problem of confronting the outlaw to oust him from town, then it will be clear to guests who have just arrived that they are viewing a Wild West sheriff's classic scene of confrontation. They will understand what is going on and can enjoy whatever new interest the actors bring to this recognizable scene without trying to figure out what it is they are watching.

If a guest arrives in the middle of this action, he or she may see the obvious figures of the sheriff and the outlaw walk to opposite ends of the street, face each other twitching their fingers over their holsters, and know what is happening. If yet another guest arrives only in time to see the outlaw being dragged off and the sheriff admonishing any other outlaws in town to be careful not to mess with him, then again it will be clear that this is a scene about a lawman confronting an outlaw. At any given moment in an encounter, it must be clear what the scene is about.

ENCOUNTERS INVOLVE NO ENTRANCES OR EXITS

Of necessity, encounters exist within French scenes; that is, they take place between the entrance or exit of a character, and the next such entrance or exit. If all the action necessary for a scene to take place can happen without anyone leaving or entering, then chances are you are dealing with a one-action problem and an encounter.

ENCOUNTERS SHOULD INCLUDE GUESTS

An encounter should always strive to include the guest on some level—as should any performance element. For instance, our shoot-out might involve several guests endowed as the outlaw's gang. The altercation could concern some of the dance hall girls, played by guests as well. Encounters are strongest when guests are utilized, especially in a way that their interaction is integral to the outcome. For this reason encounters are rarely scripted. The guest's response can never be pinpointed; therefore, an encounter must be flexible enough in the minds of the actors to adjust to whatever input the guest offers.

Encounters are fleshed out only in general terms regarding interesting activities for the guest, and the core of the scene usually remains the same. The sheriff's encounter with the outlaw may always lead to the classic shoot-out scene, even if one day the ending must change to accommodate a guest–dance hall girl's decision to jump in front of the outlaw to prevent bloodshed.

ENCOUNTERS SHOULD REVEAL CHARACTER

Needless to say, a character's activity in an encounter should reveal that character, and his or her action within the encounter ought to be consistent with the characterization. Actors must guard against the temptation to discard the characterization in favor of a momentary comic opportunity. These departures may achieve the desired reaction—laughter—but the guests will observe the actor's lack of respect for the characterization and so lose respect for it themselves.

ENCOUNTERS SHOULD NOT INCLUDE OFFSTAGE ACTION

If a scene involves too much offstage action, it will also make for a confusing encounter. This is true of any improvised scene, but even more so of an encounter. Even an overuse of pronouns, such as *he, she, it, they,* or *them,* or references to characters that are not there makes it difficult for the guest to discern what the action is about.

CHARACTERS MUST REESTABLISH INFORMATION

Reestablishing information is crucial to ensure that the audience is with you. Actors must learn to use proper names and titles far more often than in normal scene work so that those just arriving at the encounter have the opportunity to identify who is who. In the same manner, the action at hand must be stated and restated within the scene. However, this must be done in such a way as not to interrupt the smooth flow of action. Action must be restated in different ways in order not to sound repetitious. Sometimes just an additional word or phrase is enough for the arriving guest to pick up the thread of what is happening.

For instance, if the sheriff's dispute with the outlaw was over his illegal gambling practices, we would hear that early on in the scene. But newcomers would never know why this outlaw is being thrown out of town unless the sheriff reiterates it periodically by using phrases such as "this ain't a gamblin' town," " I'm throwing yer no-good gamblin' hide outta here," "so our children won't know the evil of card playin'," and "since you're not a law abidin' citizen." Guests who do not understand what the scene is about will lose interest no matter how whimsical and entertaining the characters may be, so reestablishing information is vital. (See Face Value Reestablishing Scenes and Three-Minute Scenes in *Acting Interactive Theatre*.)

ENCOUNTERS MUST HAVE RESOLUTION

It is as necessary for an encounter to have a resolution or closure as it is for a scene in a conventional play. It is not acceptable for an encounter simply to trail off, even if it is not successful. Regardless of where he or she comes into the story or how good the story is, every guest wants to know how it ends. The performers must always end an encounter!

This is not to say that a guest won't decide to move along before the ending is presented if the scene is not interesting enough. One of the unique challenges of interactive theatre is that a casually gathered audience will just as casually leave if it is not engaged by the performance.

NEW ENCOUNTER DEVELOPMENT

On the whole, encounters can be anything from the completely spontaneous to the nearly scripted. Any two characters meeting in the environment are essentially performing an encounter, even if they have no clue where they are going with it. They will most often improv their way into a single, clear conflict, include the guest, and then find closure. That is an encounter.

An encounter can also be a well-defined, tried-and-true routine that uses only a few good options and will nearly always guarantee a good response. As with most improv, the process of spontaneous discovery leads, over time, to more refined ideas and, finally, to a polished routine. Refined encounters, with their various options, can actually be rehearsed in much the same way as a script or scenario.

An experienced cast can manipulate guests into reactions and responses that lead them to a desired closure just by knowing what guests usually say. The longer an ensemble works together, the more polished bits they will be able to call upon. Some of my own ensembles have worked continually for many years and have literally hundreds of polished encounters to choose from.

New encounters are best derived from performance. In playing their character action with guests and exploring relationships with fellow characters, actors will be presented with ample, unsought possibilities. Mere writing and rehearsal alone cannot surpass the occasional gem discovered in spontaneous performance. The process should then be one of repeating and refining such raw material during subsequent rehearsal or performance.

Despite this, encounter development must be undertaken during the rehearsal process. It is not as though good encounters cannot be created in rehearsal; they can be. Of course, some will fly and some will fall. The important thing is to have an arsenal at your disposal for the opening of the production—to prime the pump, as it were.

FINDING THE PREMISE

All improvised scene work follows the same general pattern. Initially, there is the somewhat random exploration of information. Through positive assumption, the *who, what,* and *where* of the scene is established. At some point thereafter, the improvisers come to a consensus as to what the scene is about, its premise. Then the premise is developed, action is heightened, and resolution is found. The actors must follow the premise faithfully if their scene is to make sense and complete a whole picture.

If the actors don't agree on and follow the same premise, their scene may appear fragmented. The result will fall somewhere between a scene that is vaguely confusing and one that is completely unfollowable. Finding and holding the premise is the acid test for the cast's ensemble ability.

Encounters are merely improvised scenes and, as such, they go together in much the same way. One difference is that the *who, where,* and *when* are to some degree influenced by fixed choices. Another is that the encounter's premise must be a one-action problem; that is, only one thing is at stake.

In an interactive encounter, the premise puts only one character's need (ultimately its passion) at stake. The job of the interactive ensemble is to discover whom the encounter is about and then to support that scene. The theme explored will be that which belongs to this central character. When two or more characters meet to form a new encounter, they follow this process:

1. Each character follows its needs (using primary activities and relationship).
2. It finds a premise or comes to a single, clear conflict or problem (one character's passion that is at stake).
3. It expands the problem and endows and incorporates guests in an extraordinary action that reveals the subject and character theme (or extends the plot).
4. It creates resolution (finds closure).

FOIBLES AND VIRTUES IN AN ENCOUNTER

In character action, passion attainment is foiled by the foible and aided or redeemed by the character's virtue—all within the neat package of a single character's relationship with the guest(s). Where it gets complex is in the multiple-character scene work of an encounter. Foibles and virtues still affect the attainment of passion, but here again the passion to be attained is now only that of the character central to the premise—the character whose passion is most at stake. The foibles and virtues of *all* characters involved, in addition to input from the guest, interrelate to form the outcome. Which of the characters' virtues or foibles are employed and how they are used are simply a matter of what is right for the moment.

USING HIGH STAKES

One downfall of encounter work is the tendency to create the commonplace. Action is an attractive force only when the stakes are high. This does not mean necessarily that all action should bear life-or-death stakes, but the consequences must be vitally important to at least one character—usually the character whose passion is at stake.

Actors should continually ask themselves, "What is at stake?" and always be willing to raise those stakes. In real life we are conditioned to play for safety; in interactive theatre actors should be conditioned to put their character in peril. Their motto should be, "When in doubt, raise the stakes."

USING SUSPENSE

Interactive theatre plays to some of the most *uncaptive* audiences ever devised. The unengaged and disenchanted guest will merely walk away. One must continually do battle with the television sit-com attention span. Using suspense can be the most powerful weapon for holding your audience.

Try starting your encounter with something unfinished; then leave it unfinished until the end. An audience will always want to wait one more minute to see the other shoe drop. I have often seen an ingenious tease of this sort keep an audience riveted to a perfectly boring scene. I don't advise boring scenes, but a little suspense does go a long way.

The token of suspense need not even have anything to do with the scene. Hal Holbrook made brilliant use of suspense in his one-man show of Mark Twain. For almost the entire two hours he was alone onstage, Holbrook presented an unending string of subtextual, unfinished stage business that one was not so consciously aware of that it became annoying, but that made one absolutely rapt with his character. During one long discourse he pulled out a cigar, slowly unwrapped it, searched for matches, found them in the desk, carried them, put them in his pocket, pulled them out, drew a match, carried it, put it away, then placed the matches back on the desk. Later he would continue this business and finally light the match, let it burn down to his fingers, then blow it out. If I remember correctly, the cigar was not lighted until the last act. He would also do things like move a chair to the far end of the room for no apparent reason, then *not* sit down.

Whether it is passive stage business or an active element of the story that is used as a tease, the suspense must be satisfied eventually. Don't make the mistake of forgetting about it or your audience will feel cheated. (See Encounters from Attitudes in *Acting Interactive Theatre.*)

PLAUSIBILITY IN ENCOUNTERS

There are a few things to be said about how encounters relate to each other in the performance environment. The golden rule is that as the guests move from encounter to encounter, they see nothing that would give them reason to believe there is anything staged about their theatrical reality. It should have the same continuity as real life.

Guests should never see inconsistencies as a character moves from the end of one encounter to the beginning of the next. If a Wild West outlaw shoots his own foot and limps away down Main Street only to be seen moments later near the saloon dancing with the saloon girl, continuity is lost. Even if the crowd is completely dispersed from the first encounter, someone *will* see it. Many times encounters will be deliberately scheduled. Care must be taken in these cases to allow for continuity between encounters. Our outlaw might put on a bandage of some sort before he is seen next, or just limp through the next several encounters. This gives the actor more to talk about during his character action, and it adds dimension to the environment. He should see it as an asset to his performance, not as a handicap.

Many times characters make exits from encounters to specific places. If a starlet runs out of one encounter to make it to a screen test on time, it would be silly for her to rush past the immediate crowd, then slow down and begin signing autographs. As that same crowd disperses, guests will wander by her and see that she never followed through. The proper thing to do would be to exit the environment completely, then reenter at another location. It need not take long—just long enough to justify the exit. After all, she could have been too late for the screen test. The important thing is that there is a gap in the audience's connection with the character, during which anything could happen.

Characters who enter in second support of an encounter can ruin the encounter's plausibility by knowing things that they could not know within the context of the action. For instance, our starlet fires her agent for not getting her work. Then, a director enters straight from the set where his leading lady has just collapsed. He informs the starlet that he was hoping to hire her, but since she fired her agent and is not represented she can't have the job. Obviously, the director could not have known this since it just happened. He ruins the illusion by giving the impression that he, the actor, overheard the scene and jumped in to further the conflict. The same actor could have turned this overheard action to good use if he entered demanding that the agent provide a new leading lady immediately and describing our starlet exactly. Here the actor achieves the same end, but he does not assume knowledge of the starlet's actions.

BREACHING REALITIES

Spontaneous encounters can fall victim to bad second support when the entering actor does not fully understand what has been established. A group of gangsters in a Prohibition-era event plans to meet at their secret distillery and refers to a second-story window. The police chief arrives and threatens to haul them in to the precinct house for questioning and refers to the same window. A serious breach in reality has been committed, and the audience is now aware of the characters only as actors with their facts confused. This is one reason why a basic mythology of the environment is helpful.

There is a difference between a breached reality and an altered one, however. If the police chief pointed to the same window and announced that the city had purchased the building to be the site of the *future* precinct house, the boys would have an interesting new problem to solve.

Scenarios

Scenarios for interactive performance are elements that are most like the commedia dell'arte. They are improvisations within a predefined structure. A scenario is a series of predefined plot points, the sum of which make up a whole story. How each of these plot points is performed and what happens between them is the stuff of improvisation.

Interactive scenarios are essentially encounters of more than one French scene. Unlike in encounters, during scenarios characters may make entrances and exits. Action in a scenario is more complex than in an encounter; it plays out in such a way that the guest *must* see the scene from beginning to end in order to understand the story. It requires a consistent audience and a static performance location. This means that the audience must somehow be gathered before the first key piece of information is related, and then it must be retained throughout the scene. The guests must also receive the impression that this is not a casual audience situation, as in an encounter.

INTERACTIVE EVENTS AND SCENARIOS

Scenarios are the mainstays of a controlled-audience show, but they are much harder to bring off in a free-roaming-audience show. At an interactive event, setting up a well-motivated situation, in which an audience is gathered and prepared to watch before the action starts, is more difficult. Making the more complex action clear to the whole crowd also takes a big presence and precise timing. Setting reliable cues and making entrances on time can also be problematic. So scenarios are by far the most risky of the performance elements to attempt in an interactive event.

INTERACTIVE PLAYS AND SCENARIOS

Interactive plays use scenario to tell the story, connect the action, and motivate the interaction. Characters are defined by their actions dictated by the scenario. Plot points provide the disclosures that keep the story moving and supply the context for audience inclusion. Interactive plays invariably use at least one overriding scenario to guide the production.

PLAYING THE SCENARIO

Scenarios can be rehearsed so that they generally play out in a predictable way. They usually involve a number of alternatives for plot points that are susceptible to guest input and for specific points at which guest interaction can freely unfold. Actors can become surprisingly well versed in how a particular scenario will flow, even to the point of being able to manipulate guest reactions toward their desired plan.

At times, scenarios can resemble participatory theatre, in that guest response is more or less *forced* toward a specific and predetermined end. The genius in playing a scenario lies in the ensemble's ability to disclose the proper information at the right time and hit each plot point accurately, while giving the impression of a completely spontaneous happening.

A scenario might proceed somewhat like the following:

Scene One: The old prospector meets up with the sheriff in front of the saloon. He is holding a large bag of gold. He tells the sheriff that he has made an amazing strike, and that he needs to store his gold in the town's bank vault so it will be safe. The saloon girl overhears this and begins flirting with the otherwise less-than-desirable prospector. He asks her for a date;

she accepts. The prospector and the sheriff leave with the gold to put it in the bank.

Scene Two: The nasty gunslinger comes to the saloon for a drink. The saloon girl tells him that the prospector has a bag of gold, and that he and the sheriff have just gone to put it in the bank. The gunslinger thanks her, and it is obvious that the two are a team in performing evil deeds. The gunslinger then calls over his assistant and asks him to get the explosives. They are going to blow the safe. The gunslinger and his assistant leave.

Scene Three: The sheriff and the prospector reenter after stowing the gold in the safe, the saloon girl flirts with the prospector again, and suddenly a large explosion is heard. The gunslinger runs by with a bag of gold and disappears. The sheriff then quickly gathers a posse and runs in hot pursuit.

This simple scenario can be fertile ground for well-drawn, fascinating characters to create a lot of comedy and interest. The problem is that if guests walked up in the middle of it, all they might see is the gunslinger and his sidekick running off with explosives, a sheriff and a prospector showing up to flirt with a saloon girl, and a robbery taking place. All they would *know* about that scene is that somehow a robbery has taken place. They wouldn't know that it's the prospector's gold or that there was a conspiracy to steal it. Guests also wouldn't know many of the relationships in the scenario such as the pivotal character of the saloon girl and her dishonesty. None of those would be apparent because they had already taken place. In order for guests not to have missed them, they would have had to have been there from the beginning of the scenario.

How would guests be gathered there from the beginning? Some guests may just wander by as the scenario begins, but it is more likely that few would happen to be there at the right time. So our established audience would be minimal. What needs to happen is for something interesting—preferably something loud and attention getting—to take place before the first key plot point is reached that will draw an adequate crowd. Of course, this action should relate somehow to the scenario and act as an introduction, or lead-in, to the story.

In this case, the prospector might draw a healthy crowd by hooting and hollering, firing his gun, and shouting about being a rich man for about three minutes. Audiences, like most mammals, respond to sound and movement. A proper commotion before the first plot point is reached is usually all it takes to get the audience assembled. Once that is done, the next character needs to enter and begin the action. What remains is for the actors in the scene to be interesting enough to maintain the guests' attention. It is also worth mentioning here that encounters, too, can benefit greatly by using this prelude of attention-gathering action, or lead-in, before the actual scene begins.

Attractions

Interactive events and some interactive plays make use of shows within the show to add interest or to fill gaps in the action. I call these "attractions." As long as there is a plausible motive, almost any form of entertainment can be added to an interactive environment as an attraction. These usually take the form of theatrical presentations such as plays, stories, variety acts, dancing, or music. Our Wild West town, for example, may include a dance hall show at the saloon, music at the town hall, a medicine wagon rolling into town to give a show, or a rodeo. These are "advertisable" entertainments for which the audience would be deliberately gathered in one place just for that show. For attractions, the audience is endowed with the role of being an audience, albeit an audience of the period.

If the attraction is one that takes up a large area or is otherwise unmistakable, it may be presented as a happening within the interactive show itself. A carefully staged stunt show might be presented as a spontaneous shoot-out at high noon or a bar brawl might be choreographed for the saloon. The advantage here is that through carefully rehearsed action, a heightened reality can be presented as "real life."

Attractions also include any other type of diversion that may be present within the environment. Vulture Gulch may contain a row of shops that could be actual merchandise locations. The general store could sell goods and the town restaurant serve meals. The saloon could be an actual bar. Since the event is a Founders' Day celebration, period games and rides could be set up, and the local stable could serve as a sort of petting zoo.

As far as possible, every attempt should be made to establish every attraction as firmly and completely within the period as any of the characters. However, in any period environment, there will be certain logistically or legally necessary conventions that do not mesh with the time period. Many of these unavoidable conventions, such as bathroom facilities, plastic eating utensils, and so on, are familiar enough to the guests that they will easily forgive the incongruity. But any glaring inconsistency, however convenient for the producer, will affect the guests' belief in the illusion and will undo the work of the characters.

Part V

Interactive
Technique

*T*he remainder of this book is devoted to the body of techniques and ideas that I have accumulated over the years for playing the performance elements with the guests.

Relating to the Guest 16

T he way in which actors relate to guests will either create, preserve, or destroy temenos. The challenge is always to sidestep their inhibitions and trick them out of self-judgment, without their ever knowing it. Sensitivity is the key.

The Audience Is on Your Side

An actor's first experience in interactive performance can be daunting regardless of how long he or she has prepared for it. No rehearsal can duplicate the experience of actual guest interaction. Usually actors' apprehension stems from questions they have, such as "Have I made the right choices?", "Will my character be interesting and fascinating?", and "Will the guests respond positively to me?"

Actors must know one indisputable fact about the audience they are about to face: The audience is on their side. When the guests came, they came to have a great time and to see an excellent performance. When they arrive, guests are as hopeful as the actor that the performance will be brilliant; they *want* to believe that. This fact puts them on the same side as the performer. If actors understand this, their attitude toward the audience will be less adversarial. The audience is always prepared to *believe* in the actor.

Be Sensitive About Who Wants to Play

It is important for the actor to be perceptive about who wants to play and who does not. This presents some difficulty for new interactive actors, since they are not used to reacting to their audience on an individual basis. Invariably the first time out, some poor choices will be made. It is surprising, though, how quickly an actor develops the ability to perceive who is willing, and who is not. There is a "look" or a "vibe" to a guest who is willing to play along. Actors develop a sixth sense about this and naturally gravitate toward incorporating those people who are well disposed to being included.

Be Sensitive to Guest Reactions

Just as an actor develops a sense for who is initially willing to play, an actor also quickly develops sensitivity to the guests' reactions. There is a peculiar awareness gained in performance that gives the actor more sensitivity toward people's reactions than in everyday life. If a character's humor is a little too harsh, if it presumes too much in its activity, if it strikes on a sensitive subject, the actor should be aware of this and should adjust his or her performance to negate any ill effects.

Be Sensitive to the Whole Group

In relating to groups of guests who belong together, such as friends or family, the actor must also be sensitive to how the *whole* group reacts to interaction. In some cases, several members of the group will enjoy interacting while others will be anxious to move on. This is particularly true in situations in which there is an attraction they must see or a schedule they must keep. The actor is then faced with the problem of either playing with the people who are loving the play, and risking building tension within the group, or discontinuing it for the sake of someone who is anxious to move on.

Remember that the actor must always affirm the guest. In this case, the character must affirm those who wish to play *and* affirm those who wish to leave. The character must relieve the tension that would otherwise continue to build by giving the "don'ts" a reason to leave and the "dos" a reason to come back.

Service Doesn't Mean Servile

It is said that one of the things that make Americans uncomfortable when they travel abroad is being waited on by servants. The idea of a house servant, footman, or valet is foreign to the American psyche. We cling to our ideals of independence and cringe at the suggestion of service as though to *serve* means to be *servile*. But in other countries, giving good service is a point of honor. When you think about it, being an entertainer is providing a service. Actors are serving their art to the audience, and the ancient tradition of acting is a service to our culture. We must not forget that it is an honor to serve well.

If our service is declined by the audience, it is not always true that it was inadequate. We like to think that everything we do is so excellent that no one could possibly refuse it. However, we fail to take into account personal taste and preference. In every performance, an interactive character will encounter many guests who will accept and be thrilled with what it offers, but many guests will also pass. Actors must know and accept that guests have this right.

Never Force Interaction

One of the cardinal rules of interaction is not to *force* interaction. A common pitfall of the uninitiated actor is to feel that each guest must be stopped and be entertained. The feeling such actors give off is one of "Look, it's my job to entertain you, so you are going to shut up and be entertained whether you like it or not." Of course, guests wouldn't hear it in these exact words, but they would certainly feel the actor's anxious need to do his routine regardless of their reactions.

This is a hallmark of a bad interactive performance. The art of interactive theatre deals with coaxing or inspiring the guest toward interaction. A bullying or belligerent attitude is more than counterproductive; it is simply not the point. Interactive theatre is an *invitation* to play.

Make Eye Contact with the Guest

A character should always make eye contact with the guest. I instruct actors to scan the crowd by looking at eyes—not heads or torsos, noses or foreheads. This visual connection is very important because it gives the character the opportunity to reveal its likability and to invite that person to play with it. The glance must say, "I am safe," "I am friendly," "I am a person whom you would find easy to talk to." This opportunity should not be denied to any guest.

Make Contact with Every Guest

As a character walks through the performance space, it should make contact with each and every person it passes. Every guest possible should get at least a look, a nod, a wink, a hello, or a passing phrase. This keeps the character active and the actor engaged in the performance. When actors are too selective or ignore the guests around them, they come off as disinterested. This can become a bad habit.

See Through the Character's Eyes

If there is any weakness in the characterization it will show up first in the actor's eyes. This is my prime indicator as to whether an actor is "in" or "out." The eyes will reveal the actor's own thought process, worries, and anxieties, or they will reveal only the character's.

I believe that actors should visualize everything within their environment as if it were in the period depicted. They should visualize guests as they would appear to their character, whether it be in the petticoats of the Wild West or in the togas of the Romans. This accomplishes two things: It helps the "in-character" quality of the eyes, and it serves to prevent the actor from accidentally incorporating anachronisms. It provides a sort of "period filter" in the actor's perception.

Be Altruistic in Your Approach to Performance

In every aspect of the actors' relationships with the guests, they must let the audience know that they are there for *them*. There must be a built-in, friendly invitation and an unspoken message of "I won't embarrass you; you will be in control; let's have some fun together." To do this, actors must approach the work in the proper spirit and truly believe that their performance is for the guests, and on their terms.

There must be altruism in every actor's approach to interactive performance. If the actors give joyfully and unconditionally—their whole self in performance—the guests will return that gift with the gift of their attention and interest. Conversely, if the actors' relationships are conditional, and they offer self-pride or arrogance to the guests, then the road to interaction will be longer and steeper, and the return payment will be far less. The actors must decide whether they are giving to receive, or giving to give. It all works when actors take joy in the art of play.

Creating Interaction 17

ollowing the needs of the character alone will not
always bring the actor to interaction with the
guests. The techniques that follow define a path
toward getting interaction rolling.

The Good, Better, Best of Interaction

My creed for describing the value of the varying levels of
interaction is this: It is good when guests watch what you
initiate, better when they are actively involved with what
you initiate, and best when you are involved in what they
initiate. Certainly, it is not bad for guests simply to stand
and watch what is going on, but it is better to get them
involved actively and, certainly, best when they are so
absorbed in the activity that they initiate new action and
add information of their own. Some of the most exciting
encounters happen when the actors actually take on a supporting role in the scene and follow a guest's lead.

Start Small and Build Your Activity

Every actor will have expectations of excellence. These may consist of being surrounded by a huge and adoring crowd, being perfectly in tune with a fellow ensemble member, or hearing the sound of laughter and applause. These are healthy goals, to be sure, but one doesn't walk on to the sounds of laughter and applause. Interaction must be built. Rather than being ready to do whatever is needed to jar this into being, one should let it develop naturally.

To get there, an actor must start small and start with an activity. The truth is that any here-and-now activity, no matter how small, can lead to something bigger and bigger until a full-blown encounter is created. Most actors miss this point about starting small. But some of the most successful encounters can begin quite literally from the tying of a shoe or the picking off of some lint.

In interactive theatre actors may start from anywhere to build to their expectation of excellence. All they need do is start an activity and let it build. Truly unique ideas are organic. They grow from seed and take a natural course, adjusting to each circumstance as it comes along.

Repeat to Improve

Repeating bits is a good way to improve them. If a bit of free improvisation yields something interesting, repeat it the next chance you get and try variations of it until it works well. Even if it was only a so-so idea, if anything about it intrigued you, cultivate it. Let it lead you to other activities. Excellent *lazzi* and encounters are grown in this way.

Repeating shtick within the same performance must never break continuity, however. If I, as the outlaw, make a routine out of suddenly dropping my gunbelt around my ankles and struggling to secure it back on again, that activity can be repeated again and again without disturbing the continuity of the show. It would simply appear that I have a buckle that continually gives me trouble, resulting in my gun falling to the ground. Whereas, if I make a scene about having forgotten to load my gun that morning, then repeat it again and again, it would seem out of context to anyone who saw it twice. I could forget to load my gun that morning only once.

Ask Guests Questions

A great way to break the guests' initial reticence to join in is simply to ask them a question. In improvisation, asking questions is not a useful way to further action between improvisers. But the rule should not apply to guests, because it is such an effective way to initiate conversation.

Approaching Cold Contacts

A cold contact is having a character approach a guest prior to the creation of a temenos, or prior to that guest's acceptance of it. It happens most often at the beginning of an interactive show, or as a new guest first enters an interactive event. Any guest who has not yet met your character and/or has not yet seen enough other guests interacting with characters to pick up on the interactive mood is a potential cold contact. Cold contacts need to be treated differently in order for a constructive mood of play to be established.

In initial approaches, characters should do their best to let the guests know quickly that they are fascinating and then they should release them. Never let guests feel obligated to talk to you. It is more of a cat-and-mouse game, in which the characters come up and, as quickly as they can, let the guest know that they are inviting, fascinating, and safe to play with. Then, almost immediately, they give the guest an excuse or an opportunity to disengage the conversation and move on, without having anything required of him or her. They may then reengage to check the guest's level of interest.

The process is not unlike one used by Peter Falk's famous character, Detective Columbo. Columbo's interrogations of would-be criminals are rife with his stopping at the door and suddenly turning to add something else or ask just one more question, then in a very submissive way heading out the door again, only to turn and ask something further.

For interactive characters, this technique tends to take the pressure off the guests that something is going to be required of them, while still maintaining enough contact with the character to give them an opportunity to feel comfortable in responding to it. Always make the guests feel as though they are in control and have the choice of responding or not. This will keep them relaxed and will keep their inhibitions at bay so that they can be coaxed into interaction before their defense reaction takes over.

One effective technique for interactive plays and convention events, where audience and actor are abruptly thrust together, is for each character to engage each and every guest in the room within the first ten minutes. Actors establish their characters in the briefest way possible, often with only one or two lines for each group of guests they meet. They literally zoom through the room throwing around *lazzi* or endowments that establish their character and occupation for everyone they see, but allowing no one time to respond. At the end of ten minutes, nearly every guest has met each character at the event, so that every further encounter is a familiar one. This is an excellent way to begin any interactive show.

Seek to Capture Interest, Not Demand Attention

When I observe actors making a lot of unmotivated noise and movement, or running after guests to step in front of them, blocking their way in order to talk, I ask them what they are trying to accomplish. They often answer that they are trying to get the guests' attention so that they can perform. I tell them, though, that their actions should be designed to capture the guests' interest, not demand their attention.

Attention is cheap and short-lived. Attention is what a carnival barker gets when you walk by the freak show, or what a substitute teacher gets when she calls for quiet in the classroom. Interest, on the other hand, is the value the guest places on your actions. Interest is captured when a character performs an activity that inspires the guest to want to see more. It creates suspense or raises a question that the guest needs answered.

One doesn't have to get into a guest's face in order to gain his or her interest. The difference between seeking interest and attention is the difference between fishing and hunting. When you fish, you drop a lure and wait for a nibble. In hunting, you attack on sight. A beggar character scrutinizing the inside of his begging bowl will capture more interest than a beggar running after a guest looking for alms.

In these types of activities there is more implied than seen. Some actors erroneously assume that they are not being seen unless they do something big and obvious. But that is not true. In any environment, the characters will be seen by the guests. Whether or not the guests stay to watch depends upon how interesting the characters are.

There is an unspoken transaction that takes place between the performer and the guest in any interactive show. It involves the guest's viewing—or not viewing—the entertainment. The transaction follows the adage, "Never expect something for nothing." When performers demand attention only, they have given the guest nothing but their demand. In reality, it is the guest who demands, "Show me that you are worth my interest." The performer must pay in advance, so to speak.

Actors may think to themselves, "Let me get the audience first and then I will do something interesting." It's a fine sentiment, but unfortunately it just doesn't work. Characters must first do something worthy of the interest they request. Variety entertainers understand this. Once interactive performers understand it, they can use it to their advantage and not waste time trying to get something for nothing. The phrase "If you build it, they will come" applies very nicely here.

Work with Intensity and Conviction

It is essential that the character goes about its action with intensity and conviction. A half-hearted action will not garner interest. Just as interactive characters are magnified, so too must be their intensity and conviction about their actions. Imagine yourself walking down Main Street watching the gunslinger idly polishing his gun. You might think to yourself, "How interesting, the gunslinger is polishing his gun. I think I will continue on down the street." Now imagine yourself walking by the same gunslinger, who is polishing his gun with an intense focus. Picture him holding it inches from his eyes, with his face all scrunched up as though he is inspecting every molecule on the surface of the gun. Perhaps he looks at it from every angle, even peers down the barrel. Imagine that his focus is so intense that he seems completely unaware of anyone else in the world. Like most people, you will wonder if there is a reason for it, and that's the hook that may make you stop to watch.

Create Your Own Stage

Guests carry their own space, a "here-and-now, twentieth-century, guest-at-a-show space." The character's space is the temenos, the play space. When a character enters the guest's space, it is merely an actor playing a role. The challenge for the actor is to get the guest to step into the character's space. When a character captures the interest of the guest, it is as though the character creates its own stage. In that moment, a transaction takes place. The guest consents, and is willing to believe in the character's world. Actors must always seek to have the guest come into their space. That is where the character lives, and that is where the guest belongs.

Passive Interaction

I consider passive interaction to be the most powerful technique there is for creating new activity. The word *passive* refers to the fact that the character temporarily ignores the guest. It is a simple sequence involving some of the things we have just been talking about. I will describe it in two steps.

Step One: Do something interesting, a here-and-now activity, preferably a small one, that may attract the guest's interest. Go about that activity with intensity and conviction. Be peripherally aware of guests as they gather around you, but do not initially acknowledge their presence. Like fishing, you are waiting for a whole school of fish to gather around the lure. The fact that you seem not to notice guests as they gather around you will be interesting to them. It will be all the more inviting because there is no apparent interaction going on. People are just watching; therefore, it is safer. They won't be worrying about whether or not they will be the next to be talked to by the character.

Step Two: When you feel you have acquired enough audience, turn the action outward to include your onlookers. In the time it takes to gather a small crowd, you also have time to decide how to make your here-and-now activity an active choice. By virtue of their decision to step up and watch, the guests have already made the bargain of being your audience, and have stepped onto your stage.

Imagine Annie Trueheart, the mail-order bride, sitting on a bench or in the street with her suitcase opened, sorting through her clothing with intense indecision. Perhaps she folds and unfolds items, scratches her head, and quietly rehearses responses to unheard questions. During this time, the actress has focused on what it is she is doing and why. She is trying to decide what she will wear on her honeymoon. When she feels the time has come to turn the action outward, she may simply look up and ask one of the guests, "What do you think?" She may make it an even easier question to answer by asking, "What do you think? Red or purple?" From there, a discussion might ensue on the proper colors for a honeymoon, then on to proper styles, and then to other such concerns. Annie's need for the right dress might lead to her modeling the clothing for the guests and then the guests modeling the clothing for her.

These successively larger and more involved activities can grow organically from a single question. The trick of passive interaction is that the character performs a passive activity that is both interesting and easy for the guest to stop and watch. Later it is turned into a simple active choice and built upon.

Turning Passive Activity Active

There are three methods for turning passive activity active. The first is tagging into existing conversation about the character. Often guests make comments as they stand and watch, as though the character couldn't hear them. For some reason, a character who doesn't seem to notice guests will be treated as though it is not really there. At the proper time, the character responds to the comment and ties it into the activity that it is performing:

Guest: "It looks like she needs to do some laundry."
Annie: "You do laundry? Thank goodness, I've been lookin' for you."

Second, the character may enlist the guests' aid in its activity, suddenly needing their help. Again, the simpler the start, the more effective. Our mail-order bride may simply hold the garment in the air and say, "Here, hold this!" She may not even look up. The guests will likely find themselves responding without even thinking about it and take the article of clothing. Only after that may one guest discover that she is endowed as the maid of honor.

Third, the character may endow an important identity on a guest, which is integral to the situation. Our mail-order bride may suddenly ask her bridesmaid's opinion. Or she may recognize her intended husband and quickly hide her bed clothes back in her suitcase, embarrassed. Or she may recognize her mother coming to take her back home. Any of these devices is an excellent way to turn passive activity active.

Active Interaction

Active interaction is having a character seek out the guest, take focus, and initiate the action. Active interaction is not bad, but it does require careful judgment on the actor's part. Active interaction is best employed when the audience is warmed up. If the inhibitions and fears of embarrassment have been removed, and the audience knows a little bit about the characters and feels safe with their interaction, then the characters are able to be more bold in their initiations of activity.

Gossip About Other Characters

Once guests are acclimated to the idea of interaction with characters, characters should take advantage of their willingness to play along. One useful technique is to send guests on errands to other characters. One can send them off to deliver messages or search for information. This can be a great deal of fun for the guests and can create some very interesting scenes.

Also, characters can gossip about other characters to the guests. The schoolmarm can gossip about the love life of the sheriff, for instance. If she rumors to guests that the sheriff is secretly in love with the dance hall girl, this may inspire the guests to seek out the sheriff and share their tidbit of gossip with him to see for themselves how he might react.

People love to "one-up" one another. Characters can use this fact to motivate guests to initiate encounters themselves. It may happen that the sheriff does encounter a guest who suddenly accuses him of being in love with the dance hall girl. This would then be a perfectly valid assumption for the opening of a new scene.

Rumors also have the potential of opening up encounter possibilities for other characters. They are like casting seeds to the wind to see what sprouts. It may happen that guests will squeal on their source as the schoolmarm happens by, and an even more complex and lifelike connection of activities may ensue to the enjoyment of all.

Speak to Be Overheard

Characters should always speak to be overheard. If they are walking along the street window-shopping, they should be talking to themselves in such a way that they can be overheard. Even in the most private conversations, the level of projection should be such that any passerby could hear them. Interactive characters don't have private lives. All their most intimate secrets are exposed to passersby.

Picture our dance hall girl walking down a line of shops on Main Street. She might stroll along, quietly peering into the windows as any guest might do. With this choice, she would be nearly invisible to the guest and contribute little of entertainment value. However, if she were talking to herself as she walked along, it would be quite different. Perhaps she is grumbling about not having the money to buy certain items, or trying to decide which dress would look better on her, or which beau would like which type of jewelry. Now she is revealing much more of her character and providing at any given moment an opportunity for a guest to comment on what she is saying, even though she is speaking to herself.

Encourage Interaction Through Children

Children, properly approached, can be quite receptive to interaction because they have not yet learned the inhibitions that adults have. This can also be used to the actor's advantage in getting the parents involved in interaction. When a character approaches a child, the parents are usually more than happy to encourage the interaction. They may feel that as long as the focus is on their child, they may not be approached. But a smart actor will develop the situation with the child and then make an assumption that involves the parent as an integral part of it. How then can they refuse?

Choose Guests Randomly

I always remind actors to choose guests randomly for interaction. In addition to choosing guests who seem open to it, there is a tendency to choose only a certain type of guest: guests who are more outgoing, perhaps, or simply guests of the opposite sex. In many cases, the more attractive people get approached more often than others. But these kinds of choices can limit the over-all feeling of inclusivity. If surrounding guests get the feeling, if only subliminally, that only certain types are being interacted with, it will make them feel excluded. I have heard more than one guest comment, "I guess I'm not pretty enough to be talked to." Actors must choose randomly among all good prospects for interaction. This will keep their work fresh and will keep the spirit of inclusivity alive.

Playing the "Bit"   18

O nce the audience is gathered and an idea is established, the actor must work to develop the action and incorporate the guest. These rules and techniques for playing the bit will help improve the odds for success.

The Byline

The first thing presented in any bit is what is communicated through the character's semblance. This information should include occupation, period, and place and can be crystallized by the character's first words to a guest. Often characters develop a byline for their introductions to new guests, such as the Hollywood girl-off-the-bus saying, "Hi. My name is Elsie White and I'm going to be a famous movie star in an hour and a half!" or the detective saying, "Willie Ketchum, finest private detective in Hollywood."

Bylines establish the *who*, *when*, and/or *where* of the improv scene. They should properly be followed by an endowment: "Hey, weren't you the guy who sat behind me on the bus and pulled my hair?" or "I got your message, Madam Lippschtuck, and I think I can help you locate your missing poodle."

Bylines can be handy in making the character clear, but they should not be used to the point of sounding contrived. Still, if not by using a byline, the character must nonetheless make these points clear in the first few moments of the encounter.

Begin a Scene at the Middle

A scene need not always start at the beginning. In fact, a scene should start in the middle. Long exposition is unwarranted and unwise in interactive theatre. It is tedious for guests to listen to because nothing is *happening*. Beginning a neutral scene in order to introduce the conflict is not as strong as starting directly with the problem itself. It draws and holds the crowd better and adds a sense of realism to the scene. But this does not negate the need for establishing basic information. It must be tied in after the problem is established. Then the hard facts needed to understand the conflict can easily be dropped in or alluded to along the way.

Three Ways to Incorporate a Guest

One can incorporate guests in one of three ways. First, by using them as the main character, the actor assumes them into a role that is integral to the scene. Whatever the outcome, it will be a result of the guests' words or deeds. Second, an actor can use the guests in supporting roles, in which a guest has a specific identity but is not in direct conflict with the problem of the scene. Third, an actor can use guests in a chorus role, in which they share a group identity such as the jury, the fan club, or the posse.

Always Assume the Best Cooperation

There is an intangible element to getting guests to do what you would like them to do. Never consider the possibility that they might refuse. If the actor assumes with absolute certainty in his or her own mind that the guest wants to perform the action, enjoys the action, and indeed has already accomplished it, there will rarely be resistance. It is the power of suggestion.

The opposite is also very true. If a character reveals its fear or concern that the guest won't cooperate, if it has a questioning look as if to say, "Is this OK with you?" the guest will often take that as a cue to refuse. The feeling is that if this character isn't sure what it should be doing, then the guest is certainly not sure either, and he or she will play it safe and say *no*. Like your neighbor's dog, guests can *smell* fear. So never be afraid that they won't cooperate. The actor must always assume the very best from a guest's reactions.

Make Your Active Choice an Object

One of the fundamentals in playing a bit is always to involve the guest in an immediate activity, an active choice. Actors can involve a new or timid guest in an active choice by focusing on an inanimate object, not on their character directly. This draws the attention away from the guest's self-conscious anxieties or inhibitions because it is easier to relate to a thing than to a person. Once the guests are active, then include the character. As you will recall, this is how Friar Pinch coaxed the mute little girl into his world and brought about her breakthrough.

Tie Your Assumptions to the Period

Knowledge of the everyday life and values of the period must be sufficient to allow the actor to make assumptions that are consistent with that period in history. If I were playing a beggar at a Renaissance festival, I would never talk in terms of "meet me in five minutes" because during the Renaissance the concept of time was not as tight as it is today. People would not speak in terms of minutes, and a beggar would not even have a timepiece to refer to.

The character's words or actions can confirm or deny the period depicted. Certainly, an actor must guard against using words or talking about things that did not exist in that period. However, anachronisms can also take the form of actions. A gentlewoman of the Renaissance saying that she will take a shower before she goes out would be anachronistic. People of that period did not take showers. Elizabethans felt that water carried contagion and so they took baths rarely, if they washed at all. Likewise, an Elizabethan character glancing at her wrist in the context of talking about time would betray a twentieth-century actress.

Even without anachronistic words or actions, a character may still fail to conjure up the period unless it makes specific assumptions that confirm the period for the guest. It does this by expressing words or deeds that were customarily done, or could have been done *only* in that period.

Be Specific

Use specifics like names, dates, places, and topical period references in your work. Sometimes in doing scene work I will have two characters create a scene and have one or more of the actors observing write down all the items that could have been more specific. Afterward, we read off the list and replay the scene with the more specific assumptions.

Use the Environment

Actors should use what is around them in the environment. Actors should be keenly aware of their surroundings, and use every object or set piece to inspire them or support their activity. Something as simple as a bench, a bookcase, a stick of wood, or a pile of dirt can become the focus of a fascinating situation. Actors must never cease searching their environment for new things to play with.

Assume What the Guest Says Is True

Always assume that what is said to you is *true* as you play with guests. Those who are inspired to play along and make an offer of information do not always make as useful an assumption as a fellow actor would. An actor may tend to overlook or ignore guest assumptions that aren't expedient choices, but this is detrimental to the spirit of interaction.

There should always be a feeling of "the customer is always right." Actors must remember that they are playing a game of improv with the guest, and when the guest is inspired to play, they must play back and not forget the rules of positive assumption. If they do forget, they run the risk of giving guests the impression that *their* ideas are not as good, and this will cause them to clam up, fold their arms, and refuse to take part.

I've worked this idea in scenes by having one or more characters encounter a mock guest, whose intent is to make absurd, incongruous, or unreal assumptions for the scene. The character's task is to affirm and incorporate those assumptions, and still further the scene in a constructive and interesting way. Naturally, there is a difference between a guest giving a difficult assumption with good intent and one who is deliberately trying to make the situation difficult for the actor. The latter must be dealt with differently. I am speaking here of a guest who truly wants to partake but falters in the attempt.

Leave the Guest Room to Respond

A character's exchange with a guest should be a two-way street. There should be a give-and-take between character and guest. Actors must remember to give guests opportunities to react to what they give them, and then allow them to contribute. A bad habit can develop when actors continually throw their performance at the guests but, through a lack of trust, never leave them an opportunity to react or respond. If they can't react, they can't interact. A character must throw the ball to the guest and wait a few beats to give him or her an opportunity to respond.

If guests are feeling comfortable and involved, it is likely that they may add an idea of their own. This might take a few beats longer than the actor is used to in passing focus with fellow actors. The guest will be slower to formulate his or her response than would be another actor. By giving the guest time, it allows him or her to be more involved, and ultimately the actor will have more material to work from. People have a natural tendency to want to fill a pause anyway, so when an actor is looking to coax responses from guests, a simple pause for their response provides a cue for them to speak.

Have Energy

An interactive actor must have more energy than any guest in the space. Characters should have an underlining intensity and enthusiasm about everything they do. It is not only an important aspect of making the character larger than life, but energy itself is infectious and pumps up the guest. An audience that feels that energy will respond to it and will interact more readily. I have tested this idea empirically. I have asked a cast to perform a set just as they normally would, but with half their normal energy level. I then had the same cast perform another set, putting all they had into it. The difference in the level of interaction was astounding. The "power set" created an atmosphere of fun and abandon, which made the guests incredibly receptive.

There is also a threshold of energy needed by the cast, at which the audience generates its own atmosphere of excitement. It is up to the cast to commit to full energy at the beginning of the show or set. The audience then creates its own energy, which the cast then feeds off of. This energy circulates and feeds itself so that the actor no longer feels the output as a strain but as an exhilarating flow.

Play for the Scene

Actors have a responsibility to their fellow players to provide material and to set up the laugh for each other. A short-sighted improviser plays only for him- or herself, manipulating the scene to give only his or her character the best possible opportunities. Actors who play for the betterment of the scene, or of their fellow players, create better opportunities for their own characters as well as for the scene at large. The audience, of course, receives the greatest benefit of all. There is also the added thrill the audience gets from witnessing the harmony and cooperation between the performers. Like any good basketball team, the players can't score as many points unless they work together and set up the shots.

Entertain the Guests, Not Each Other

A pitfall for even the most experienced interactive actor is to fall into the trap of entertaining his or her fellow actor. For a novice, this comes out of insecurity. For a veteran, it can simply be a case of too much fun to resist. But comedy in performance must never be internal comedy. Inside jokes don't work and only serve to alienate the audience. Activities performed for the purpose of seeing a fellow actor's reaction to them are not constructive performance.

This type of playing can seriously undermine trust in an ensemble over time. If actors begin to play selfish games with one another on set, they will eventually acquire a defensive mind-set onstage, always wary of the prank and questioning each other's motives. It won't matter if the games are intended in a playful way; it will impede their ability to psych into the other actor and cash in on the genius of their cooperation.

Never Break Character, Ever

The biggest crime an actor can commit in interactive performance, or in any other for that matter, is that of breaking character. One would think that it wouldn't be necessary to remind an actor not to break character. It just isn't done. But there is something about interactive performance—the casualness of it perhaps, or the proximity to real people—that makes it easier to drop character. Sometimes the intimacy with real people can lure an actor out of character. Sometimes an exceedingly funny moment or a particularly unsuccessful encounter can break the character. Even having a great time with a fellow actor can lead to the characterization being broken.

There are degrees of breaking character. It is not just a matter of being "in" or "out" of character. There can be a *thinning* of characterization resulting from any of the types of distractions just named. When a characterization thins, it is like a double exposure in a photograph; the ghost of a secondary personality peers through. When you look into the character's eyes, you see the actor behind them. You see the actor's thoughts and motivations under the characterization. The physicalization becomes more muted; the character voice is less defined. The extraordinary and magnified nature of the character is diminished, and what remains is little more than "normal." It is often a matter of laziness on the actor's part, though sometimes it can happen without the actor being aware of it. Whatever the case, it always compromises the performance.

Actors should think of not breaking character as they would think of not breaking an object of great value, something crafted by their own hands that they put a lot of time and care into. This is precisely what their characterization is, a creation of their own that they have put a lot of time and care into. Why then would they want to compromise a work of art that they have labored over so carefully?

Moreover, the audience really doesn't want to see the character broken, even though guests often do their best to break a character. It is like watching a magician perform an illusion. The observer may beg the magician to explain exactly how the trick is done, but the magician knows that the moment he does, the magic is gone.

Guests are likely to ask characters to break by asking how much they are paid, or how they are hired for their job, or what school they went to, or what their real name is. If an actor succumbs to these requests, he or she will invariably see disappointment in the guest's eyes—not satisfaction. Some guests are quite deliberate about it, viewing it as a battle to be won, but once they win, there is no more magic in the show.

When characters break, they break more than their own characterization. They also break the illusion of the entire show and, in so doing, indirectly break all the other characters as well. From a guest's point of view, if one character breaks and becomes an actor playing a part, then by association all the other characters also become just actors playing their parts. It breaks the suspension of disbelief for the entire production. When actors break, they betray the trust placed in them by the production and by their fellow cast members.

The Sanctity of Bits

As character bits develop throughout the cast, each actor must be aware and respectful of bits developed by other characters.

Sometimes an actor consciously or unconsciously absorbs a routine of another actor. I call this "bit osmosis." The problem for the production is not only the repetition of the same sorts of bits, but the trepidation on the originator's part of letting it be performed by other characters. Although sharing and building on ideas together must be strongly encouraged in an ensemble, sometimes character-specific routines are best left to their originator. The often-delicate balance to be struck is sharing a creative process on the one hand and having the ensemble be protective of its material on the other.

For instance, the outlaw Ned Beazzle might find a way of getting his spurs tangled and tripping himself to great comic effect. But if the prospector character begins using the same bit, it becomes a matter of concern for the actor playing Ned Beazzle and for the director in seeing such an obvious duplication of routines. The director should counsel the prospector character to try to develop a different sort of routine that gives him the same effect.

Even then there may be some concern as to who thought of it first, and who has the right to do the bit. Smallness may creep in and make interactions between those two actors more difficult. Certainly, ideas must be shared in creative ensembles, but by the same token I don't want to give the impression that absolutely anything goes in duplicating what others have created. If mutual respect, support, and cooperation are practiced and reinforced, then there is usually no problem. It is simply a matter of one ensemble member being respectful of another's creativity. (See Guest Scenes in *Acting Interactive Theatre*.)

Street Staging *19*

Street staging is not as static an affair as it is on-stage. It is a dance in which the actors scoop up the most concentrated focus they can while exploring their routines. Although no actor can preplan his or her blocking in this type of performance, there are a number of basic rules that allow the actor to focus the audience's attention properly and create an active and engaging environment.

Stage Position

Street staging is not unlike staging for theatre in the round. Characters should never face each other squarely, but should stand slightly skewed, so that the right foot of one is more or less in front of the right foot of the other, rather than stand toe-to-toe. This allows the people behind each actor to see at least one of the two clearly. It also gives a more inviting body language because the characters will seem less closed off to outside listeners.

Finding the Light

Often a character's audience is concentrated to one side. In this situation actors need to learn to direct their conversations toward their strongest side, that is, toward the side with the most onlookers. Since the audience in a street situation does not always stay in the same place, the actors may have to shift their staging as the crowd moves about them. This takes a little practice. In interactive performance, the eyes of the audience become the stage lights for the actors. Good actors learn to adjust their position so that they can be seen by the largest number of guests, and so find their light.

Splitting the Crowd

Actors can form a crowd where they want it formed, and can consolidate or adjust it for any disruption. Sometimes a crowd of dubious focus or scattered placement can be concentrated by being split. This is done by one or more actors crossing into the thickest part of the crowd, getting to the backside of that crowd, and continuing with the routine across the distance. This requires the crowd to separate and spread apart so that everyone can see both characters. It tends to sharpen the audience's focus on what is going on. This can also be accomplished by actors entering the scene, but from behind the thickest part of the crowd.

Finding a Weenie

Another strong audience-focusing technique is "finding a weenie." This is a matter of using a particularly interesting set piece as a backdrop. Actors begin a planned encounter or even a free-improv in front of a building face or set piece. This is more eye-catching to guests and also gives the impression of a planned event, which might better prompt guests to investigate. For instance, Streetmosphere characters often used the antique cars that were once a part of Hollywood Boulevard as backdrops for their routines. Characters looked more a part of the environment, and it tended to collect more focus than a routine that began in an open area.

Magnifying Your Distance

Another rule of street staging is that conversational distances between characters should be three times their normal distance. Characters must fill a larger space and make whatever interactions they have with each other open to guest reaction. If I were having a normal, friendly conversation with someone on the street, I might stand two or three feet away from that person. But if I were an interactive character, I would have the same conversation, with the same sense of intimacy, standing six to nine feet away.

Likewise, instead of standing squarely in front of the person as I might in a normal conversation, I would open my stance and cheat toward the largest number of guests. This extra distance makes the characters easier to see, and it invites the guests to eavesdrop on what is being said—perhaps even to join the conversation. It comes down to a simple matter of body language, by which the character always seems to invite approach.

It is important to keep the intended level of intimacy. This presents a vocal challenge to the actor of sounding intimate while standing beyond that circle of intimacy. There is often a tendency to scream in a large interactive environment. When this happens, the environment becomes a sort of screeching sideshow, with a lot of bellowing characters that make one wonder why they don't just quiet down, approach one another, and talk normally. Remember that the intent in interactive theatre is always to magnify and heighten, not to distort.

This idea of holding a greater interpersonal distance for a given level of intimacy can be quite effective when taken to extreme. Characters speaking conversationally over a long distance tend to create a sense of intimacy within the environment. It is also an effective means of gathering a crowd if people have to walk through their conversation.

Picture our Wild West town with two characters conversing from rocking chairs on the porch. Now imagine the conversation from two porches on opposite sides of the street. In the latter, everyone who walks by is privy to the conversation and has the choice of stopping and listening. This lends a greater sense of township. Moreover, situations with a character speaking from the street to a second-story window are also quite a focus catcher, not because of the distance involved, but because of the different elevations and the sight of characters being physically connected to the setting.

Clumping

Of bad habits, one of the most insidious is what I call "clumping." This is the tendency for interactive actors, particularly new and less secure ones, to huddle in a clump with other characters. The effect is that characters eventually end up facing each other in a circle, performing to one another and thereby cutting out the audience entirely. The first mistake here is performing for another character, and the second is facing inward and away from any guest who might be watching. This not only negates the idea of inviting interaction, but it actually fosters the opposite by delivering the message, "Stay away from us; we are interested only in speaking to each other."

Clumping can be a symptom of the rehearsal process, in which it is difficult, if not impossible, to perform for real guests. In rehearsals, actors often substitute for guests and so perform with—and for—each other. The habit may then carry over into actual performance. It also happens that actors clump out of fear or reluctance to interact. They feel it is safer or more fun to interact only with their ensemble buddies. These actors have not yet realized the power and joy of guest interaction.

The Three Rule

The remedy for clumping is a rule I call "the three rule." In character action there should never be more than three characters involved in the same action in one place.

In any improv situation, the focus should be on only one character at any given moment. In a two-character scene, the other character can be the object of the focus or the support for the focus when it's on a guest. Three characters in a scene add another level of complexity to the focus, but not an impossible one. Three is a stable number, and a scene with three active characters can provide an interesting variety of focus while still being clear to the guest. With more than three characters, it will seem as if there is always one character contributing nothing to the scene. This character can be better utilized somewhere else in the environment, working alone or with one or two other characters.

Clumping is contagious. If left unchecked, one character after another will join the clump until there is an absurd number of characters standing in a circle, leaving the rest of the environment empty. This is another reason for the three rule. The simple mathematics of it is that, with fewer, larger groups of actors, there is less activity within the overall environment. However, the same-sized cast working in groups of no more than three engenders many more active scenes at any given time.

For example, our Wild West Main Street has thirty characters currently performing on it. One walks through the street and sees three clumps of activities, each involving ten or so characters. Walk up to one of those activities, and you will see that only two or three characters are engaged in the activity of the scene. The rest are standing in support but contributing very little. When you look over the whole street, you see only three things going on.

Now imagine walking onto Main Street with the same thirty characters, but with ten or fifteen separate pieces of activity going on in various parts of the street, each one involving only one, two, or three characters. Each scene that you now view fully utilizes the characters within it. The street is now teeming with activity and looks like an environment come alive, rather than a mostly empty set with a few islands of activity.

It can be hard for actors not to sidle up to an activity when they are not needed, particularly when the activity is successful. There are few things more tempting to an actor than the sound of an encounter in which the audience is laughing and enjoying itself. But if there are three characters already involved, the actor's involvement will more likely be that of another spectator and not a contributing character.

Focus is also more difficult to keep clear when there are more than three characters in a scene. Where there are four or five characters vying for focus or trying to contribute ideas, the scene usually suffers for it. So in addition to few scenes, clumping engenders poor scenes as well.

Physical Contact with the Guest

Proper physical treatment of guests is very important. Their personal space must always be respected. If an actor approaches a guest and the guest takes a step backward, that is an indication to the actor of what interpersonal distance the guest is comfortable with. The actor should not step into that space once the guest has so defined it. Again, this has to do with the guest feeling in control and unthreatened.

Actors must never physically force, pull, grasp, or restrain guests. Their hands should never close on a guest's arm or shoulder. They should always offer an open palm. It is all right for a character to touch a guest. Physical contact can work wonders in relieving inhibitions and encouraging guests to be comfortable with characters. While there are, of course, limits to physical contact with guests, an open hand on a shoulder or back is usually acceptable. Touching on the arms and hands is usually all right too. Much of what is "acceptable" is a judgment call on the director's or producer's part, and will be guided by variables such as the style of show, type of clientele, geographic location, and prevailing social attitudes.

However, any kind of abrupt physical contact, such as slapping a guest on the back, should be avoided. One never knows when guests may have a physical infirmity that might cause them pain, like a sunburn or a sore shoulder. In any physical contact with a guest, a character should always telegraph that contact beforehand to give the guest an opportunity to react to it. It should never be a surprise.

If a character is to place its open hand on a guest's shoulder in a gesture of friendship, the hand should be in the air an extra beat longer so that the guest is aware of what is going to happen. If the guest shies away, then the actor must abort the move. When a rapport is already established with a guest, the actor can know what liberties can be taken. The rule of thumb here, though, is, "If in doubt, don't try it."

Moving Guests

Often a character needs to move a guest from point A to point B, such as a guest who is singled out of the crowd to perform some task or to play a leading role in an encounter that requires some staging. The best technique for this is elbow leading. Elbow leading is the actor inserting an open hand between the guest's ribs and elbow and gently drawing the elbow away from the body in the direction the character would like the guest to move.

When the character pulls the guest's elbow away from his or

her body, the tendency will be for the guest to close the gap. In order to do this, the guest will have to move his or her body in the direction of the elbow. In this way a character can lead a reluctant guest in any direction. It is also subtle enough so that the guest is never aware of it, but it nonetheless works.

To enhance the move, the character engages the guest's conscious mind by speaking to him or her at the same time, and focusing his or her attention on the place the character wants the guest to go. The character can also gesture with its free hand where it wants the guest to go. A combination of gesture, gently guiding, and speaking to the guest will succeed in bringing even the most reluctant guests out of their shell and into motion without their having to be dragged—which of course you wouldn't do.

Ignore Distractions as Long as Possible

There are bound to be distractions and unexpected interruptions in an interactive performance environment. It is best for actors to ignore distractions as much as possible and to play into them as little as possible. Many actors, annoyed by a distraction in their encounter, will turn their attention to it, feeling that if they are distracted, the guests certainly must be, so they may as well address it and deal with it.

It must be remembered that whenever the character turns its focus away from its activity, the guests will follow. A character once distracted distracts its entire audience. The truth is that most interruptions are short-lived, and if the character doesn't seem to notice them, neither will most of the audience.

An actor who maintains his or her concentration in the scene will regain most of the audience's attention when the distraction ends. The actor who does not gives the scene over to the distraction, then struggles to recover. Actors must hold their concentration for as long as possible. Only the point at which the distraction *cannot* be ignored is the time to identify it, affirm it, release it, and continue the encounter.

The Streetmosphere show at Disney was regularly interrupted by loud parkwide announcements. The cast dealt with them by finding a neutral, nonverbal, activity within the context of the scene until the announcement was over, then resuming the scene as if the actors had never heard the announcement. The guests accepted this convention quite readily. If, on the other hand, a child entered the scene with an autograph book and would not be denied, the characters were to incorporate that into the scene, sign the book, and release the child.

Own Your Space

There is never room in interactive performance for a tentative choice. Actors must learn to love the stage they are on. When they are onstage, they *own the space,* and must continue to do so until they are completely offstage. Interactive performance is like being the host of a party. Each character is hosting its own party in its own living room and has the responsibility for making sure its guests have a good time. Often actors do not realize the power they have when they are on the interactive stage.

Fill Your Space

Characters must choose their space and *fill it.* In vocal projection and in presence a character must always be aware of how large a field of influence it needs. Actors must mentally choose that field as though it were the radius of a circle and everything within its arc lives inside them. Whatever its size, they must fill it completely. If they don't pay attention to the sphere of influence, their choices may be too small—or too large—for the given situation.

Two Wild West characters converse from their porch chairs, each on opposite sides of Main Street. Each actor knows that his sphere of influence must at least reach that chair on the other side of the street. Both voice and presence must match the distance. Likewise, if the two characters are having an intimate conversation side by side on the same porch, they must again choose their sphere of influence. In this case, they would want to choose one greater than the distance between them in order to include guests passing in the street. Then they must fill that space completely.

Be Great

One of my colleagues encourages his actors to *be great.* He says, "Life does not encourage you to be great. Life encourages you to be 'at least as good as someone else.' Don't strive to be good, be great." There is no reason for artists to set their sights any lower than greatness. This is not to encourage self-importance but to allow actors to break away from letting themselves be defined by someone or something else. When actors are free from defining their work by other people's work, they become genuine and so open the pathway for real greatness. Learning to judge oneself on one's own terms rather than on other people's terms is the first step in becoming a truly original artist. (See Guest Environment in *Acting Interactive Theatre*.)

Survival Tools 20

_T_his chapter contains tools to navigate through the performance day. These tricks of the trade will help keep the interactive performance healthy and productive.

Performance Preparation

We all carry baggage with us from day to day, the everyday stress and worry that is part of our existence. We need to leave this baggage behind before we go to the theatre to perform. On the conventional stage, the effect of performing the same lines and the same blocking each night help to displace the actor's conscious anxieties. But an interactive show is spontaneous. So much is drawn from your own psyche that extra care has to be taken not to allow your own personal baggage to affect the performance process.

I use exercises to prepare actors for interaction. They consist of a five-step process. The individual exercise techniques can change, but the following five basic steps are always observed in them.

The first is to calm your mind, to clear the noise and

static of your thoughts, and to find a stillness. This can be done by breathing deeply and using a concentration exercise.

Second, take stock of your feelings and anxieties. Do a personal inventory of your baggage. Include things like deadlines, bills, getting the car fixed, the argument this morning, and all of the anxieties, fears, worries, frustrations, sadness, anger, and regrets that are rolling around in your mind and heart. Do nothing with them. Do not attempt to solve them, but simply identify them by giving them a visual image or symbol.

Third, after identifying your feelings and anxieties, collect them together and visualize jettisoning them. There are a number of visualizations that can be used for this, but you essentially lock away, vaporize, or transmute these symbols or images and make a mental affirmation that they are now gone or set aside for the duration of the performance.

Fourth, you make the affirmation to yourself that at this point in time there is nowhere else that you need to be and nothing else that you need to do except the performance. Affirm to yourself as well that all of the problems, worries, and anxieties you have jettisoned will still be there to be dealt with or discarded at the end of the day's performance. But, for now, you have all that you need in front of you. So relax and play.

Fifth, you must think well of the expectant audience and remind yourself that people have come from their homes and places of work for the express purpose of seeing you perform. If they have paid to see you, take that as a vote of confidence and belief in you. Accept the responsibility of meeting or exceeding their expectations.

Dealing with Negative Emotions in Performance

Sometimes in performance you just cannot get around a bad mood. When that baggage does find its way into your performance and you are depressed, angry, or upset, and you find that this mood is impeding your performance, don't try to suppress it. Identify the mood, accept it, and try to work through it *as your character.*

There are some cautions here. If you find yourself angry, for instance, projecting your anger onto guests or fellow cast members will not be in the best interest of the performance. But if you are angry or sad and you play that mood as an *objective* in your performance, using those feelings in the proper context of your character and the show, you can deflate its effect upon you personally.

For instance, you are playing the mail-order bride and find that you are in a very sad mood because you just broke up with your boyfriend. You have tried to jettison the feeling, but it is too strong, and you find yourself having to perform all day. It may be constructive, then, for you to choose to play that emotion of sadness in your character. Perhaps she is sad because she is broke or lost her money or ruined her best dress. I would not recommend playing the emotion too close to reality and saying that the reason for her sadness is that she just lost her husband. I would play the *emotion*, but play it in a different light. Playing the sadness will connect the actor to the character, and as the bride is cheered up in the course of play, the actor may be cheered as well.

Obviously this must be done responsibly, but it is a way to get over and through the mood. Often actors can then move on to other objectives and have a normal and constructive performance. Actors who try to suppress strong emotions in interactive performance can often end up with a miserable performance day.

Maintaining Concentration

When concentration wanes and you find your characterization slipping, try to keep your conscious mind occupied with an activity—a very here-and-now, denotative activity—even if it is scraping paint off a wall or digging in the dirt. Keeping your conscious mind occupied, even with a simple, repetitive task, can help refocus and reenergize you so that you can tune back into your character.

Escaping Self-Judgment

Sometimes a run-in with a mean guest or a series of bad choices in performance can get you down and make you doubt yourself. It is then that you need to remember that nothing you do can be denied once you do it. There is no going back. If something is done poorly, it is nonetheless done, and it cannot be undone.

Focus your attention on letting it go, and continuing. Don't judge yourself as doing good or bad, right or wrong. That's the audience's job! Your job is to believe in the character! When bad choices happen, rather than beating yourself up over something that is probably already forgotten by the guest, turn your attention instead toward your own belief in your characterization, and leave the judgment to the audience.

When inspiration fails, an actor must look to the choices he or she has made and *follow the character*. When there is no inspiration in sight, there is still a considerable landscape of specific needs created when your character was originated. Follow the needs and passion of the character, and just *be*. Working organically in this way will always lead you to new discoveries.

A playwright once told me his secret for getting around writer's block, that corner a writer paints himself into when he just doesn't know what will happen next. He said, "Ask the characters; ask what *they* would do next." The characters, if well drawn, will tell the writer exactly what happens next. It is the same with interactive characters. If you don't know what to say or do next, ask your character; then do it.

Develop Your Character's Routine

As actors follow the character in performance, letting it lead them from one activity to the next, they may find patterns developing. Characters have a way of creating their own routine, repeating what they like to do or stops they like to make within the performance environment. That is a good thing. Try to develop a character's routine because it gives the actor a better understanding of the character and makes it seem more real. The character's routine can become a framework for repeating successful *lazzi*.

For example, the outlaw Ned Beazzle's daily routine might be as follows: He walks into town and goes to the watering trough, first thing, and washes himself. The actor may find this opens him up to some slapstick opportunities. After exploring them, Ned may decide to go to the saloon for a drink, where the actor may launch into a number of already established saloon *lazzi* and encounters. His personal objective may be to leave the saloon when he manages to get himself thrown out. He may then wander down toward the corral where he endeavors to find the horse he lost in a drunken stupor the night before. Lining up the character's routine like this is a way for the actor to spread himself throughout the environment and capitalize on previously established and successful patterns.

Use the Language of the Period

The language of the period is a powerful tool. Know it and use it. I constantly motivate my actors to play with language and to learn more of its vernacular and use it in their performance. It is an ongoing process, like learning a foreign language. The more facility an actor has with the period language, the more clearly fixed the character will be historically.

Disarm Aggressive Behavior

Not often, but occasionally, a guest will respond with negative, even aggressive behavior. The *last* thing a character should do is meet aggressive behavior with aggressive behavior. The only possible result is an escalation of aggression. The character must instead disarm aggressive behavior by affirming it, even agreeing with it.

For example, let's imagine Sheriff Weston confronting a large, muscular, macho guest who has several women around him to impress. Our sheriff decides to endow him as Black Bart and tell him that he ought to watch himself. To which our macho guest replies something to the effect of, "I can break you in half. Go ahead and pull the trigger. Your bullets don't hurt me. I run this town."

For the sheriff to challenge this guest or call his bluff would avail little. He would only set up a situation in which the guest feels he has to prove himself, and the sheriff would get more of the same behavior, and worse. Instead, the actor playing the sheriff might disarm the behavior by suddenly being impressed with the guest's bravery and strength. He may attempt to coax him over to his side of the law, deputize him, and explain how he became a sheriff only because the girls really went for it. At this point, it may be fun for our macho guest to play along with the sheriff to show him how *he* impresses the ladies.

The sheriff might also take a different tack and present him with the keys to the town. He could tell him that, indeed, he *does* run the town. This, after all, would be accepting the guest's assumption. The mayor has just given the town to him because he is so afraid of him.

Any of these behaviors would create an enjoyable situation for the guest, who clearly wants the upper hand. The actor can easily give the macho guy what he is looking for and develop action that would be just as much fun for the people around him. When confronted by an aggressive assumption from the guest, the actor has no good reason to "stick to his guns."

It doesn't matter whether the character wins or loses. What matters is that the guest's choices are affirmed, regardless of what those choices may be (within reason and safety). I should also point out that, as a guest type, the big macho guy is generally a pussycat, as long as you allow him his macho. The truly tough guests are adolescents, especially males. They have such a need for acceptance that they would do almost anything, particularly when they are with their peers, to achieve it or to keep from losing it.

Some characters will be more vulnerable to aggressive guest types than others. One of my favorite Streetmosphere characters was the girl-off-the-bus, the little girl from Hometown USA who arrives in Hollywood with suitcase in hand to become famous. This character type was particularly susceptible to aggressive adolescents because of the girl's young age and her naïveté.

One of my favorite actresses playing this role was a tiny woman who, although in her twenties, appeared to be twelve or thirteen years old in costume. She had developed some rather ingenious ways of dealing with adolescent boys. Usually they would follow her around, make rude comments, and try to help her out by carrying her suitcase, which of course was a guise for running off with it.

When it got bothersome, the actress would pinpoint the dominant one in the group and "fall in love" with him. She would ask him if he had a girlfriend, ask if she could be his girlfriend, tell him he had pretty eyes, ask to hold his hand, or tell him she will follow him around forever. This always turned the tide from aggressive behavior to one of defense. When the other adolescents smelled vulnerability in their peer, *he* would become the focus of their torment. Unable to bear the deadly peer pressure, the boy would either settle down or turn tail and run. This again is how actors stay in control by lowering their dominance.

Changing the Subject

Sometimes guests choose a troublesome line of conversation, conversation that continually undermines the illusion by referring to the character as an actor in the show, asking about the production, or pointing out anachronisms that may be present. Sometimes these troublesome lines of conversation are presented innocently by guests, and sometimes they are a deliberate attempt to make life difficult.

Whatever the motivation or line of conversation, the best technique for getting out of that kind of trouble is the time-tested practice of changing the subject. It works just like it does in real life. Innocently changing the subject, and then not allowing the guest to respond until well into the new topic, is usually effective in escaping an undesirable conversation. It is even better when you can end with a specific question to the guest. Changing the subject rarely needs to be used more than once or twice. If it doesn't work, the next option may be to find closure and leave the situation. The least desirable choice is to take on the guest in a challenge. At that point, you would be fighting on the guest's turf, and you will *never* win on those terms.

Dealing with Anachronisms

Anachronisms are inevitable. Rarely, if ever, will you be blessed with a completely seamless environment. Modern safety and fire codes alone almost ensure it, and there will always be something that a guest who knows the period will look at and say, "This does not belong here!" Likewise, it is inevitable that a character will make a slip of the tongue or be presented with something anachronistic, such as a wristwatch in King Arthur's court.

The rules for dealing with anachronisms are quite simple. The first rule is never to deliberately seek out or use anachronisms. This may seem obvious, but to the novice, seeing a camera dangling from a guest's neck cries out to be addressed *because* it is so out of context. The contrast will seem to invite an exchange: the novice will be amazed by the camera, will ask questions about it, but will then suddenly find him- or herself in a losing game with an anachronism. Anachronisms put the player in the world of the guest, when the point is to place the guest in the realm of the character. The novice can make the choice of not noticing the camera dangling and thus get around the problem by never getting into it.

Actors must remember that from the guest's point of view, anachronisms are not as obvious as they may be to the actor. An actor may spend much time studying what modern devices were not invented in the 1860s, but guests will more readily take their anachronistic possessions for granted.

Despite how carefully an actor may turn a blind eye or deaf ear to anachronisms, there will be times when they are inescapably thrust upon them. Situations arise in which a guest offers an anachronism by way of asking a question, presenting an object, or pointing out a discrepancy in the environment.

Here the next rule is to deal with the anachronism as your character would deal with it. If the actor *thinks* like a person from the 1860s and *reacts* accordingly, he or she can't go too far wrong. The point is that what would seem unusual, implausible, or impossible to a real person of the 1860s would be taken that way by the character. It is also perfectly acceptable for a character not to understand.

If a guest hands the actor that camera and asks, "Do you know what this is?" a reply must be made. Perhaps it is something "newfangled" and difficult for the character to understand; it may have to have the guest explain it. In most cases, the character can then either believe the guest is crazy, or walk away having learned something new. In this case, the actor would know that photography had been invented by 1860, but that at that time it was very crude. He may either assume that, being in the wilderness, he would not have heard of the latest in photography, or he would know enough about it to inquire where the rest of the camera had gone. This may still result in a relatively uninteresting exchange of technological facts. So the actor will want to change the subject as soon as possible and get on to something more related to his character's primary needs.

The most entertaining way to deal with an unavoidable anachronism is to *translate* it. This rule is never to deny what you can translate. Translating involves seeing the anachronism through the historic filter of the character, but then making a strong assumption about what it is, within the scope of the character's understanding.

A guest may approach a character in King Arthur's court and ask, "May I take your picture?" To which the character might pat his pockets and reply, "I have no picture." A guest may ask, "Do you like Madonna?" and the character might reply, "I love the virgin mother and pray to her every night." Or a guest may inquire, "Do you know what a motorcycle is?" "About twenty-eight days, I think." Some actors are better at translations than others, but a guest can have a ball trying to get a character to understand something that is quite out of its reach. I have seen actors come up with some clever and plausible explanations for anachronisms. If it's good enough, guests will accept the character's explanation over their own.

Code Words

Sometimes performing interactive theatre is like the boy who cried wolf. With so much extraordinary action going on, it may be difficult to tell when something really does go wrong. Therefore, in all my shows, I choose a particular word from the period lexicon and reserve it for emergency use only. I pick an antique word, one not likely to be used except deliberately, and ordain it to mean, "I am not performing, I really mean what I am saying." In this way the cast can express important information without having to drop character, or have the guests realize what is being said.

For my Renaissance shows I use the expression *in sooth,* which means "in truth." If an actor says, "In sooth, my lord, I am ill and must retire," I know I have a sick actor. In Streetmosphere I used the word *frankly.* "Frankly, I got a lost kid here" would let anyone who knew the code know that the actor wasn't just making another assumption.

Other code words can be devised as the need arises. When a Renaissance maid calls another actor or stage manager "good cousin," there is a drunken guest pestering her. "Ben's Chili Bowl" was a euphemism for backstage in Streetmosphere. When performers referred to taking lunch at Ben's Chili Bowl, they meant it was time to leave the set for their break. The Streetmosphere cast came up with its own code word for their director. I was referred to as "the Mayor."

Dealing with the Media

Actors often seek advice on how to deal with media attending the show. An inevitability of performance, it seems, is the presence of a television news camera or a newspaper reporter doing a review or article on the show. These people will unabashedly approach characters in mid-encounter and ask them pointed twentieth-century questions about the production.

The rule for the media is the same as with the guests. Ignore anachronisms as long as you can. Do not notice or bring to attention the microphone under your chin. This will come across on tape only as trite and unoriginal in the extreme. If in view of the guests, answer the questions as a period character would: unruffled and calmly uncomprehending of anything out of context. The interviewer will soon get the idea and ask only in-context questions.

Much of this problem can be alleviated by management arranging out-of-character interviews backstage and making it clear to media visitors that the actors will not break character in performance. Also, actors should never seek out or mug for photo publicity because it always looks amateurish and makes for a bad show.

Exit Lazzi

As time goes on, the sheer probability of failure will catch up with an actor, and a bit will fall flat. What is needed in these situations is for the character to find clean closes that fit the character and can be utilized in a variety of ways. A standard "Close it, and get out of there" that fits the character can be a handy thing for an actor to have in his or her bag of tricks.

When inspiration falters, or when one improvises one's way into a corner, a stock closer can wrap up an unproductive encounter in a comic and revealing way. Exit *lazzi* allow the actors to cut their losses and escape relatively unscathed, and should be carried as one might carry Mace on a key chain—just in case.

Pace Yourself

Interactive performance can be an exhausting experience. Often the effects of performance are felt only after it is over. The performance itself is so exhilarating, and the energy exchange between performer and audience such a fulfilling one, that the actors hardly notice their fatigue until afterward. But if they are not careful to pace themselves wisely, they will expire vocally or physically before the performance is complete. An interactive environment, particularly a large one, requires a great deal of energy to fill. Actors need to pace themselves so that they sustain the entire performance time and do not diminish their actions toward the end.

Follow Your Intuition

Interactive characters are constantly faced with making performance choices. I insist on their being guided by their own intuition. They will more often than not make the best choices automatically. Over time, interactive actors develop an uncanny instinct about what will or will not work in a given situation. This makes them powerful performers in any type of theatre. My rule is, "When in doubt, let go and follow your intuition."

Above All, Have Fun!

I would like to close with one of my most important rules of interactive theatre. As a character, the actor should be having as much fun as the guest. If you are not having fun, you're not doing it right. People smile at this rule, but I am quite serious about it. You cannot spread the joy of play without feeling it yourself. If actors become too caught up in following the rules and techniques of interactive theatre, and constantly judge themselves as to how well they are living up to them, they will not be projecting the essence of what interactive theatre is all about: play. You will know it when it works, because it feels wonderful.

Transcending Interactive Theatre

It may seem inappropriate to end a book on interactive theatre by suggesting that the sum of the technique comprises something more important than the theatre it describes, but I believe this to be true. I would be remiss not to point out that this process touches the human condition on a more profound level than is plumbed by even the great tradition of the theatre. My own experiences on this journey have shown me on many occasions that this process—this temenos, this natural actualization of self, this community of minds and spirits—has a deep power to heal. I have even seen it save lives.

Repeatedly, actors return to the Sterling Renaissance Festival—my first and best laboratory—to play a role again. They call it recharging, or getting grounded again, or reconnecting to their art, or to themselves. Their second year back, they don't care if they get the stage role they want. Their third year back they don't even care what occupation they play: "I'll do anything you choose for me; just take me back—I have to be there!" If not the roles, then what is the lure? Somewhere in this interactive technique lies the answer. Perhaps my next quest will be to find it. Perhaps it will be yours as well.

I hope that the process outlined in this book not only will be useful to every kind of artist, but will also have meaning for the teacher, the therapist, the behavioral scientist, the parent, and the healer. The power and potential of the art of play touch many walks of life.

My love has always been for the magic of the theatre. I have endeavored to create theatre that everyone can touch and share together. In achieving it, I cannot escape the notion that I have touched on something much greater. In my blitheness, perhaps I have tapped the power of a thunderstorm to turn a pinwheel, but what a pretty pinwheel it is.

Have fun!